THE HISTORY OF
15TH THE KING'S HU

1914-1922

GENERAL SIR WILLIAM PEYTON, K.C.B., K.C.V.O., D.S.O.
COLONEL OF THE 15TH THE KING'S HUSSARS, 1916–1931

THE HISTORY
of the
15TH THE KING'S HUSSARS
1914-1922

BY

LORD CARNOCK, M.C.
(late 15th Hussars)

WITH A FOREWORD BY

BRIG.-GENERAL A. COURAGE, D.S.O., M.C.
(Colonel 15/19th Hussars)

ILLUSTRATED BY

CAPT. C. SHAW
(late 15th Hussars)

FOREWORD

THE publication of this History of the Regiment has been made possible in consequence of the generosity of the past and present officers of the Regiment.

I wish to place on record my very sincere thanks to them. Their generosity has enabled the book to be sold at a price considerably below cost price, thereby bringing it within the reach of everyone who has passed through the ranks of the Regiment.

The thanks of everyone connected with the Regiment are due to Lord Carnock who has written the History, no small task as it involved a careful research and compilation as well as literary ability. I am sure everyone who peruses its pages will agree that the result is a very faithful and pleasing record.

Our thanks are also due to Major F. W. Tomlinson, late The Buffs, of the Historical Section of the War Office, who has reviewed the work with meticulous care.

There has been added a series of most excellent sketches, drawn by the late Captain Charles Shaw of the 15th Hussars, and our thanks are due to his widow, Mrs. Shaw, for giving the sketches.

A. Courage.
Brig: General
Colonel 15/19th Hussars.

AUTHOR'S PREFACE

THE History of the 15th The King's Hussars from the time the Regiment was raised on 21st March, 1759, until 17th January, 1913, has been written by Colonel H. C. Wylly, C.B.

The following pages continue the story of the Regiment to the year 1922, when owing to various reasons, it was found necessary to reduce the number of cavalry units, and the 15th Hussars after over a century and a half of independent life found themselves merged with another unit.

In the first volume, the history of the Regiment has been most ably detailed. Its achievements, the part it played in British history, its difficulties, and the various vicissitudes through which it passed, make a story which cannot fail to interest.

Colonel Wylly finished his history with the following words :

" It is beyond all contradiction that enough has been recorded in the latter-day pages of these annals to convince all who may be interested in the doings of the Regiment, that those who have served in it of recent years, have been inspired by the splendid traditions that have been handed down to them. It is equally indisputable that those who are honoured by a place in its ranks at the present day are imbued with a similar inspiration, and that they are firmly resolved to pass on these traditions unsullied to future generations, being assisted in the attainment of this object by a fixed determination to live up to the time-honoured and deeply reverenced Regimental Motto

" MEREBIMUR."

These words had hardly been penned, and the ink was scarcely dry on the pages, when the 15th Hussars were once again asked to prove their mettle on the old battlefields of France and Flanders.

The fight was to be more fierce perhaps than any battle their ancestors had known, and engines of war were to be employed undreamt of by the old Hussars. Nevertheless the Regiment did its best to uphold the old traditions, and to fulfil the prediction of Colonel Wylly.

In the following pages the adventures of the 15th Hussars are recorded as faithfully as may be. But the doings of a small unit like a cavalry regiment, in a war in which whole empires were engaged, can of necessity only interest a limited public.

AUTHOR'S PREFACE

No one can pretend that the various actions of the 15th produced any effect in the drama of the world conflict ; and the earnest student of military history will, therefore, learn little by the perusal of the following pages. But perhaps the reader will here find a record of duty well done, of valour and self-sacrifice, of hardships uncomplainingly borne and of a faith and esprit de corps which neither disasters nor disappointment could shatter.

When at length the victory was won, all ranks could feel that they had done their best, and that their ancestors, watching over the destinies of the Old Regiment, would have no cause to be ashamed of their descendants.

C.

Cavalry Club,
London,
May 27th, 1932.

CONTENTS

APPENDICES

LIST OF ILLUSTRATIONS

LIST OF MAPS

THE HISTORY OF THE 15TH THE KING'S HUSSARS 1914-1922

CHAPTER I

RETURN FROM SOUTH AFRICA TO THE EVE OF THE BATTLE OF MONS

WHEN the 15th Hussars landed in England towards the end of 1912, after fourteen years of foreign service, they were disappointed to find themselves quartered at Longmoor Camp, originally built during the South African War, and for the last few years used as the Mounted Infantry School. The Regiment took over the tin huts and the Mounted Infantry cobs from the defunct school, and at first all ranks complained bitterly about their remounts ; but in the course of time the cobs gained high favour, and in the stern test of war proved their great value as cavalry troop horses.

Directly they arrived in the Aldershot Command the 15th Hussars were detailed as Divisional Cavalry, and were the first cavalry regiment to be allotted permanently to infantry divisions. The practice heretofore had been to detail squadrons for this duty from various cavalry brigades for manœuvres only, but the 15th Hussars were permanently allotted to infantry divisions. A Squadron was attached to the 3rd Division, B Squadron to the 2nd Division, and C Squadron to the 1st Division.

The work of a squadron of divisional cavalry differs very materially from the work of a squadron which forms part of a cavalry brigade, and requires special training. In 1913 there were unfortunately no British text books dealing exclusively with the duties of a squadron of divisional cavalry; in consequence at first the use of the squadrons and their co-operation with the other arms was largely of an experimental character.

The 1st and 2nd Divisions were stationed at Aldershot, and therefore B and C Squadrons were enabled to do all their training with their own divisions. During the greater part of the training season of 1913 B and C Squadrons were at Aldershot. By the end of the season all ranks were convinced that they thoroughly understood their new duties, and also felt that the infantry commanders trusted and relied upon them. A Squadron on the other hand, whose division was on Salisbury Plain, only had the opportunity to work with it on manœuvres.

The work of divisional cavalry consists chiefly in reconnaissance. At this period the Royal Flying Corps had not reached that stage of development which it attained later, nor was the Signal Service very elaborately equipped and organised. A commander therefore relied to a considerable extent, both for his information and for his inter-communication, on his squadron of divisional cavalry.

In 1914 the development of divisional cavalry was carried out in even greater detail. Each battalion of infantry whilst undergoing training had a few Hussars attached to it. Thus by the middle of the summer the squadrons had become an integral part of their divisions and felt competent to carry out their work under all conditions.

On 23rd July, 1914, the whole of the 15th Hussars were encamped at Nursery Camp, Aldershot, and took part in a field day, where they worked together as a regiment, the first occasion they had done so since leaving South Africa. By midday on Friday, 24th July, the field day ended, and at the conclusion of the operations the Regiment marched back to camp. There was no sign of a war cloud on the horizon, and not a soul realised that the next occasion when the Regiment would march together would be to the sound of the guns in the dreaded Ypres Salient. Everyone anticipated a short period of leave after the strenuous training of the last few weeks, and before marching off to the Grand Manœuvres. The storm clouds were gathering but no one realised the fact.

The European crisis became acute a few days later. All leave was suspended, and the 15th Hussars awaited impatiently their orders to mobilise. They had not long to wait, for on 29th July the preliminary orders to mobilise were issued, and on 1st August the Regiment returned to Longmoor.

A considerable number of troops had been collected round Aldershot in anticipation of the coming manœuvres, and all of these were now ordered back to their stations. The sight of marching troops was familiar enough to the quiet countryside about Aldershot, but on this August evening, as the long khaki columns wound their way by main road or quiet country lane, and through the sleepy villages, the cottagers hurried to their doors to watch the troops as they went by, for all were strangely stirred, and realised that the passing regiments were about to take part in a great and terrible adventure, and that many of the cheerful singing soldiers, who so gaily swung along the roads, were destined never again to see their homes.

The details of mobilisation were familiar enough to everyone, for they had always been a favourite question at all examinations ; and it proceeded with the greatest ease and celerity. The reservists arrived punctually, equipped and accoutred to the last button ; splendid horses joined—many from famous hunt stables ; waggons, ammunition and stores of every description were drawn, and in a very few days the Regiment could report that it was ready for war.

As much time as possible was spent on the range, for the short Lee-Enfield Rifle was a new weapon to some of the older Reservists.

The actual date on which the Expeditionary Force was to sail was kept a secret ; and on several occasions squadrons paraded ready equipped to march away, only to return to barracks. But eventually it was known that during the night of 15th–16th August the Regiment would move to its port of embarkation. For the last time at Longmoor all the officers of the 15th Hussars assembled round the mess table at dinner. Those about to venture forth were dressed in their war khaki, and round the table were many officers called up from the Reserve, dressed in the uniforms of peace ; in time their turn would also come, to fill the gaps caused by those who had fallen in the service of their country.

From the walls the portraits of the former commanding officers looked down upon this memorable scene, and upon the table still glittered the gold and silver plate, the heritage of former generations.

A final stirrup cup was taken, those for the front buckled on their equipment, the last goodbyes were said, and one by one they passed out into the night and the unknown.

Meanwhile on the barrack square the men formed up in the darkness, and by the light of electric torches the roll was called.[1] The order to mount was given, and the 15th The King's Hussars marched away to battle. C Squadron marched at midnight 15th August, followed by B Squadron at 4 a.m. on the 16th, and A Squadron at 9.30 a.m. the same day.

Headquarters did not leave England until some weeks later. The 15th Hussars, as will be related further on, were not assembled together as a regiment until well into 1915, and therefore the headquarters took no part in the earlier stages of the war. The Machine-gun detachment also did not leave England with the rest of the Regiment, and did not join until the battle of the Aisne.

It is now a matter of history that the British Expeditionary Force left the shores of Great Britain without pomp or parade, and few people were aware of its departure until it had sailed. The arrangements at Southampton had all been well thought

[1] For strengths on marching out, see Appendix E.

out beforehand, and during Sunday, the 16th and the following night, the squadrons embarked without let or hindrance, A Squadron on the *Manchester Engineer*, C Squadron on the *Siptah* and B Squadron on the *Orion*. By dawn on the 17th the loaded transports were awaiting in Southampton Water the orders to sail, and a few hours after daylight the passage across the Channel began.

The day was beautiful and the sea calm, the long columns of crowded transports steamed across an unruffled ocean. During the passage the messages from H.M. The King and Lord Kitchener were read aloud to the troops. The map boxes were broken open and their contents sorted and distributed. In the afternoon and evening the various transports reached Havre, where orders were received to proceed to Rouen.

The ships conveying the Regiment formed units of a long column, which steamed slowly up the Seine. The inhabitants crowded to both banks of the river and gave vent to their enthusiasm by continuous cheers, fireworks, and patriotic songs. The men remained on deck far into the night and responded energetically. The stately column of transports was a fine sight, and from ship to ship echoed the strains of God Save the King, Rule Britannia, the Marseillaise, and perhaps more topical songs, not excluding Tipperary.

The three squadrons reached Rouen on 18th August, and marched to a camp at Bruyeres. The camp was at this time in a fairly chaotic state, as it had been hastily formed and was contracted into a very confined space. Units of all branches of the Service kept pouring in as they disembarked from the transports, and a certain amount of confusion was inevitable. The three squadrons were here encamped together, and many months were to elapse before the squadrons would once again bivouac in the same field.

Here, too, the Interpreters from the French Army joined, and at first were supplied on a lavish scale, one to each troop.

The bicycles were drawn for the Cyclist Companies which were to be attached to each squadron. It had always been intended to supplement each squadron of divisional cavalry by a company of cyclists, but on the outbreak of war no establishment of cyclists had as yet been authorised for the Regular divisions, and these had now to be improvised.

As the squadrons arrived at their forward concentration areas, they were joined by officers, N.C.O's, and men drawn from the various battalions of the divisions to which the squadrons belonged, who took over the bicycles and became part of the Divisional Mounted Troops.

If in the following pages there is but little record of the doings of the Cyclist Companies, the reader must not imagine it is because they played an unimportant part. Far otherwise, for in every engagement the cyclists played a most decisive role, and fought side by side with their hussar comrades in many a bitter fight. On numerous occasions they fought independently of the squadrons, and the story of their achievements is well worthy of record. But this is a history of the 15th Hussars, and a chronicle of their doings alone. Nevertheless it is only right and proper that a due recognition of the services of the Cyclist Companies should be made, and the great debt of gratitude which the 15th Hussars owe to them should be placed on record.

During the 19th August the three squadrons entrained at Rouen for an unknown destination. Entraining began long before daylight, aided by the dim glimmer of hand lanterns, and at first proceeded slowly, for the French horse-boxes were still unfamiliar to most British soldiers, but in a short time the gaily-decorated trains were speeding across France towards the battle front.

The reader must realise that, in the battles and marches about to be described, the 15th Hussars never fought together as a unit, and that it was seldom indeed that the squadrons fought as squadrons. The men were employed as a rule in small parties and patrols covering their infantry divisions. To follow the movements of each patrol, or to record the action of every small detachment is manifestly impossible, and therefore the history of many very gallant deeds, and many stories of heroic endeavour, must of necessity remain unchronicled.

It was said of the Rifles during the Peninsular War that the first shot and the last shot of every engagement were fired by a rifleman, and perhaps the same might apply to the 15th Hussars during the retreat from Mons. For in the dim light of the early morning as the long grey columns of the enemy began their march, the patrols from the 15th Hussars were hovering about them to watch their every movement ; and when, after the sun had set, the tired German troops settled down to snatch a few hours rest, they were still watched by the scouts from the Regiment.

This was not the first occasion on which the 15th Hussars had taken part in a great retreat, for the Regiment had formed a unit of the rear guard to Corunna, and the action of rear guards, in whatever century or whatever clime, bears a certain resemblance.

The railway journeys of the three squadrons were all uneventful. At the wayside stations, wherever the trains stopped, refreshments were available for the men. The sight of troop trains crowded with British soldiers was then a novel spectacle in France, and the populace crowded to the stations to do all in their power to show the men how much France appreciated the arrival of her Allies.

A Squadron detrained at 3 p.m. on 20th August at Aulnoye, and C Squadron on the same day at Le Nouvion. B Squadron did not detrain until 4 a.m. on the 21st at Vaux-Andigny, whence after a short halt it marched to Noyelles, close to La Groise.

Day and night the various units of the British Expeditionary Force, which consisted of the Cavalry Division (1st, 2nd, 3rd, and 4th Cavalry Brigades), the 5th Cavalry Brigade, and the 1st, 2nd, 3rd and 5th Divisions, were hurrying across France as quickly as the railways could carry them, and as the different units detrained, they marched to the forward concentration areas. From these jumping-off positions the advance into Belgium was to commence on 21st August.

In accordance with these arrangements after detrainment, A Squadron marched from Aulnoye to Goegnies Chaussée, where it joined the 3rd Division ; and C Squadron marched to St. Hilaire.

From this place patrols were sent from C Squadron to the French Army. For the 1st Division was on the right of the British Army, where it connected with the French. It was thought advisable that the French troops should be shown the British uniforms, and should realise that the Expeditionary Force had really landed, and was coming up in line with their Allies.

On 22nd August the British Army advanced, crossed the Belgian frontier, and took up its stand on the left of the French Army, with its centre about the mining town of Mons. The day was fine, the sun shone from a cloudless sky and beat down perhaps a little too fiercely upon the long columns of khaki troops as they toiled along the straight paved roads. Once again after the lapse of almost exactly a century, the countryside of France and Belgium echoed to the tread of the marching soldiers of Great Britain, and once again the roll of British drums woke the sleepy towns and villages of the Low Countries.

The spirit and the morale of all ranks were at the highest pitch, and loudly the men sang all the popular songs of the period, as they swung along the dusty roads. A better trained, a better disciplined, or a force more imbued with real esprit de corps, had probably never before marched to battle.

As the troops crossed the frontier into Belgium, they were received with acclamations. Amongst all the inhabitants of Belgium the terror of the advancing armies of Germany was very real indeed, for well they knew what misery this invasion would entail. For days past they had seen a constant stream of refugees passing their doors, and had heard accounts of destruction and death, pillage and terrorism, which filled everyone with horror. But the sight of the British Army advancing to their relief at once restored confidence, for now at last they felt help was at hand, and they no longer stood alone in an attempt to stay the torrent of the enemy's onslaught.

It can be well imagined what the feelings of the population must have been, when a few hours later they stood at their doors to watch their protectors from Great Britain rolling back in retreat, and leaving them at the mercy of the invader.

The British Army was now about to test on the battlefield the lessons that had been learnt, not only on the manœuvre ground, but in many a hard-fought action in all parts of the world.

The German and French Armies had not met since 1871, and it was but natural that the lessons of this last great European war, fought forty-four years before, deeply influenced the strategy, training and tactics of all Continental armies.

The British Army, of all those engaged on the Western Front, had at this period the greatest experience of the power of modern weapons. For there were few of the senior officers who had not taken part in the South African War. It might therefore be suggested that the training of the British Army was in many respects far in advance of that of the other Powers. It is moreover a well-known fact that the rifle-fire of the British cavalry and infantry was far superior to that of any other troops who took the field in 1914. There has probably never been an army whose rifle-fire was so deadly as that of the old Regular Army of 1914; and probably there never will be again. From the very earliest times British battles have been won by the steady shooting of the rank and file.

A document captured from the Germans just before the Battle of Mons described the organisation and methods of warfare adopted by the British Army. In this document special stress was laid on the fact that the British fought in thin lines, and relied on the shooting of the rank and file to stop the enemy's assault. This document further went on to say that behind our thin firing lines there were no reserves, so that once the firing line had been pierced the British Army was helpless.

This was all very true, but what the German document failed to point out was that in all the wars of the past this line had practically never been broken. It was the rank and file at Crecy and Agincourt who by their steady shooting with the long bow, broke to pieces the chivalry of Europe. Napoleon's columns in the Peninsula, and at Waterloo, the Russians with their dense masses in the Crimea, the onslaughts of many thousands of fanatical savages, had practically in every instance failed to break the steady "Thin Red Line." And now, although the thin line was khaki, it was still able to check any

LED HORSES, AUGUST 1914

attack, no matter how fiercely pressed, and this fact the German Armies were about to discover.

As far as the 15th Hussars were concerned, the march into Belgium on 22nd August did not entail any contact with the enemy. On the right of the Expeditionary Force, C Squadron formed the advance guard to the 3rd Infantry Brigade, which led the 1st Division. The squadron left St. Hilaire at 4 a.m. and the route led through the fortress of Maubeuge. French Territorials were busily engaged in digging trenches, putting up wire entanglements, and placing the surrounding villages in a state of defence. To those as yet unacquainted with the power of modern artillery, the fortress and its approaches gave a great feeling of strength and security. Yet in a short time this strong place was to fall to the Germans like a ripe plum. Shortly after crossing the frontier, the headquarters of the 1st Division went into billets in a fine old chateau at the village of Rouveroy. C Squadron turned into a large and commodious farm near the chateau. Meanwhile patrols sent out from the squadron had gained touch with the 5th Cavalry Brigade about Binche, and had further sighted some patrols of Uhlans, with whom they had not become engaged.

The 2nd Division had also advanced into Belgium, and B Squadron covered its advance, marching at an early hour from La Groise, and thence by Le Quesnoy to Bavai. This squadron sent out strong detachments to block all the approaches through the Forêt de Mormal.

The 3rd Division received orders to take up a line from Villers St. Ghislain through Nimy (1½ miles north of Mons) to the Mariette Bridge on the canal (4½ miles east of Mons). Whilst this march was in progress, and the troops were manœuvring to get into position, A Squadron covered the operation and their patrols gained touch with the flanks, and with our cavalry, who were already engaged with the enemy about Bray. By nightfall A Squadron was bivouacked about Hyon, and all units of the British Army were engaged in entrenching themselves, and in preparing the bridges over the canal near Mons for demolition, in anticipation of the attack which all felt sure would develop the next day.

The reader will find some difficulty in following the narrative of the doings of the three squadrons during the operations which are about to be recorded. When the Army stood in line at Mons, the first Division was on the right, in touch with the French, on the left of the 1st Division came the 2nd, and on the left of the 2nd stood the 3rd Division. This order never changed until after the Battle of the Aisne, when the British Army was moved into Flanders. In order therefore to make the story as simple as possible, the narrative of each squadron will be related from day to day, detailed from right to left : C Squadron, B Squadron and A Squadron, each in turn.

The various patrols from the squadrons returned to billets during the evening of 22nd August. They had all gained touch with our cavalry, who had become engaged with the enemy during the day.

Our cavalrymen, flushed with success from their first encounters with the Germans, were all most optimistic in their reports, and recounted how the enemy had advanced in dense masses against our rifle-fire, offering the most splendid targets, and marching to their own destruction.

During the night orders were issued for the operations on the following day.

The following officers left England with the original Expeditionary Force during August and September, 1914.

Headquarters. Lieutenant-Colonel H. A. Tagart, D.S.O., Major H. D. Bramwell, Lieutenant H. F. Brace (Adjutant), Lieutenant B. Osborne (Machine Guns), Lieutenant and Quarter-Master F. C. Marsh.

A Squadron. Captain O. B. Walker, Captain R. P. Wells, Lieutenant C. H. Whittle, Second-Lieutenant J. C. Rogerson, Second-Lieutenant C. M. Hoare, Second-Lieutenant E. H. Rouse-Boughton.

B Squadron. Captain the Hon. W. A. Nugent, Captain C. Nelson, Lieutenant J. M. Tylee, Second-Lieutenant C. H. Liddell, Second-Lieutenant G. H. Straker.

C Squadron. Major F. C. Pilkington, Captain A. Courage, Lieutenant F. A. Nicolson, Second-Lieutenant C. J. Stanhope, Second-Lieutenant the Hon. E. C. Hardinge.

Staff. Major P. O. Hambro (Headquarters Staff, Cavalry Division), Lieutenant J. Arnott (A.D.C. to G.O.C. Cavalry Division), Lieutenant J. B. Wheeler (Signals, Cavalry Division), Captain F. W. Barrett (Staff Captain, 2nd Cavalry Brigade), Captain F. H. Sykes (Temporary Lieutenant-Colonel Commandant R.F.C. Military Wing), Captain the Hon. J. D. Y. Bingham, Captain B. Ritchie, Captain E. H. Bald joined the Regiment on the Aisne.

Chapter II

THE BATTLE OF MONS AND THE RETREAT

THE orders for the British Army were as a matter of fact very simple. They were required only to hold their own, and offer as much resistance as possible to the advance of the enemy.

The right of the 1st Division, and therefore the right of the British Army, rested on the little village of Peissant, and between this place and the left of the Fifth French Army there existed a gap of a few miles, to watch which the 2nd Troop of C Squadron, and a proportion of cyclists were sent. Lieutenant C. Stanhope's troop was ordered to watch the front of the outpost line about Binche and Merbes Ste. Marie. If the enemy advanced in any force he was to fall back on the outpost line. The troop formed up just before daylight, and as they awaited their final orders, the stillness of dawn was suddenly broken by the roaring of the guns, and the majority now heard for the first time in their lives artillery speaking in real earnest.

The patrols from C Squadron advanced through the outpost line to take up their various positions. Shortly after leaving the shelter of our outpost system, Lieutenant Stanhope and his men came upon the enemy, who was lining a bank at the edge of a wood, and a heavy fire was directed against the troop, which was forced to withdraw and take cover, after suffering a few casualties. Lieutenant Stanhope then moved to the left, and joined forces with Lieutenant Nicolson, who by this time had reached the edge of the village of Villereil-les-Brayeau.

This small force never became actively engaged ; a squadron of German cavalry approached the edge of the village, and the two troops opened fire upon it at long range, whereupon the enemy retired. Hostile patrols continued in observation, but made no serious effort to advance.

The men of the squadron who had been sent to gain touch with the French succeeded in doing so, and were rewarded with a magnificent view of the German attack, but they themselves never became involved in the battle.

Throughout the day C Squadron took no further action, for the enemy contented himself with watching the 1st Division, and confined all his attentions to the left flank of the British Army.

Shortly after dark the troops retired back through the outpost line, and returned to their previous billets at Rouveroy. The attitude of C Squadron throughout the Battle of Mons had been little more than that of spectators.

To turn now to the adventures of B Squadron. The 2nd Division on the evening of 22nd August was some way in rear of the rest of the Army, and had before it a considerable march until it could come up in line with the remainder. At 3 a.m. on 23rd August Captain the Hon. W. A. Nugent received the following order: "The Divisional Mounted Troops 2nd Division will march at once on receipt of these orders, and will occupy the line Bray–Mons, both inclusive." The order also went on to state that they were expected to be in position by 6 a.m., and that the rest of the division was marching at once. As soon as possible the mounted troops turned out, and began a forced march along the cobbled roads, which tried the horses exceedingly, and proved most exhausting to the cyclists. After pushing on as rapidly as possible, Bray was reached shortly before the hour named. This town was found to be already in the occupation of the 3rd Division, and here also the greater part of A Squadron was found, having received orders to carry out a task almost identical to that of B Squadron. The two squadrons therefore joined forces in order to work together, and perform their allotted duties as much as possible in company.

The 2nd Division had left their billets very early in the morning, but did not reach Mons until about midday. At this time the real situation was not understood, and it appeared that the 3rd Division was already in position in front of the 2nd, the latter Division was therefore ordered to billet where it was.

Before any action was taken further orders arrived, which directed the troops to move forward, and take up a position between the 1st and 3rd Divisions. The men were thoroughly tired by their long march on a hot day, over the unaccustomed *pavé* roads, and were quite exhausted before ever they reached the battlefield. B Squadron after a short halt to breathe the horses, marched in company with a few men of A Squadron to Villers St. Ghislain, where about 8 a.m. they took up a position. Patrols were pushed forward to hold the bridges at Obourg, Havré and Thieu.

These positions were taken up without any difficulty, but shortly afterwards the German advance commenced. The experiences of these advanced posts were almost identical. The enemy, in more or less close order, advanced against the bridges, only to be met by the fire of the men holding them.

The Hussars were at first delighted at the excellent targets their opponents offered, and at first imagined that they had a very easy task before them. But as a matter of fact the drama had only just commenced. For the enemy, after a short halt, once again advanced to the attack ; but this time in extended order, and supported by artillery. The attacking troops consisted of the 17th Jaeger Division. They advanced in a series of short rushes, supported by heavy covering fire.

The handful of men holding the bridges were soon driven from their positions, and about 11 a.m. fell back upon the rest of the squadron, in position about Villers St. Ghislain. The Germans did not delay very long in following up their initial success, and a strong column of all arms deployed against the village. Captain Nugent with the majority of B Squadron and a few men of A retired to a position on the high ground just south of Villers St. Ghislain, whilst Captain C. Nelson[1] remained with two troops to hold the village as long as possible.

The attack against the village now commenced, in the initial stages the Germans disdained the support of their artillery, but they soon found that they were unable to advance against our rifle-fire ; they then rapidly brought up their guns, and renewed their attacks with the support of their artillery, which succeeded in clearing a path for the infantry.

The ground in front consisted of fields, which had just been harvested, and the cut corn, packed in stooks, covered the whole countryside. The enemy advanced in short rushes, taking every advantage of these corn stooks, which at any rate covered him from direct observation ; he thus soon built up a thick firing line, and Captain Nelson had to abandon the village.[2] The troops retired upon the rest of the squadron, who, as already narrated, were in position on the high ground south of the village. The small rise, which the handful of Hussars were now prepared to hold, proved to be a death trap, for the place had only been lightly entrenched by Belgian civilians, and at this time our men had with them no entrenching tools with which to improve the defences.

It was not very long before the whole position was smothered by enemy shells, the led horses stampeded, and the bicycles of the cyclist companies smashed to pieces. The Germans were enabled to bring up field guns, and fire over open sights, for at this time none of our own guns were in a position to offer any support. From all sides the hostile infantry advanced, and there was nothing for it but withdrawal. This was eventually

[1] Now Major C. Nelson, D.S.O

[2] In this action Second Lieutenant J. M. Tylee was killed, and thus the first officer of the 15th Hussars fell in battle.

effected, but not without great difficulty, for the men were almost pinned to the ground by the hostile fire. The squadron withdrew in scattered parties and the majority were collected at Harmignes. The led horses, after their stampede, had galloped to this place, where nearly all of them were recovered.

Whilst this engagement was taking place, Lieutenant C. H. Liddell with his troop had been sent to Bray, and so was not engaged with the rest of B Squadron. This detached troop, nevertheless, was also forced to fall back before the advance of the Germans, and joined the rest of the squadron before dark. When night fell, B Squadron collected at the ninth milestone on the Maubeuge–Mons road, and bivouacked in the open fields.

It is very difficult indeed to follow the actions of A Squadron during the Battle of Mons. For one reason the squadron was broken up into numerous small detachments, and for another, owing to the number of casualties which occurred later, there are few records available.

The 3rd Division was ordered to hold the outpost line in strength, and to resist the enemy's advance as long as possible. This task was a difficult one, because of the pronounced salient at Nimy, and the enclosed nature of the mining villages round Mons, with innumerable small cottages and buildings. Added to these difficulties of terrain the 3rd Division was asked to withstand the assault of the greater part of the German Forces arraigned against the British Army.

A Squadron received orders to reconnoitre the villages of Havré and Bray. Early in the morning of 23rd August, two troops under Captain R. P. Wells[1] started out on this mission ; Lieutenant C. M. Hoare's troop went to Havré, and Lieutenant J. C. Rogerson's to Bray.

Lieutenant Hoare soon met the enemy, and only extricated himself by hard fighting, falling back to the village of St. Symphorien, from which he was also summarily ejected by the enemy. Lieutenant Rogerson and his troop joined forces with B Squadron, and fought with them.

During the withdrawal of this squadron Lieutenant Rogerson was wounded, and was evacuated with others to the fortress of Maubeuge. When this place fell, he became a prisoner, and was sent to Germany.

As soon as it became apparent that Captain Wells and his men were in difficulties, the rest of A Squadron was sent to his support. This tiny reinforcement could not offer any material opposition to the hostile advance, and after suffering considerable

[1] Now Lieutenant-Colonel R. P. Collings-Wells, D.S.O., O.B.E.

losses, the remnants joined B Squadron at Villers St. Ghislain. Whilst this retirement took place Captain Wells fell wounded.

It was impossible to evacuate the wounded and those unable to move, as they lay scattered all over the stubble fields, and thus perforce they had to be left to their fate. Captain Wells was very lucky, for the place where he fell happened to be near the high road, he was picked up by a civilian car which was passing at the time. The kindly Belgians, in spite of the danger, carried him back to the British lines, and after terrible hardships he was evacuated to England.

Whilst the Hussars were fighting to hold the outpost line, and it must be owned without much success, the infantry arrived and took up their various positions. The German attacks increased in severity, and finally, after very severe fighting, the infantry in their turn were forced to retire. The salient at Nimy was at the best never very favourable, and as the enemy's pressure against it developed, it became apparent that the position was untenable. At about 1 p.m. orders were issued to evacuate this salient, and for the 3rd Division to occupy a position south of Mons.

The retirement was not effected without considerable fighting, and Lieutenant E. H. Rouse-Boughton with a proportion of A Squadron, found themselves engaged in a rear-guard action, which took place on either side of the Hyon–Mons road. As the shell-fire was particularly heavy about this spot, the led horses were found to be too exposed, and were sent away, the men joining the infantry and fighting entirely on foot. Towards dusk the enemy attacks ceased their pressure, and the fighting died down.

An effort was now made to collect the scattered details of A Squadron, but before many men had been assembled a fresh order was issued. It appeared that the enemy had pierced our line, and Lieutenant Rouse-Boughton was once again sent forward with the men who had been collected to the Bois de Haut, near Hyon, where one of our batteries was in danger of being surrounded. A brief fight took place in the darkness, but eventually the battery was safely brought out of action. It was not until far into the night that the various patrols and detachments of A Squadron assembled at Nouvelles.

At dawn the following morning the squadron was ordered to Frameries, but as a matter of fact, it was not until some time after daybreak on the 24th that the squadron reached this place, where the various scattered detachments rejoined.

Meanwhile, during the night, Captain O. B. Walker, who commanded A Squadron, had been despatched on a special mission. He was never heard of again, and his fate remained uncertain until the end of the war. Some time after the Armistice, his body was found, where he had been reverently buried by the enemy. That evening, as soon as it became evident that Captain Walker was missing, Lieutenant C. H. S. Whittle assumed command of A Squadron.

By nightfall on 23rd August C Squadron was in billets at Rouveroy. It had suffered few casualties, and had not been engaged to any great extent. B Squadron was bivouacked by the side of the road. Its casualties had been fairly heavy, but the squadron as a whole was intact. A Squadron was collecting at Nouvelles, and the men were very scattered, the various detachments coming into headquarters during the night.

It is now necessary to return to the chronicle of what took place with C Squadron on the right of the British Army.

The men had only just settled into billets, when about 10 p m. on the 23rd orders were received for two officers' patrols to proceed forthwith and reconnoitre the movements of the German troops, and report at daybreak in what direction they were moving. In compliance with these orders Lieutenant F. A. Nicolson and Lieutenant the Honourable E. Hardinge moved up the Binche–Givry road, passed through our outpost line, and as soon as day broke proceeded towards the enemy positions, in an attempt to carry out their mission. Lieutenant Hardinge with his troop reached the village of Estinne au Mont, where he was enabled to hide his men and horses in the cottages, whilst he himself with a few picked men climbed into the steeple of the village church.

From this point of vantage they obtained an excellent view of the German troops as they broke up their bivouacs at daybreak. They could see the hostile infantry forming up, and marching away in a north-westerly direction, and were enabled to report on the position and movements of the artillery and cavalry. During this reconnaisance a squadron of German cavalry entered the village, but luckily failed to detect the presence of the British troops. The enemy left a few cavalrymen in the village to guard the roads, and the rest of the squadron formed up in a hollow north of the village, whence patrols were sent out to watch the movements of the British Army. At this juncture in the proceedings Lieutenant Nicolson and his troop, on their way back from their reconnaissance, passed through Estinne au Mont, and came in contact with the German troopers. A few shots were exchanged and the Germans galloped off to join their own squadron. The two troops of Hussars were now enabled to withdraw without difficulty. The information which Lieutenant Hardinge had obtained was of vital importance and he was awarded the D.S.O. for this fine performance.

During the night orders were received for the retreat of the British Army. These orders, as far as the I Corps was concerned, came as a terrible surprise. The corps had so far not been very heavily engaged, and on those occasions when our men met the enemy, the result had always been in our favour. Yet the orders were to retreat, and most inexplicable these orders seemed at the time. All ranks comforted themselves with the thought that the retrograde movement was in accordance with some elaborate military manœuvre, and did not signify anything in the nature of a real retreat.

By 4.30 a.m. on 24th August, C Squadron was in position, covering the rear guard of the 1st Division. The patrols on the right were privileged to watch the attack of the German forces against the French rear guards. They watched the movements of the enemy from very close quarters, and when the retreat commenced they found themselves isolated ; it was only with some difficulty, and after a certain amount of galloping, that they were enabled to extricate themselves from their position, and rejoined the squadron.

The rear guard of the 1st Division was not pressed, the Uhlan patrols constantly felt all along the line, but never actually closed in any strength. The division was therefore enabled to fall back slowly and unhampered. The retreat continued past the outer forts of Maubeuge, which at the time seemed to offer a wonderful haven of refuge, and about 7.30 p.m. C Squadron reached its billets at Feignies.

The orders for the retreat also came as a great surprise to B Squadron, in bivouac at the side of the road.

Before dawn patrols were out in front of the rear guard of the 2nd Division, and throughout the day were employed in the uncongenial task of covering a retreat. The route of the division led across the old battlefield of Malplaquet to Audignies. Although the enemy did not interfere to any great extent with this retreat, it was not until long after midnight that the tired men were enabled to snatch a few hours' rest.

It is true the 2nd Division had not so far been very heavily engaged, but the men had marched and dug, and marched and dug again, until all were almost exhausted. Large numbers of the men were already footsore, owing to the *pavé* roads, over which they had not been accustomed to march. By midnight, 24th August, C Squadron was billeted at Feignies and B Squadron at Audignies, both squadrons were tired but otherwise intact.

With A Squadron matters had not gone at all well on this day. As the 3rd Division at the Battle of Mons had been forced to meet a far heavier attack on the part of the enemy than either of the two divisions of the I Corps, it was natural that A Squadron had suffered in consequence heavier casualties than the other squadrons.

It is true that owing to the pressure of the enemy the 3rd Division had been forced to give ground, and that during the night Germans had occupied Hyon, but all ranks felt that the enemy had suffered severely for his temerity, and were confident that they could hold on to their new positions indefinitely. It was therefore with bitter disappointment and surprise that orders were received for the division to abandon its positions and to retreat.

The 3rd Division retreated in two columns, one marching by Genly and the other by Eugies. The right column of the Division was in touch with the 2nd Division, but between the left column and the 5th Division there was a considerable gap, as this division marched west of the Bois de Montroeul. A Squadron received orders to bridge this gap, and to open up communication between the 3rd and 5th Divisions during their retirement. In accordance with these orders, A Squadron marched at 8.30 a.m. from Frameries to near Blangies. A report was received that the 5th Division was retiring on Athies. Lieutenant Whittle therefore ordered Lieutenant E. Rouse-Boughton with his troop to proceed direct to this place, and get in touch with the 5th Division. This troop, after two encounters with the hostile cavalry, succeeded in reaching the town, and in gaining touch with the 5th Division. Primed with all the latest information they returned to rejoin their own division, which they succeeded in doing just before evening. When they reported to the Headquarters of the 3rd Division, they were informed that the rest of the squadron had been practically annihilated.

Shortly after Lieutenant Rouse-Boughton's troop had left for Athies, the remainder prepared to follow in the same direction, but at this moment the flanking patrols galloped in, with the information that strong parties of hostile cavalry were on the move in all directions. A further reconnaissance, however, showed that directly our Hussars appeared the enemy patrols retired into the village of Blangies, and were seen to pass through this village and collect in Offignies, which hamlet was a continuation of the larger village. Whilst the patrols were collecting this information, the squadron moved towards the enemy, and halted in a small wood near Blangies. The inhabitants, escaping from the villages, as they passed by the squadron waiting in readiness, confirmed the information brought in by the patrols. The maps issued at the time did not show clearly that Blangies and Offignies were in fact one village, and it appeared therefore quite feasible to gallop the former place.

All ranks were filled with the greatest desire to meet the enemy with cold steel ; Lieutenant Whittle gave the order to draw swords, the squadron formed line of extended files, and galloped for the village of Blangies. As was anticipated, the place was not held by the enemy. When the enthusiastic horsemen reached the edge of the village, it was found necessary to alter the formation in order to proceed down the main street, for the houses were surrounded by enclosed gardens, the squadron therefore formed column of fours, and galloped through the village. On reaching the northern edge, it was found that the street continued, and that it was quite impossible to deploy. Nevertheless, the excited column continued to sweep on, until the leading files reached a barricade which had been erected across the village street. A check now ensued, when suddenly from the surrounding houses a deadly machine-gun-fire was opened upon the unfortunate squadron. Caught in an ambush, escape was impossible, and the men were shot down in the narrow street like rats in a trap. In a few seconds the road became blocked by fallen men and horses. Here and there a few men were enabled to leap the barricade and gallop on towards Offignies, but the enemy had a second barricade behind their first, which accounted for those who escaped.

Sergeant F. Hannam, who saw what had happened, was enabled to check a few men of the rear troop, and with them took cover behind some houses, and later these few were able to withdraw, but the squadron had suffered so severely that to all intents and purposes it ceased to exist. Lieutenants Whittle and Hoare both fell at the head of their men. Sergeant Hannam retired with the survivors to Bavai, where Lieutenant Rouse-Boughton, the only officer left alive, took over the command of the remnants.

In order to avoid needless repetition it may be as well to describe how the three squadrons of the 15th Hussars carried out their duties during the great retreat. Although each day brought new situations and fresh complications, the method of performing the rôle of divisional cavalry to the rear guard was always more or less the same.

At least one troop remained at divisional headquarters, as escort to the G.O.C. The signal companies were also supplied with orderlies. The remainder formed a thin screen between the enemy and the infantry rear guard. Their duty was to prevent this rear guard from surprise. Reconnaissance entails dispersion, and fighting means concentration. The squadron leaders therefore always tried to keep a small formed body together, as a rallying point for the patrols, and to use for fighting if this became necessary.

Long before daylight on 25th August, the long columns of the British Army continued their retreat. The enemy was quickly on the heels of the rear guards. But luckily for the

AUGUST 1914

Expeditionary Force, the Germans suffered under a delusion, for their higher commanders imagined that the British were retiring on to the Channel Ports. This misconception was a great boon to us, and strangely influenced the movements of the enemy, who never closed very vigorously with our rear guards, and at first felt his way forward in the wrong direction.

The retreat was nevertheless carried out with some difficulty, as the roads were all blocked by French Territorial troops, who had become involved in the general retirement. The very large number of refugees, who crowded every road and lane, caused even greater delay, and their presence was most trying for the troops. The problem of the civil population, in full flight before an invasion, had never been considered on manœuvres.

The fighting troops were thus delayed for hours, whilst along the roads there filed a sad and piteous procession. Whole families fleeing from their homes, with their household goods stacked on vehicles of every description. Young and old, healthy and infirm—all trudged along the roads leading south.

The spectacle of the inhabitants fleeing from the enemy must have been familiar enough in all wars of the past, as indeed it became in this last great war. But familiarity did not breed contempt, and this sight never failed to bring home to all ranks the real horror of war and of invasion.

C Squadron with its patrols covered the retirement of the rear guard to the 1st Division, which on this day, 25th August, was found by the 1st Guards Brigade ; nothing worthy of record took place, and towards evening the squadron was ordered to retire to Taisnieres, and there spend the night. On its way it picked up a long column of transport, which consisted of waggons, limbers and led horses, belonging to every unit of the division, and included the whole of its own baggage.

During manœuvres at home in England, it had often been found that when the divisional cavalry returned to its bivouacs after dark it was fired upon by its own outpost line, and special precautions were therefore taken to guard against such an accident. This night the squadron passed safely through the outpost line, and continued its march without any thought of danger to its destined bivouacs. As in the darkness the long column of horsemen and transport approached Taisnieres, a heavy and unexpected fire was opened upon them. In a few moments the whole of the transport stampeded, and the greatest confusion ensued ; the mistake was soon discovered, and the fire ceased, but not before considerable damage had been caused. The reason for this incident was not far to seek. During the retreat parties of Uhlans had broken through the rear guards and had threatened the flanks of the columns. Even divisional headquarters had been menaced by the presence of the ubiquitous German cavalry, and had been forced to defend themselves. In consequence every unit had been ordered to arrange for its own protection during the night, and it was the outpost line, put out for the protection of the G.O.C. and headquarters staff, which had fired on the squadron as it returned to its bivouacs for the night.

Earlier in the day, as soon as it became apparent that the hostile cavalry was through our lines, Captain A. Courage[1] had

[1] Now Brigadier-General A. Courage, D.S.O., M.C. (Colonel of 15th Hussars).

collected a small body of men from the squadron with the object of protecting divisional headquarters. This escort had some fighting with the enterprising hostile patrols, but drove them off.

In the darkness it was found impossible to collect the scattered transport, which had to be abandoned. It must be owned that during the night there was a certain amount of confusion. Reports and rumours of an alarming nature were circulated, which at the time seemed hardly credible, but which had in them a certain modicum of truth, for the situation at the time was, to say the least, rather grim.

The bivouacs which C Squadron was enabled to occupy at this hour of the night were utterly horrid, and the squadron was not too cheerful.

On 25th August the 2nd Division continued the retreat under the same conditions as the 1st Division. The rear guard was found by the 6th Infantry Brigade, covered by B Squadron.

The greater part of the route of this retreat led past the Forêt de Mormal, and B Squadron found it a very difficult task to reconnoitre this wood, and in consequence was forced to break up into numerous small detachments, in order to watch the rides and paths which intersected the forest. Once clear of it, the squadron was able to concentrate at Pont sur Sambre, and fall back as a unit on Noyelles. No sooner was this place reached than orders were received to occupy the bridges round the town of Maroilles, and to hold these bridges until relieved by the infantry.

In the darkness, and with tired men, it was very difficult to make adequate arrangements for the defence of these bridges. Captain the Hon. W. A. Nugent took a troop to the bridge nearest the town, and Lieutenant G. H. Straker[1] was sent to hold the one just north-west of Maroilles. About 8 p.m. the enemy commenced an attack in some force against both these bridges. These attacks were pressed with determination, and at the spot occupied by Captain Nugent the Germans brought up artillery, and their guns opened fire at the closest range upon the men holding the position. The bridge was approached by a long causeway, and it was found impossible to take cover from the storm of shells. The men hung on grimly for a short time, but finally, under the combined fire of artillery and machine guns, they were forced to abandon the position. The enemy at once occupied the bridge, and was thus enabled to cross the canal. The position of Lieutenant Straker's troop further to the west was thus rendered most precarious, as his

[1] Now Major G. H. Cradock, M.C.

flank was turned. Private Price plunged into the canal, and by swimming down it, avoided the Germans, and reached Lieutenant Straker, whom he warned of his danger.[1] The troop was thus enabled to withdraw before being entirely surrounded.

The loss of these bridges was considered at the time most serious, and during the night numerous attempts were made by the infantry to recapture them. Every effort failed, for the Germans were very strongly posted and in spite of the most heroic endeavours repulsed every attack. Although the efforts of the infantry were not crowned with success, the enemy retired from the positions he had gained before dawn. The German histories have not explained the reason for this retirement, and it was lucky for the 2nd Division that the enemy never took advantage of the success he had achieved.

So far as B Squadron was concerned, this engagement had without doubt proved a failure. The discomforted Hussars fell back on to Maroilles, where they spent what was left of the night by the roadside.

Whilst this fight was taking place about the bridges near Maroilles, the Germans were also attacking our outpost line about Landrecies, which was held by the 4th Guards Brigade. The result was naturally never in question, for at this spot the enemy met the flower of our Army and experienced in consequence a great defeat. The roar of this battle could be heard by the squadron throughout the night.

The 3rd Division on the left of the I Corps continued the retreat in two columns, the right by Villereau to Audincourt and the left by Solesmes to Caudry ; but A Squadron was by this time hardly in a position to afford it much support, the disaster of the day before had left it lamentably weak, and only able to find a few patrols and an escort to the G.O.C. By 3 a.m. on 25th these columns were on the march, and a few patrols from A Squadron covered their rear guards.

It was not until long after dark that the tired units of the 3rd Division struggled into their bivouacs and billets, after a most trying time. During the whole of their retreat the enemy was close on their heels, and in the effort to escape the troops had a very long and exhausting march. The men of the 15th Hussars were never seriously engaged, but the patrols were in constant touch with those of the enemy, and skirmishing continued throughout the day.

Of this division there were in fact many men who obtained no respite at all, for without any rest they found themselves involved the next day in the Battle of Le Cateau. About mid-

[1] For this act of gallantry Private Price was awarded the D.C.M.

night A Squadron halted for a short time in a field near the town of Le Cateau.

The night of 25–26th August was for all ranks of the 15th Hussars one of great uneasiness, for no one knew exactly what had happened, and all feared that our outpost line had been pierced, and that the British Army was in a position of great danger. It can thus be well imagined that during the hours of darkness there was a certain amount of agitation, and little sleep for anyone. During the whole night it poured with rain, which added considerably to the other discomforts.

On 26th August the I Corps on the right continued the retreat without much difficulty. Both C and B Squadrons were on the move long before dawn, resuming once again their task with the rear guards. B Squadron marched to Landrecies. This place showed the effects of the fighting which had taken place during the night, but the squadron entered an empty and deserted town. Throughout the day both squadrons fell back slowly : C Squadron to Oisy and B Squadron to Etreux. This retirement was not altogether peaceful, for the rear guards were constantly engaged with the enemy, whose patrols at this time displayed the most discomforting initiative.

One incident which took place on this day impressed upon all ranks the fact that the military situation could not be too favourable. The supplies were dumped on the side of the road, and as the men passed, they were told to take what they wanted from these dumps, and the rear guards had orders to burn what was left. This method of issuing rations was quite a new one to all ranks, and it indicated only too clearly that all was not well with the British Expeditionary Force.

This order to burn the large accumulation of stores left behind during the retreat produced perhaps a slight feeling of depression. It was therefore inevitable that the 15th Hussars were not in the best of spirits when they marched into their bivouacs. The 5th Cavalry Brigade had been in rear of the I Corps during this march, and in consequence the squadrons were relieved of much of their duties, so on the whole they had an easy day.

The 15th Hussars played but a small part at the Battle of Le Cateau, and it is therefore hardly necessary to give a very detailed account of the action. Nevertheless, A Squadron formed part of one of the divisions who fought in this historic battle, and their movements must be recorded.

Le Cateau was perhaps one of the most important engagements ever fought by the British Army, for it was one in which a portion of the Regular Army was forced to turn at bay, and fight most desperately for its very existence. This battle has already been written about and discussed in many pamphlets and books; but to those who were with the II Corps during the retreat, it seemed inevitable that the time had come when they were forced to face the Germans and fight.

The pressure of the enemy upon the rear guards had become so great that it was found impossible to continue the retreat; the II Corps therefore halted, turned about, and fought on the Audencourt–Caudry position.

After a very severe bombardment, the enemy attacked with the greatest determination, but as far as the 3rd Division was concerned, the attack failed everywhere. On the flanks of the division, however, certain units had been forced to give ground, and in consequence the division was compelled to conform to their movements, and during the afternoon had to break off the engagement and retire.

It has always been found very difficult to withdraw from a battle with order and decency, nevertheless the units of the 3rd Division were enabled to extricate themselves. A portion of the covering troops failed to receive the orders for the retirement, and hung on to their positions until they were isolated; they continued to fight and were eventually annihilated.

The majority of the division withdrew from the battlefield and retired to Beaurevoir, where they spent the night. A Squadron did not play an important rôle during the battle, for the majority only guarded the divisional train. Numerous patrols were engaged, and became involved in the general fighting. As no records exist it has been impossible to narrate their adventures. Some time after dark A Squadron bivouacked for the night near Jeancourt.

C Squadron of the 15th Hussars was the one which so far had been the least seriously engaged, but on 27th August the rear guard of the 1st Division became involved in a severe fight with the enemy, and in this encounter C Squadron played a fairly conspicuous part.

Long before dawn the men were all in their battle positions, the rear guard to the 1st Division being found on this day by the 1st Guards Brigade. No sooner had the patrols from the squadron moved forward towards the enemy's night bivouacs than they discovered that the Germans were advancing in considerable strength, and closing in on all sides upon the rear guards.

Shortly after the sun rose, C Squadron was distributed along the whole front of the 1st Guards Brigade, with a strong detachment at Chapeau Rouge, another with the Munster Fusiliers at Fesmy, and a third with the flank guard, which operated between the 1st Division and the French. These latter consisted mainly of territorial troops, who had retreated with a speed which was much more rapid than that of the 1st Division, and were by this time many miles south of the British rear guards. The right of the 1st Guards Brigade was therefore completely in the air.

The reserve troops of the squadron were sent to protect both flanks, and by 9.30 a.m. the whole of the squadron, together with all the Cyclists, were strung out in the form of a thin screen between the rear guards and the enemy.

Lieutenant Stanhope and his troop were on the left, and his patrols very soon became involved with the enemy. The German cavalry, which covered the advance of the infantry columns, was no match for our men, when it came to dismounted action. Near Ribeauville two small detachments of 15th Hussars, under Corporals Durnford and Appleton, held up the German cavalry for some considerable time, until in fact the infantry arrived, brought up in motor lorries, and forced these two small detachments to retire.

By 10 a.m. all the patrols from C Squadron had been driven in. The enemy now deployed in some strength, and thick lines of infantry advanced across the fields against our positions, supported by the fire of their guns. As soon as the Germans discovered that the opposition to their front was too strong for them, they began to envelop our flanks, and pressed with remarkable determination upon our right flank, against which they advanced through the woods of La Queue de Boue, whence they even threatened for a short time the corps headquarters. By midday the whole of the rear guard was fiercely engaged.

The strenuous opposition offered by the 1st Guards Brigade thoroughly fulfilled the duties of a rear guard, for the remainder of the division were enabled to make good their retreat, and at 1.30 p.m. orders were issued for the rear guard to break off the action and retire. It is well known that one of the most difficult operations in war is to break off an engagement, once the troops have become thoroughly involved. Nevertheless three battalions of the Guards Brigade were enabled to shake themselves free of the enemy and retreat.

Unfortunately the motor cyclist who was conveying the order to the Royal Munster Fusiliers was killed, and the order never reached this battalion, which was fighting about the villages of Fesmy and Bergues, on the extreme right flank. Upon the retirement of the rest of the 1st Guards Brigade, this gallant battalion was left isolated and alone, to bear the brunt of the

German attack, which later proved to have been launched by the whole of the advance guard to a German Army. So far the 1st Division had never had a real fight with the enemy, although they had been in retreat for several days, and all ranks were filled with the most ardent desire to try conclusions with the Germans. Although there can be little doubt that the Munster Fusiliers were well aware of the retirement of the rest of the rear guard, they were determined in the absence of orders to fight on. These brave Irishmen therefore refused to budge, and without direct orders to the contrary, no other course could be expected from their gallant commander, Major P. A. Charrier.

As the battle developed, and the cavalry patrols were driven in, Major F. C. Pilkington[1] collected the squadron together, so much of them as he was able, and formed up under cover in rear of the infantry, there to await further developments.

Brigadier-General I. Maxse,[2] the commander of the rear guard, as soon as it became apparent that the Munster Fusiliers were in danger of envelopment, asked Major Pilkington to do what he could with the squadron to extricate the battalion, whilst the rest of the brigade continued the retreat.

The squadron leader therefore sent out three patrols, to gain touch with the Munsters, and discover what their situation actually was. These patrols were unable to carry out their mission, as the battalion was almost hemmed in. Nevertheless, although it appeared that the party of the Munsters in Fesmy were completely surrounded, there was still hope of saving those in Bergues, for about this place there still existed a small gap, where the enemy had not yet completely effected their envelopment, and if only this gap could be kept open long enough, it was possible that some of the battalion might escape through it.

The greater part of the squadron therefore dashed for this gap and a fierce fight now ensued at the outskirts of Bergues. The men galloped into action at the closest range, and attacked the enemy with fierce determination. The Germans were surprised at this sudden onslaught, and a few men of the squadron entered the village. The Munster Fusiliers were thus enabled to withdraw, covered by the fire of the dismounted troopers. Sergeant Papworth, who commanded the Hussars at this spot, exhibited the greatest skill and gallantry in carrying out this difficult operation, and he was awarded the D.C.M. for his action.

It was now a question of holding on long enough to enable the Munsters to get away, 170 of whom had retired from the village. For a short time a fight took place at close quarters,

[1] Now Lieutenant-Colonel F. C. Pilkington, D.S.O.

[2] Now General Sir Ivor Maxse, K.C.B., D.S.O., C.V.O.

whilst the infantry made good their escape. As soon as this was accomplished the withdrawal was ordered, but the firing line had a most difficult task in extricating themselves and reaching their horses, and the few devoted men who covered this withdrawal were all either killed or captured; the majority were however enabled to reach their horses, and gallop clear of the enemy. In this action Lieutenant the Hon. E. Hardinge, D.S.O., who was most gallantly leading his men, fell mortally wounded at the head of his troop.

About 3 p.m. the greater part of the squadron were collected at Oisy, where a number of men of the 4th Hussars who had lost their regiment put themselves under the orders of Major F. C. Pilkington.

About this time the enemy commenced to make a flank movement by Villers-les-Guise, which threatened the retreat of the squadron. Captain Courage took the men of the 4th Hussars and some men of the 1st and 2nd Troops to ward off this attack. He succeeded in checking the advance of the enemy, and by 3.30 p.m. the squadron fell back, fighting a rear-guard action the whole way, until about 7 p.m., when it reached a ridge near La Mont Rouge, north of Lesquielles. The enemy, still fighting with the Munster Fusiliers, did not press the squadron after this point was reached, and its withdrawal was continued unmolested. About 11.50 p.m. the tired men marched to a bivouac near Origny Ste. Benoite.

At the time the loss of the greater part of the Royal Munster Fusiliers seemed a terrible disaster, but it is probable that the action of this battalion saved the 1st Guards Brigade from a most difficult position, for the enemy were trying to force a wedge between the rear guard and the main body. Although many German battalions were engaged, they all seemed fascinated by the battle surging round the Munsters, and closed in upon this battalion from all sides, without seriously threatening the rest of the rear guard, and as late as 7 p.m. the Irishmen were still holding out in Fesmy.

The squadron could see that the Germans had brought up their artillery to surround our infantry, and had batteries in position facing north, with their backs to the retreating British, in action against this battalion.

The men of C Squadron were very tired when they struggled into bivouac about midnight—a bivouac which proved only to be a wet field by the side of the canal; they were only able to snatch a brief moment of rest, for by 3 a.m. the squadron was once again on the move.

Except for this bitter rear-guard engagement, the 1st Division was able to carry out its retirement unhampered by the enemy. On its left the 2nd Division also escaped unmolested.

B Squadron found the usual patrols for the rear guard, which marched in two columns, one by Venerolles and Bernot, and the other by Guise to Mont Origny. On arrival at their bivouacs there was a rumour that St. Quentin had been occupied by the enemy. This would have placed the division in a very difficult position. In consequence the squadron had no rest during the night, being employed on outpost duty, whilst the division entrenched. As a matter of fact, the rumour was quite unfounded, but it had the result that the already tired troops were deprived of their night's rest.

As has already been narrated, the 3rd Division having managed to shake itself clear of the enemy after the Battle of Le Cateau continued its retreat on the 27th. A Squadron detailed a few patrols with the rear guard, and these had a certain amount of fighting with the enemy. The squadron, however, reached Ham without any incident worth recording, and bivouacked there for the night.

By this time there was a certain amount of confusion in the Expeditionary Force. Numerous small parties of men, belonging to every unit of the Army, were wandering about with all sense of direction lost, and quite in ignorance as to what had happened to their units.

There were many cavalry troopers among them, some of the 15th Hussars who had lost their horses, and wandering about on foot, joined the nearest infantry battalion, with whom they fought and in some cases were killed. On the other hand, there were a certain number of infantrymen (ex-mounted infantry) who had found spare horses, and mounting them took their place in the ranks of the cavalry. It was not until the Battle of the Aisne settled down to trench warfare that these men were sorted out, and sent back to their own regiments.

To those who took part in the Retreat, the situation at the time appeared grim and ominous. The spirit of the men was excellent, and although many were dispersed and scattered in all directions, every unit, however tiny, clung together, and all ranks were still full of fight.

The 28th August dawned with a clear sky and a fierce sun, and the Army continued the retreat. The enemy did not impede the retirement on this day, nevertheless the march was most tiring and exhausting to the troops. All day long the pitiless sun beat down on the toiling columns. The men were parched with thirst, and choked by dust. The march was also very much hampered by the interminable stream of inhabitants, fleeing from the invasion, who blocked every road, and whose presence was anything but inspiring.

The three squadrons each found their usual quota of patrols to the rear guards, and were engaged on nothing more serious than a continual bicker with the enemy, but the hostile patrols never closed on our rear guards with any determination. It was not until very late at night that the tired troops reached their billets—C Squadron at St. Gobain, B Squadron at Servais, and A Squadron near Pontoise.

For the reader of this account of the doings of the 15th Hussars it will probably be most difficult to realise after the lapse of time how exhausted everyone had become at this stage of the retreat. Accounts of battles and of marches, written some time afterwards, do not adequately portray the real physical and mental strain which they entailed. In addition, all ranks were quite ignorant of the real situation, and to them it appeared at the time that the British Army was left alone to stand the brunt of the enemy attacks, attacks launched in every case in overwhelming force.

It can therefore hardly be a matter of surprise that everyone experienced a feeling that can best be described as bewilderment at the course the campaign was taking, and a feeling of exasperation at the continued retreat, which gave the troops no opportunity of showing their real metal against the enemy.

When the orders were issued for a halt on the 29th they were received with the profoundest relief, for this was the first day's leisure which any one had enjoyed since landing in France.

In nine days the men had marched about 200 miles, and a rest was in reality most urgently needed. The majority of the horses had not been unsaddled since the Battle of Mons, and all equipment needed a thorough cleaning and overhaul. The morning was in consequence a very busy one for everybody: every article of equipment was cleaned and repaired as quickly as the time allowed; the waggons were unpacked, and the loads readjusted; the horses were shod up, and all traces of the wear and stress of the last few days were, as far as possible, removed. But towards the afternoon it appeared that the welcome rest was not to be of long duration, for urgent orders arrived that all the wagons were to be repacked immediately, and the transport to be sent to the rear. Furthermore, strong patrols were ordered forward at once. C Squadron occupied the bridges at La Fère, with cavalry and cyclists. B Squadron pushed out patrols in front of the outpost line; these detachments soon came in touch with strong reconnoitring parties of the enemy, who rapidly drove them back on to our outpost line. This outpost line was not continuous, and there were large gaps in it, through which the enemy could have advanced if he had made the effort.

A Squadron was also disturbed during its rest, and about midday marched to Cuts, where, however, the night was passed undisturbed.

The retreat was resumed at 4.30 a.m. on 30th August. It is true that the day's rest had been a godsend to all ranks, but many found on resuming the march that they were remarkably stiff and sore, and this march was perhaps the most tiring of all. The day was exceptionally hot, and clouds of dust choked the unfortunate infantrymen as they toiled along the *pavé* roads leading towards the south ; many were quite unable to continue the march, and were forced to fall out. As the rear guard troops came upon these unfortunate individuals, they did all in their power to make them move. The Hussars dismounted and the infantry packs were loaded upon the horses. In some cases the exhausted men were hoisted on to the troop horses, and in this way as many soldiers as possible were saved from falling into the hands of the enemy. C Squadron about 6 p.m. reached the chateau at Pinon, where it was billeted for the night. This castle was one of the most magnificent in France, and the squadron was most sumptuously housed, but unfortunately on this night the transport failed to arrive, and in consequence there were no supplies and no food. Something to eat and a less gorgeous billet would have been more appreciated.

By some mischance B Squadron received no orders in the morning, but the sight of the infantry battalions forming up and marching away, made it quite clear what was taking place. The squadron therefore without further orders slipped into its place with the rear guard. The orders at first issued detailed the 2nd Division to retire south of Soissons, but the men were so exhausted that it was found impossible to carry out the full march.

In consequence just before dark the division halted where it happened to be at the moment, and B Squadron spent the night at Coucy le Chateau.

A Squadron before dawn sent out patrols, and these remained in observation for some time, finally retiring on to the rear guard as the enemy advanced. The whole squadron crossed the Aisne and bivouacked during the night at Montoise, near Vic-sur-Aisne.

None of the three squadrons encountered the enemy in any force, and the rear guards were never seriously pressed.

The retreat on 31st August was almost a repetition of the march of the day before, hot, dusty and very tiring to all concerned. Towards the evening the I Corps crossed the Aisne.

The 1st Division passed over the river at Soissons. Whilst the bridge was being prepared for demolition, C Squadron remained on the far side, protecting the engineers whilst they carried out their mission. During this operation the enemy patrols moved cautiously forward, but never ventured too close. When all was ready our patrols galloped back across the bridge, and as soon as the last Hussar was safely over the bridge was blown up.

The transport horses of the squadron were now quite worn out by overwork ; but when the humble bivouac at Croix de Fer was reached, a French farmer was found who willingly handed over two fine cart-horses. These two horses proved to be most excellent, and remained with the squadron for a considerable time.

B Squadron crossed the Aisne at Pommiers, but not until late in the evening, and it was long after dark before the tired troopers could snatch a few hours rest at Cutry.

A Squadron had an uneventful day, although a tiring one, and eventually bivouacked at Vauciennes.

With the usual monotonous regularity the various patrols from the Regiment were in their positions by dawn on 1st September, and once again the weary columns began their march.

After the Expeditionary Force had left the mining country round Mons, the retreat had led across the usually peaceful and quiet agricultural countryside of France, which in this part consisted of rolling plains of unenclosed land, nearly every inch of which was devoted to cultivation. At this time of the year the crops were already cut and standing in stooks, and only awaited carting away. The country was thickly populated. Prosperous small towns and villages were to be found in large numbers. Interspersed between the villages were many rich chateaux and comfortable farms, and it seemed indeed a tragedy to abandon this rich and smiling country to the horrors of war and the ravages of invasion. As the rear guards retired from ridge to ridge, an excellent view could be obtained of the surrounding country ; and the patrols had no very difficult task to locate the advance of the enemy. For in the distance the sight of the burning farms and villages could clearly be discerned, thus the attack of the invading hosts was marked by fire and flame.

But on this day the route led through the woods about Villers Cotterets. The patrols with a certain feeling of anxiety entered the wood, and scouted up the rides and through the thick glades of the forest.

This feeling of uneasiness was not without foundation, for

about 10 a.m. the patrols from C Squadron reported that the enemy was advancing in some strength against the left of the 1st Division.

B Squadron had marched at 3 a.m. to Soucy, where the rear guard to the 2nd Division formed up, from there patrols were sent forward towards Chelles. Soon these patrols came tumbling back with the information that strong columns of the enemy, composed of all arms, were advancing against the rear guards. The enemy had very little difficulty in driving back the patrols from the 15th Hussars, and C Squadron retired on to the 1st Guards Brigade, whilst B Squadron also fell back on to their division.

The Germans shortly afterwards developed their attack. The full weight of it was directed against the 4th Guards Brigade, who were covering the retirement of the 2nd Division, but the rear guard of the 1st Division on their right also became engaged. It seemed almost incredible that the enemy could have closed so quickly, for at dawn our patrols had seen no sign of them south of the Aisne, and this sudden arrival of the Germans was as disturbing as it was unexpected. But apparently, as far as the enemy was concerned, the encounter was also more or less a chance one.

The force which met the I Corps was composed of the cavalry of Von Marwitz's 9th Division, and of infantry of the III Corps, brought up in motor lorries ; they were not actually directed against our I Corps, but were making a flank march, when they stumbled against the British rear guards.

Fighting now took place at close quarters in the depth of the forest. The 4th Guards Brigade had taken up a position west of Rond de la Reine, and here the battle was extremely fierce. It became very difficult for the divisional cavalry to carry out its duties. The enemy guns fired down every ride over direct sights, and mounted men only moved with difficulty through the thick undergrowth and amongst the trees of the forest. The roar of the rifle-fire was absolutely deafening, and echoed amidst the trees, whilst leaves and twigs fell on all sides in a continual shower, brought down by the storm of lead which swept through the branches.

Never perhaps in the history of the British Army was the good shooting and the steady discipline of the rank and file more effective than on this day. The officer commanding the Irish Guards thought that the fire of his men was becoming too wild ; the " Cease Fire " was therefore sounded, and this order was instantly obeyed and not a shot was fired until the order to recommence was given, although at the moment the Germans were only a few yards away from the firing line. So steady and so well controlled was the fire discipline that the enemy were actually mown down like ripe corn. They imagined they had encountered machine guns, whereas it was the British private soldier and his rifle which had devastated the German ranks.

Whilst this fight was in progress C Squadron collected behind the firing line, and a section of artillery was attached to it. Their orders were that, in the event of the rear guard of the 2nd Division becoming too heavily engaged, they were to attack in order to relieve the pressure on this rear guard.

The squadron was never called upon, the 2nd Division extricated themselves without any difficulty—in fact, they left behind them a shattered and broken enemy.

As already narrated, the patrols of the 15th Hussars were flung back by the Germans. B Squadron in the same and identical manner as C Squadron retired through the infantry line, and re-formed behind the left flank of the Irish Guards.

Although both squadrons found themselves involved in a certain amount of skirmishing in the wood, the 15th Hussars were never very seriously engaged at Villers Cotterets.

The enemy attacks eventually failed. The 4th Guards Brigade were enabled to extricate themselves, and the rear guard of the 2nd Division retired through the 6th Infantry Brigade, which had taken up a position to cover this retirement. B Squadron conformed and fell back with the rear guard, after they had thrown out a screen of scouts, to cover the 6th Infantry Brigade.

This retirement began about 3.30 p.m. Patrols from C Squadron under Lieutenant Stanhope were still watching the enemy in the forest, but eventually they were ordered to retire. The whole of the rear guards thus withdrew without much difficulty. C Squadron about 7 p.m. took up a position at La Ferte Milon watching the Germans. At 11 p.m. they retired to Mareuil, when it was quite evident that the enemy was not advancing. In a similar manner B Squadron slowly retired to Antilly.

The men of both squadrons, by this time thoroughly tired, were only enabled to snatch a few moments' sleep under the trees, before they were once again on the move.

Whilst the I Corps was fighting this rear guard action in the woods about Villers Cotterets, the 3rd Division was enabled to continue the retirement without much difficulty, for in this part of the field the hostile pursuit seemed to have slackened considerably. A Squadron retired by Levingnen and Fresnoy to

Villers St. Genest ; the squadron was far too weak in numbers to take any active part in the operations, and the men reached their bivouacs without being seriously engaged.

The fight at Villers Cotterets was the last action of any importance to be fought during the Retreat from Mons.

Up to this time, it appeared to the members of the Expeditionary Force who were taking part in the Retreat, that the British Army had been left, alone and unaided, to withstand the whole weight of the German attack. But the reader must understand that at the time everybody was in absolute ignorance of the general situation, and only knew of what was taking place to their immediate front.

After 1st September all ranks realised that there was a subtle change in the whole atmosphere, and that somewhere in some place movements must be taking place which were altering the strategical situation, and which reacted on the enemy troops pressing our rear guards. The marches, although still long and tiring, were conducted with some consideration for the comfort and convenience of the troops. No longer were the men on the alert day and night, ready to turn out at any moment in order to retire before the advancing enemy, nor did overpowering columns of Germans continuously threaten to overwhelm the rear guards.

The 2nd September was a fairly quiet day, as far as the 15th Hussars were concerned. It is true that the various patrols bickered all day with the Uhlan detachments, but there was no real fighting.

The 1st Division retreated through Beauval, where the rear guard entrenched ; whilst this operation was taking place, C Squadron formed a line of observation facing the enemy. About 3 p.m. the retreat continued to Meaux, which place was reached just before the sun set. Patrols remained out far in advance of the outpost line until long after dark, when finally the last Hussars were withdrawn.

The day was quite uneventful for B Squadron, their retreat led through Etreux and Villenoy, and the squadron spent the night in a chateau near Chauconin.

A Squadron retired without any adventure to Monthyon.

The march on 3rd September can hardly be considered as a retreat, for the British Expeditionary Force in reality only closed up and readjusted the line.

The greater part of the army crossed the Marne on this day, and destroyed the bridges behind them as they passed over. The patrols from the 15th Hussars remained on the far side until the last moment, and when the Hussars had galloped back, there were a series of tremendous explosions, the bridges crumbled into dust and sank into the stream.

The 1st Division crossed at La Ferté sous Jouarre, and late that night C Squadron bivouacked at Le Grand Glairet. B Squadron marched through Meaux and Trilport to bivouacs about Les Lacquais.

A Squadron crossed the Marne at Meaux, and bivouacked at La Haute Maison.

A new difficulty now arose, and one which as a matter of fact had not been unforeseen. Although a large supply of maps was brought over from England, they did not include the country over which the squadrons were now working. The Regiment was bound to find numerous patrols, and it was essential that the leaders of these patrols should have in their possession maps of the country they were asked to reconnoitre. Maps were produced somehow—many torn from old railway guides—but for many days this shortage was a source of great difficulty, and very great embarrassment.

At an early hour on 4th September, the I Corps continued its march. Although many of the bridges over the Marne had been destroyed the night before, some had purposely been left intact. Before dawn, therefore, strong patrols of the Hussars, both from the 1st and 2nd Divisions, were sent to watch these untouched bridges, and to report directly the enemy attempted to cross them.

A patrol from C Squadron went to Mery. B Squadron sent patrols under Captain Nugent to Sammeron, Lieutenant Straker to St. Jean, and Lieutenant C. H. Liddell[1] to La Ferté.

Although at this latter place the bridge had been destroyed, in a remarkably short time the enemy succeeded in repairing it, and by 8.15 a.m. his advance guard commenced to cross. Some of the patrols sent out by both B and C Squadrons were very nearly captured, for the enemy crossed in their rear, by means of the bridge at La Ferté. It was only by hard galloping that the patrols escaped capture. The Uhlans were far more intent on looting the shops and houses in La Ferté than on pressing forward, and this gave the Hussars time to slip away.

The marches of the Expeditionary Force on this day were neither very long nor very tiring. The rear guards were never seriously pressed, as the enemy did not cross the Marne in very great numbers. Nevertheless there was a certain amount of skirmishing, and a patrol from C Squadron was enabled to prevent a wounded officer of the 20th Hussars from falling into the hands of the enemy.

C Squadron retired to Coulommiers. B Squadron remained

[1] Now Major C. H. Liddell.

in observations until 3 p.m., and then retired to Villeneuve Farm. Both these squadrons reached their billets at a comparatively early hour, and the men had a good night's rest.

The 3rd Division remained halted, except for some movements to readjust its line, and thus 4th September was a day of rest to most of the men of A Squadron. It was found necessary to send out a few patrols to reconnoitre in front of the outpost line, and patrols from both sides exchanged shots, but there was no real fighting. As soon as darkness set in, A Squadron fell back to La Chapelle, where it halted for a short time, and continued the retreat through the Forêt de Crecy.

The 5th September was the last day during which the British Army retired. As far as the I Corps was concerned the march was short and pleasant, the day was fine, there was no sign of the enemy, and billets were reached in good time.

C Squadron billeted at Rozoy, and B Squadron at Marles.

A Squadron had a certain amount of fighting on this day. The 3rd Division, after its night march, threw out the usual outpost line, and the patrols from the divisional mounted troops covered the position. Until 2.30 p.m. this duty was carried out by the Cyclist Company, the cavalry relieving them during the afternoon.

The patrols received orders to push forward as far as possible, and to act with boldness. The Hussars made every effort to carry out these orders. A small patrol from A Squadron, commanded by Sergeant Scarterfield, encountered a detachment of the enemy, which consisted of at least two squadrons. This detachment attacked at once, and by dismounted fire, combined with shock action, attempted to annihilate the tiny British patrol. There was nothing else to be done but to retreat, and the Hussars mounted their horses and galloped as hard as they could for safety. In jumping a small ditch the horse ridden by Sergeant Scarterfield fell, and the rider lay pinned underneath it. In spite of the heavy fire and the close proximity of the enemy, Corporal Garforth returned, extricated the sergeant from underneath his horse, placed him upon his own, and the pair escaped.

This was not the only gallant action performed by Corporal Garforth, for at the Battle of Mons, whilst A Squadron was falling back on to Villers St. Ghislain, a wire fence held up the retreat of the squadron. The enemy had placed machine-guns in such positions that they fired directly down this fence. In spite of this fact Corporal Garforth rushed forward and cut it in several places. Through the gaps he had thus created, his squadron were enabled to gallop to safety.[1] For these two acts of bravery Corporal Garforth was awarded the Victoria Cross. He was one of the first soldiers to be thus honoured during the war.

By this time A Squadron only mustered forty rifles all told. They fell back to Chartres, and bivouacked there for the night.

One of the effects of the fairly leisurely retirement of the past few days which was most appreciated was the fact that the men were enabled to indulge in a cooked meal from time to time. Cavalry have no cookers, and fires had to be lighted and the food prepared for the men after their arrival in bivouac or billet. But when troops do not reach their resting place until long after midnight, and are on the move again before daylight, tired men have no time for cooking. In consequence the 15th Hussars lived almost entirely on cold bully beef and biscuits, without even a cup of tea to cheer them.

THE RETREAT, 1914

[1] Lance-Corporal G. Ball dashed to the fence with Corporal Garforth, and helped to cut the wire. As Lance-Corporal G. Ball was taken prisoner shortly afterwards, this is the only place where his gallant action is recorded.

Chapter III

THE BATTLES OF THE MARNE AND THE AISNE

DURING the night of the 5th/6th September, the squadron leaders were summoned to their different headquarters, and the real situation was explained to the officers commanding the various units. This was the first time that subordinate officers were informed of the true state of affairs, or of what was taking place outside their immediate vicinity. To those persons privileged to take part at these conferences, the scene must always be a most dramatic memory. The situation of the German Army, the position of the French Armies, and the plans for the future were explained. A great and decisive battle was about to be fought. In tiny schoolhouses and small estaminets throughout the billets occupied by the Expeditionary Force, orders were issued, which made it clear to everyone the tremendous issues involved. So clear were the orders that the humblest soldier understood that he was about to engage in operations which would decide the fate of whole nations. Not a single man doubted the result of the great battle about to be fought.

The reader can well imagine with what delight the three squadrons heard that on the next day they were to advance, and that at length the British Army was to attack. As far as the I Corps was concerned, the last few days of easy marches had quite rested the men. Everyone was in the best of spirits, ready for the advance, and as fit as when they left Aldershot. The 3rd Division, it is true, had been involved in very severe fighting, had suffered heavily, and was more disorganised than the divisions of the I Corps, but the men's morale was in no way impaired, they were still eager for a fight, and were prepared to carry out any task allotted to them.

It was with light hearts and full of confidence that the three squadrons of the 15th Hussars marched forward at daybreak, to take up the various positions with the advance guards of their divisions.

In the earlier stages of the war it seemed inevitable that on Sunday something important was bound to happen. It therefore caused no surprise that it was upon a Sunday, 6th September, that the British Army turned about and advanced.

The movements of the three squadrons will now be described in detail.

The patrols from C Squadron were in position before dawn, when the advance from Rozoy commenced. The men had scarcely left the friendly shelter of the outpost line, when they encountered the hostile rear guards. The enemy at once opened a heavy fire of shrapnel, and machine-guns played along the whole front. The patrols were forced to gallop back behind cover.

The infantry columns which formed the advance guard, deployed into open order, and began an attack against the enemy positions. Unfortunately, for various reasons, the troops on either side of the 1st Division were not in a position to advance, and, in consequence, the 1st Division was ordered to halt. The advance guard therefore proceeded to entrench on either side of the Rozoy–Vaudoy road, on the ground which they had already gained. The patrols from C Squadron remained in front of the troops who were digging in, and continued to feel the enemy's position. This activity only led to increased shelling, so that later on, at the request of the infantry, the Hussars were withdrawn. Thus the 1st Division remained halted, awaiting further orders.

The adventures of one patrol from C Squadron are perhaps worthy of record. This patrol, commanded by Corporal Mackay, passed right through the German rear guards and got amongst an enemy column near the village of Le Plessis. It may seem incredible, but none the less it is a fact, that this patrol from the 15th Hussars actually marched along the same road and in company with the German troops, and was never discovered. They thus had ample opportunity of observing the enemy, and the handful of Hussars were enabled to make good their escape, and return to headquarters with the information. This information was naturally of vital importance. The major-general commanding the division personally congratulated the corporal, who later received his commission as an officer.

The 1st Division eventually received orders to advance, but it was not until 3 p.m., by which time the German rear guards had commenced to retire, covered by Jaeger cyclist battalions, and as soon as our patrols commenced to move forward, the grey-clad figures leapt to their feet, rushed to their bicycles, and hurried away as far as they could pedal.

C Squadron suffered but few casualties. The hostile shell fire had at times been very heavy, but it was confined chiefly to the roads, which mounted men could easily avoid. The cyclists on the other hand suffered somewhat more severely.

Vaudoy was reached about 7 p.m., where the squadron bivouacked, sending one troop out on outpost duty during the night.

To turn now to the 2nd Division, and follow the adventures of B Squadron.

The 2nd Division by dawn on 6th September was on the line Marles towards Lumigny, with the 4th and 5th Infantry Brigades in front, and the 6th Infantry Brigade in reserve about Charbuisson Farm.

The advance of this division was delayed, for it also had to await a forward movement of the troops on its left flank. B Squadron nevertheless received orders to break through the enemy rear guards, if they could, and to locate their main columns.

In accordance with these orders, the squadron advanced, covered by three strong patrols, and reached the vicinity of Pezarches. The enemy was found to be in considerable strength, and batteries of artillery were located about Touquin.

The 15th Hussars now engaged in a fight round about the village of Lumigny. The enemy contested every inch of ground, and B Squadron lost about fifty per cent. of men and horses without making any real headway. This fighting lasted till about 4.30 p.m., when the whole of the 2nd Division began a general advance. Directly the enemy rear guards saw the lines of infantry commence their forward movement, they broke off the action, and promptly retired. No very great advance could, however, be made before dark, and the division bivouacked on the line Pezarches–Touquin–Rigny. B Squadron bivouacked at Rigny.

The 3rd Division conformed to the general advance. They did not meet with any very formidable opposition. But the hostile rear guards fought obstinately, and made every effort to delay the forward movement.

A Squadron's numbers were so weak that they could scarcely do more than find a few patrols for the infantry advance guards. The day passed in continual skirmishing, and a slow advance. Towards evening the squadron was collected together, and received orders to billet for the night at Faremoutieres. As the advance patrols approached this village they were fired upon by the enemy. The squadron knew that this village was to be their billet for the night, and they were quite determined to occupy it. In consequence they engaged in a short scrimmage for their night's lodging, and eventually drove the Germans out of the village, and occupied the billets the Germans had just abandoned.

A Squadron did not spend a quiet night, for its patrols were ordered to keep touch with the German outpost line. During the night the Hussars and the enemy were continually exchanging shots and there was little rest for anyone. About midnight the cyclist company came up, and with the greatest gallantry rushed a bridge at the point of the bayonet, and thus gained a very important point for the operations on the following day.

The following account of the operations of the 15th Hussars will hardly convey to the reader the fact that the Regiment was engaged in one of the decisive battles of the world—the Battle of the Marne. In these pages it is scarcely possible, or perhaps desirable, to enter into the details which brought about the retreat of the Germans, nor to elaborate the strategy and tactics of the great battle. The plain unvarnished record of the movements of the 15th Hussars is all that can be chronicled. The majority of the British Army were at the time quite ignorant of the terrible struggle in which our French Allies were engaged on either flank, although the steady unending roar of the guns in the distance could be clearly heard.

There is an old aphorism, that the British never know when they are beaten. But this the German Higher Commanders had forgotten, and they imagined that the British Force had ceased to count as a fighting unit. They were entirely wrong. Obsessed by this idea, they only covered their retirement opposite the advance of our troops by a cavalry and cyclist screen and some Jaeger battalions. A screen which was, however, well provided with machine-guns and artillery. These rear guards were thus enabled to offer a considerable amount of resistance. In consequence the British Army at first made but slow progress.

It must be remembered that since the opening of the campaign our troops had performed no other movement but that of a continual retreat. To change directly from a retirement which seemed unending and inevitable to a vigorous advance, required a complete alteration of perspective, and this takes time to accomplish. It will thus be readily understood why the advance was at first both slow and cautious.

The British Expeditionary Force on 7th September resumed the advance along the whole front.

C Squadron on the right, as a matter of fact, had very little fighting. But the operations of the 2nd Troop of this squadron will show what a cavalry patrol can do when intelligently and boldly led.

This troop was sent forward about 10 a.m. with orders to seize and hold the cross roads about St. Eloi, and there await the arrival of the infantry advance guard. From the map this position appeared to be one of importance, and the patrols approached the cross roads with due caution. The scouts reported that the enemy was holding this tactical point and estimated his strength as a squadron of cavalry, dismounted and in position. The troop of the 15th dismounted and, crawling up unperceived to within decisive range, opened a sudden and accurate fire ; they made very short work of the German cavalry, whose led horses stampeded at the first discharge. The surviving men fled in all directions, only to fall victims to the British cavalry who were advancing on their flank.

It was a curious coincidence that the squadron of enemy cavalry belonged to the 4th German Hussars, and it was into the arms of the British 4th Hussars that they fell as they abandoned their position.

The troop of the 15th Hussars collected the majority of the enemy's led horses, all fully equipped and the best of these eventually took their places in the ranks of C squadron. They were all chestnuts, rather weedy, but all beautifully trained.

About midday the men were relieved by the infantry advance guard, but were, however, ordered to push forward to Choisy and to reconnoitre Jouy-sur-Morin. They moved forward without incident as far as Rebais, where they encountered the enemy in considerable strength, and were forced to retire back on to the squadron, which they rejoined without difficulty, together with all the patrols, about 5.30 p.m., and the squadron bivouacked at Choisy.

Whilst halted in this tiny village, the squadron for the first time received news as to what had happened to the rest of the Regiment. No real and authenticated information as to the operations of the flank divisions and the rest of the Army had so far reached the officers and men. Thus the plight of A Squadron was only known on this evening. Captain Courage was ordered to rejoin A Squadron and take over the command.

There is not very much to record about B Squadron on 7th September. It formed part of the advance guard to the 2nd Division and marched by Saints and Chilly. By dark the 2nd Division occupied a line La Vanne–St. Simeon–Les Grands Bordes, and B Squadron bivouacked at La Vanne.

A Squadron marched along the banks of the Grand Morin and through Coulommieres. One patrol, proceeding on reconnaissance duty, penetrated to a considerable depth amongst the enemy's columns, where it encountered two German motor lorries, making the best of their way back to the rear. Sergeant Lewis, who commanded the patrol, attacked the enemy at once. Unfortunately for the 15th Hussars, upon each lorry there was a machine gun, and with these the enemy opened fire upon the adventurous patrol. As can well be imagined the Hussars sustained considerable casualties. Corporal Garforth, already recommended for the V.C.,[1] took up a position under cover, and his rifle fire completely held up the German lorries in spite of their machine guns, and gave time for the wounded to be withdrawn.

Except for this encounter the squadron was not engaged, and billeted for the night at Coulommieres. The men were all tired but optimistic when they settled into the various billets and bivouacs that night.

At 4.30 a.m. on 8th September the Regiment was aroused from its slumbers, and once again the squadrons took up the march.

Both the 1st and 2nd Divisions experienced some difficulty in forcing the crossings of the Petit Morin. The German rear guards were liberally supplied with machine-guns. These were well hidden and very hard to locate, they caused considerable casualties and made it very difficult and costly to advance.

The 1st Division advanced on the right of the British Army ; a troop of C Squadron was as usual with the advance guard of this division. This troop (commanded by Lieutenant Stanhope) succeeded about 9 a.m. in crossing the Petit Morin at Bellot without much difficulty, but immediately came under very heavy fire from parties of the Germans, who were holding the high ground on the northern banks of the river.

A detachment of French cavalry had also succeeded in forcing the passage, joined in the combat, and vigorously attacked the enemy. Unfortunately the combined Allied cavalry patrols were not in sufficient strength to achieve any decisive result. Nevertheless they were enabled to pin the Germans to their position, and to locate in detail their strength and how they were disposed.

The leading battalion of the advance guard arrived very soon after the cavalry had become engaged. This was a battalion of the Black Watch, which so far had not suffered very severe casualties. The Germans never had a chance : how could they when opposed to this gallant regiment ? After an hour and a half of fighting the Germans were utterly routed, and left about fifty prisoners in our hands. This small batch of prisoners was the first capture of any importance to be made by the 1st Division in the campaign. Although the fight had been slight and unimportant, it nevertheless had a great moral effect. Everyone anticipated that the Germans would make a determined effort to hold the line of the Petit Morin, and the comparative ease in which this stream had been crossed raised the spirits of all ranks.

[1] See p. 38.

After this episode, a short march took the squadron to Flagny, where billets were reached about 7 p.m.

B Squadron formed part of the advance guard to the 2nd Division, which on this day was found by the 4th Guards Brigade. The march lay through Rebais to Le Tretoire. Hardly had the advanced troops entered this latter place, when shell after shell burst amongst them. They were under direct fire from enemy batteries posted on the high ground about Boitron.

In spite of the shell fire B Squadron determined to advance, but very soon came under the fire of machine guns, supported by enemy infantry, in occupation of roughly constructed trenches. It was impossible to continue the advance mounted. An attempt was therefore made to push forward dismounted. The hostile fire, however, was far too heavy, and in a short time the squadron found itself pinned to the ground unable to advance or to retire, and for a time its situation was uncomfortable in the extreme.

It was not long before the Guards Brigade arrived, the artillery of the advance guard unlimbered, the infantry deployed for battle, and in a short time a determined attack was launched against the hostile rear guard. The British artillery after a short but intense duel with the enemy guns drove them off the field. The German infantry proved to be most obstinate, and a fierce battle soon developed. B Squadron only played the part of spectators, except for the patrols it sent out on either flank. Although the Germans were not supported by their artillery, they refused to give way. In consequence the whole of the 4th Guards Brigade was forced to deploy as well as part of the 5th Infantry Brigade.

It is only fair to record the splendid spirit of heroism and determination displayed by this enemy rear guard, for the Germans literally fought almost to the last man. Although tremendously outnumbered, they even attempted to counter-attack. In the end they were nearly all killed or captured, and but few escaped.

After this engagement the division could only make a short advance, and B Squadron billeted for the night at Boitron.

A Squadron also became involved in the fight for the crossings of the Petit Morin.

At dawn the squadron marched to Rebais, where Captain Courage took over the command. Second Lieutenant Rouse-Boughton was the only officer left since the disaster. Officers had, however, been sent up from the base as quickly as possible, and Lieutenant K. North (4th Hussars), Lieutenant J. H. Cornwall (R.F.A.) and Lieutenant D. C. Lawrie (8th Hussars) joined on the 3rd, 5th and 8th September respectively. A small draft of men and horses also joined A Squadron as it marched through Rebais.

The 3rd Division had to fight for its passage across the Petit Morin, and encountered the same kind of opposition as the divisions of the I Corps. As the scouts from A Squadron approached the village of Orly, they were met by heavy rifle and machine-gun-fire, and they were soon compelled to retire. The whole of the 8th Infantry Brigade was forced to deploy, and later part of the 9th Infantry Brigade was brought forward to support them. After a considerable amount of fighting, the German rear guard was driven off the field.

In consequence of this fight, the 3rd Division could not advance very far. A Squadron billeted for the night at Bussieres.

The Expeditionary Force resumed the advance at daylight on 9th September. Everyone anticipated that there would be considerable fighting on this day, because the line of advance lay across the river Marne. It was but natural to expect that the enemy would offer a vigorous opposition to the passage of this river. As a matter of fact the resistance was very slight and the Marne was crossed without much difficulty.

The orders received by C Squadron were to march direct to La Chapelle. A section of artillery was attached, and they left their bivouacs at dawn.

The rendezvous was reached without any difficulty and from here there was a most magnificent view over the whole of the valley of the Marne. As the sun rose and the mists which clung to the valley lifted, lines of cavalry could be observed riding up the northern banks of the river. It was imagined at first that these horsemen were German, and the guns unlimbered prepared to shell them, but as the light improved, it became quite evident that it was our own cavalry, and it was then realised that the passage of the Marne had been effected.

The squadron therefore moved to Saulchery, and without any difficulty crossed over the bridge at this place.

The line of march lay through the vineyards. The sky was cloudless, and the countryside appeared a dream of beauty. It was almost impossible to imagine that amongst these ideal surroundings a state of war existed. On reaching the high ground above the Marne, orders were received to halt. An outpost line was thrown out, and the men lay on the ground, basking in the bright sunshine and revelling in the luxury of a rest.

B Squadron joined the 6th Infantry Brigade advance guard to the 2nd Division, and marched to Charly-sur-Marne. The advance patrols from the squadron approached the bridge at this place with commendable caution, but as they entered the town they found it deserted, and the bridge intact. The Germans had built a strong barricade across the bridge. This barricade was so solidly constructed that it took a considerable time to remove. Bit by bit it was taken down, and the patrols managed to slip across. No sooner had they reached the further bank when they encountered the patrols of hostile cavalry. A certain amount of skirmishing took place, but directly the infantry columns appeared the enemy retired. By 8.15 a.m. the whole of the advance guard was over the river. Nevertheless until the situation became clearer, the artillery was kept on the southern bank.

About this time the 2nd Division also received orders to halt. The squadron therefore dismounted, and formed the usual outpost line. This long halt, during which many small parties of Germans came in and surrendered to the patrols of the 15th Hussars, was thoroughly enjoyed by all ranks, although no one in the Regiment at the time knew the reason for it. All sorts of rumours were circulated as to the cause of this pause in the operations, but the men did not bother their heads about the why and wherefore, they lit their fires and cooked a good midday meal, and made the best of the opportunity.

The passage of a river by large forces in the presence of an active and enterprising enemy is always a difficult and ticklish operation. Long columns of the enemy had been located by the aeroplanes reconnoitring on the right flank of the I Corps, and it was feared that the Germans might be contemplating an attack whilst the British Army was in the process of the passage of the Marne.

At the moment everyone was surprised at the ease with which this river had been crossed, and all suspected that the enemy had some sinister design in store. Until the destination of these hostile columns had been definitely settled, it was decided that no risks could be taken. This wise decision was the reason of the long halt which has been very adversely criticised by certain foreign writers. As a matter of fact, the Germans had no surprise up their sleeve ; they were everywhere retreating, and the passages of the Marne were practically undefended. But at the time this fact was hardly realised. It was not until fairly late in the afternoon that orders were received for the march to be ontinued.

B and C Squadrons reached their billets without any incident taking place. C Squadron spent the night at Beau Repaire Farm, and B Squadron at Couprou.

As far as A Squadron was concerned, it was still too weak in numbers to take any very active part in the operations. The 3rd Division had probably a severer struggle in forcing the Marne than either of the divisions of the I Corps.

The passage was effected at Nanteuil, where the patrols from the squadron found the bridge intact much to their surprise. The 9th Infantry Brigade, which formed the advance guard to the division, was thus enabled to cross the river without much difficulty, but found the enemy entrenched on the far bank, with a certain number of batteries of artillery in position.

The advance guard at once attacked, and after considerable fighting the enemy withdrew, and the 9th Infantry Brigade proceeded to form a bridgehead. Since, however, on its right, as has already been narrated, the I Corps remained halted, it was hardly possible for the 3rd Division to advance, and it did not resume the march until the I Corps moved forward.

Eventually orders were received to continue the forward movement, but the enemy rear guards were extremely obstinate, and continual fighting took place. The advance in consequence was not very rapid, and it was not until far into the night that A Squadron was able to find a bivouac, near Champressy Farm.

During the early period of the war, when the Armies were in constant movement, the divisional cavalry was daily faced with a difficult problem. Each day after the operations the squadrons as a rule bivouacked somewhere in the vicinity of divisional headquarters, which were naturally located some distance in rear of the outpost line. This entailed a long march for the squadrons when they eventually received orders to retire for the night. Furthermore, they had to retrace their steps at a very early hour in the morning in order to take their places in front of the advance guard. As the divisions always started some time before dawn, the unfortunate 15th Hussars were forced to march at a very early hour indeed.

On 10th September C Squadron, in order to be in position up to time, was forced to break bivouac and move off before receiving orders for the march.

The original orders were for the 2nd Infantry Brigade to form the advance guard, and to advance along certain roads. Shortly after C Squadron had left its bivouacs fresh orders were issued, which changed the direction of the march. Messengers were dispatched across country to recall the scattered patrols and the various details of the squadron were forced to counter march across country and re-arrange themselves into their new positions, which entailed some hard galloping. The march had hardly commenced before the German patrols were encountered.

These made no effort to fight, but retired slowly before our advance. Small parties of Uhlans retreated in front of each patrol from the squadron, halting from time to time to observe their movements, but whenever chased or fired on, they galloped away. Full of ardour, the 15th tried to close with the enemy, but the Uhlans were too elusive, and would not be drawn into a fight.

As our leading patrols approached the little village of Priez, the German horsemen suddenly cleared our front, and galloped away to a wood about two miles north of Priez, where they could be seen collecting. This action of the German rear-guard cavalry was very suspicious, and made our patrols most cautious.

On the north, the village of Priez was overlooked by a ridge, and at the bottom of this ridge a small stream ran through the village, which was crossed only by a single bridge. The position was an ideal one for a rear guard, which from the ridge above would overlook the village and watch its pursuers forming into columns in order to pass through the village and over the bridge. C Squadron was, however, not to be hoodwinked, and located the enemy in position along the ridge above Priez.

Acting upon the information sent in by the squadron, the G.O.C. commanding the 2nd Infantry Brigade deployed the brigade under cover, and advanced against the enemy in extended lines.

To the German commanders on the field it must have been a bitter disappointment as they saw the British advance guard moving forward in battle formation, covered by their artillery, instead, as they no doubt anticipated, of catching them in column in the streets of the village, or as they were crossing the bridge.

As the British line of assault advanced up the slope towards the enemy position, the German guns let fly. The 1st Division, which so far had only encountered the comparatively innocuous shell fired by the ordinary field gun, now met for the first time the German heavy artillery; it was thus a most unpleasant surprise when shells of a far heavier calibre began to burst amongst the assaulting troops. They were nicknamed at once, and in the bivouacs that night they were called "Jack Johnsons" or "Black Marias" on account of the heavy black cloud they gave out on bursting.

As soon as the infantry battle became engaged, the various detachments of the squadron withdrew to the flanks, there to await eventualities.

In their endeavour to advance the 1st Division was forced to deploy the whole of the 2nd Infantry Brigade and part of the 1st Guards Brigade, and the assault almost reached the proportions of a battle. Eventually the Germans were driven off the ridge, and retreated about 4.30 p.m.

Directly the enemy retired, half C Squadron received orders to move forward, as far as the railway line, just north of Neuilly St. Front. Inhabitants warned the advance scouts that this village was held by the enemy. The order to dismount was therefore given, and the men advanced towards the village with every possible precaution. The Germans were found to be in occupation of the school house and yard in the centre of the village. Only a few shots were exchanged, whereupon the Germans surrendered. They expected to be slaughtered on the spot, and when they found that their lives were to be spared their joy was absolutely ludicrous.

This was the first haul of prisoners taken by C Squadron, and the men were much amused by their capture. A private of the 15th was noticed trundling a wounded German towards the dressing station in a wheelbarrow, whilst behind walked another German prisoner carrying the Hussar's rifle ! Among the captures was a German staff car, with a well-fitted luncheon basket, unfortunately empty of food or drink.

Leaving a small guard over the prisoners, the troops pushed on to the railway, where they encountered about half a company of Germans. Both sides opened fire, but the enemy broke and scattered into the woods. The fighting died down by dusk, and at 8 p.m. the detachments of the squadron were withdrawn to Priez, where they spent the night.

The 2nd Division also were not able to advance this day without some fighting. The 6th Infantry Brigade formed the advance guard, with B Squadron attached as usual. The march lay through Marigny towards Noroy.

As the leading scouts from the squadron approached the village of Bussieres, the Uhlan patrols who during the whole march had been hovering about in front of the advance guard suddenly dismounted, and attempted to drive away our patrols by rifle-fire. The whole of B Squadron with the cyclists at once moved forward in support of the advanced detachments, and the enemy skirmishers were forced to withdraw. The enemy retired very slowly, and continual fighting took place. It was quite evident that the Germans were most reluctant to give ground, and apparently they were attempting to cover some column. Outside the village of Hautevesnes the opposition became so obstinate that the mounted troops were unable to advance. The 6th Infantry Brigade, however, was close at hand, and after a short struggle carried the village of Hautevesnes.

As soon as the village was in our hands, B Squadron continued the advance, but had hardly left the village before the scouts encountered a long column of the enemy, chiefly composed of transport, moving from west to east across our front, from the direction of Vinly to Grisolles. Officers from the squadron galloped back to the artillery and informed them of the excellent target which was awaiting them. Battery after battery galloped into action and in a few moments our shells were bursting in the middle of the long column of German transport.

The German transport did not move without a strong escort, and in a short time the covering troops had to be reckoned with. There soon debouched from the tiny hamlet of Vinly extended lines of grey-clad German infantry, who in spite of our heavy fire advanced to and occupied a sunken road, which gave them excellent cover, whilst at the same time the German artillery opened fire. The 6th Infantry Brigade now advanced to the attack, in order to drive away the covering troops, and capture the transport column, which by this time was in the greatest confusion, as our shells burst continuously amongst the waggons. As battery after battery of the advance guard deployed into action an artillery duel developed, but the enemy guns were soon silenced and driven off the field.

The 1st King's Royal Rifles now advanced straight to their front, on the right of the Rifles were the 1st Royal Berkshire, whilst two companies of the South Staffords continued the line on the left. The Germans attempted to put up a stubborn resistance, but they had now to withstand a real British attack. So deadly was our rifle-fire, that they were quite unable to meet it, and in a short time they were pinned to the ground, unable either to advance or to retire. The enemy then surrendered, although our assaulting line was still about seven hundred yards from the hostile position. A few did manage to creep away, only to fall into the hands of the 3rd Division.

After this brilliant little action the advance was resumed, and B Squadron, still acting as advance guard, marched through Chezy en Orxois to Monnes, where it billeted for the night.

Although both divisions of the I Corps had some fighting on this day, A Squadron with the 3rd Division fought no very serious engagement. Throughout the night the men of A Squadron had been engaged in constant skirmishing with the hostile detachments, but by daylight the enemy withdrew, so that when the patrols moved forward at dawn they met with no opposition.

Shortly after the advance had commenced, the 3rd Cavalry Brigade appeared, and as it had the priority of the roads, the squadron halted by the roadside to let it pass. As the advance was now covered by this brigade, the squadron was relieved of much anxious work, but not for long ; the cavalry Brigade soon became engaged with the enemy, and in consequence the advance guard of the 3rd Division deployed, in order to support it if necessary.

The information brought in by the flanking patrols and the roar of artillery soon conveyed the news that the 2nd Division on the right was engaged in an action of some importance. The patrols from A Squadron were ordered forward to Vinly, where they also came in contact with the enemy rear guards, with whom, as already related, the 2nd Division were by this time heavily engaged.

In consequence of the fight which was already in progress, the 3rd Division halted for some time, but directly the enemy had broken and fled the advance was resumed. A Squadron had the satisfaction of capturing a number of prisoners, for the whole countryside was covered by small parties of Germans, who seemed only too anxious to surrender.

Late that night A Squadron halted at Dammard.

To the 15th Hussars as they marched forward on this day it seemed that the enemy was retreating in some disorder. The sight of transport abandoned by the side of the road, of discarded equipment and of hastily evacuated bivouacs gave the impression that the German Army was in full flight. There was a feeling amongst all ranks that a great success had been won, and that the British Army was advancing to the final stages of absolute victory.

It was a very pitiable spectacle to see the villages and the farms which the enemy had evacuated in his retreat. Every house had been looted, every door broken open, every cupboard ransacked, and the contents scattered in hopeless confusion on the floor. It appeared inconceivable that anybody would have either the time or the energy for such useless destruction. It seemed such a meaningless outrage, deliberately to tear up the sheets, bedding and linen of the peasants, and to break up all their crockery and furniture. The people themselves appeared quite dazed from what they had gone through, and sat helpless and listless in the midst of the destruction.

There is not very much to record about the advance on 11th September. The British and French Armies were closing in on each other, and in consequence the roads became congested with marching troops, which from time to time entailed a long halt by the roadside. The majority of the men, however, were enabled to reach billets fairly early in the day. This was very fortunate because the weather changed and during the afternoon it began to rain in torrents.

C Squadron passed long columns of French soldiers, all in the best of spirits advancing forward in pursuit of the enemy ; the spectacle of these troops was most inspiring. By midday C Squadron was comfortably housed out of the wet of Coincy.

B Squadron, delayed for some time by the congestion on the roads, eventually billeted at Beugneux.

A Squadron had a particularly easy day, did not start until 7 a.m., and by noon was in billets at Grand Rozoy.

On 12th September the British Army crossed the Vesle. The 1st Division had no difficulty in effecting this passage. The enemy made no real attempt to delay the advance ; his artillery sprinkled the roads over which the division advanced with shrapnel, and C Squadron had no fighting.

At certain points the enemy did indeed offer some slight show of resistance, but directly our advance guard prepared to attack the enemy retired. The Vesle was crossed at Bazoches, and our advanced troops pushed on to Vauxcere. On the high ground about this place the hostile rear guards did attempt to stand, but the British advance soon forced them to retire, leaving their wounded behind them. The various detachments of C Squadron were recalled after dark to Bazoches, where they remained for the night. During the greater part of the day rain fell in an almost tropical torrent, and everybody was soaked to the skin ; the rations also failed to turn up, so that taken on the whole, the night was a very uncomfortable one for all concerned.

On 12th September the 2nd Division had some difficulty in forcing the crossings of the Vesle. At dawn B Squadron joined the 5th Infantry Brigade, which formed the advance guard, and marched by Quincy towards Courcelles.

On this day the 4th Cavalry Brigade operated in front of the advance guard, and became involved in a certain amount of fighting, as the hostile rear guard only retired when forced to do so. The patrols from B Squadron also became engaged in this fighting. Eventually the 4th Cavalry Brigade succeeded in entering the village of Courcelles, only to find that the bridge over the Vesle had been destroyed. The destruction, however, was not complete, a few planks were intact, which still spanned the river, and as soon as the infantry of the advance guard came up, they commenced to pass over in single file, and eventually managed to occupy the far bank.

As it was impossible for the cavalry with their horses to cross at this place, B Squadron was ordered to march to Braine, where it was reported that the bridge was undamaged. When this latter place was reached a fierce struggle was found to be in progress for the possession of the town. The Germans were obstinately defending the crossing, and the 1st Cavalry Brigade was fighting hard, in an attempt to seize the bridge. After some time the Germans were forced to retire, which they did in such a hurry that they failed to destroy the bridge, and the 1st Cavalry Brigade was enabled to secure the bridge-head. B Squadron crossed over the Vesle with the rest of the cavalry.

It was found that the 2nd Division would take a considerable time to cross the Vesle at Courcelles in single file, especially as the bridge could not be repaired very quickly. Consequently the whole of the 2nd Division (less the advance guard) marched to Braine with orders to cross the Vesle at this place.

The original orders issued in the morning were for the division to advance forward on to the river Aisne. But the delay in crossing the Vesle had been considerable, and it was already becoming late. In consequence orders were issued for the division to advance no further and to halt where it was. B Squadron spent the night at Vieil Arcy.

A Squadron marched at dawn with the intention of crossing the Vesle at Braine. As has already been narrated, the 1st Cavalry Brigade became engaged in battle for this town, and A Squadron, owing to the fact that the 1st Cavalry Brigade was in front, had very little to do, and took no important part in the fighting ; they halted outside the town where they awaited the result of the battle.

Meanwhile the whole of the advance guard of the 3rd Division deployed ready to assist the cavalry if necessary. Their assistance was not however required, except for artillery support. As already recorded, the cavalry secured the crossing, and the 2nd Division was ordered to cross at Braine. In consequence the 3rd Division halted at the side of the road until their time came to cross over. Finally they were ordered to remain where they were for the night.

A Squadron bivouacked in the chateau grounds at Braine. Rain fell in torrents all night, and everybody was soaked to the skin, but as it was not cold nobody was much the worse.

As in the growing light of the early dawn on 13th September the 15th Hussars formed up to take their places in front of the various advance guards, all anticipated that before the sun had set there would be some hard fighting, for it could hardly be expected that the enemy would allow the British Army to cross the Aisne without a battle. It is true that the Germans had offered no very stubborn resistance to the passage of the Marne, but the Vesle had not been crossed without a fight, and it was quite evident that resistance was stiffening.

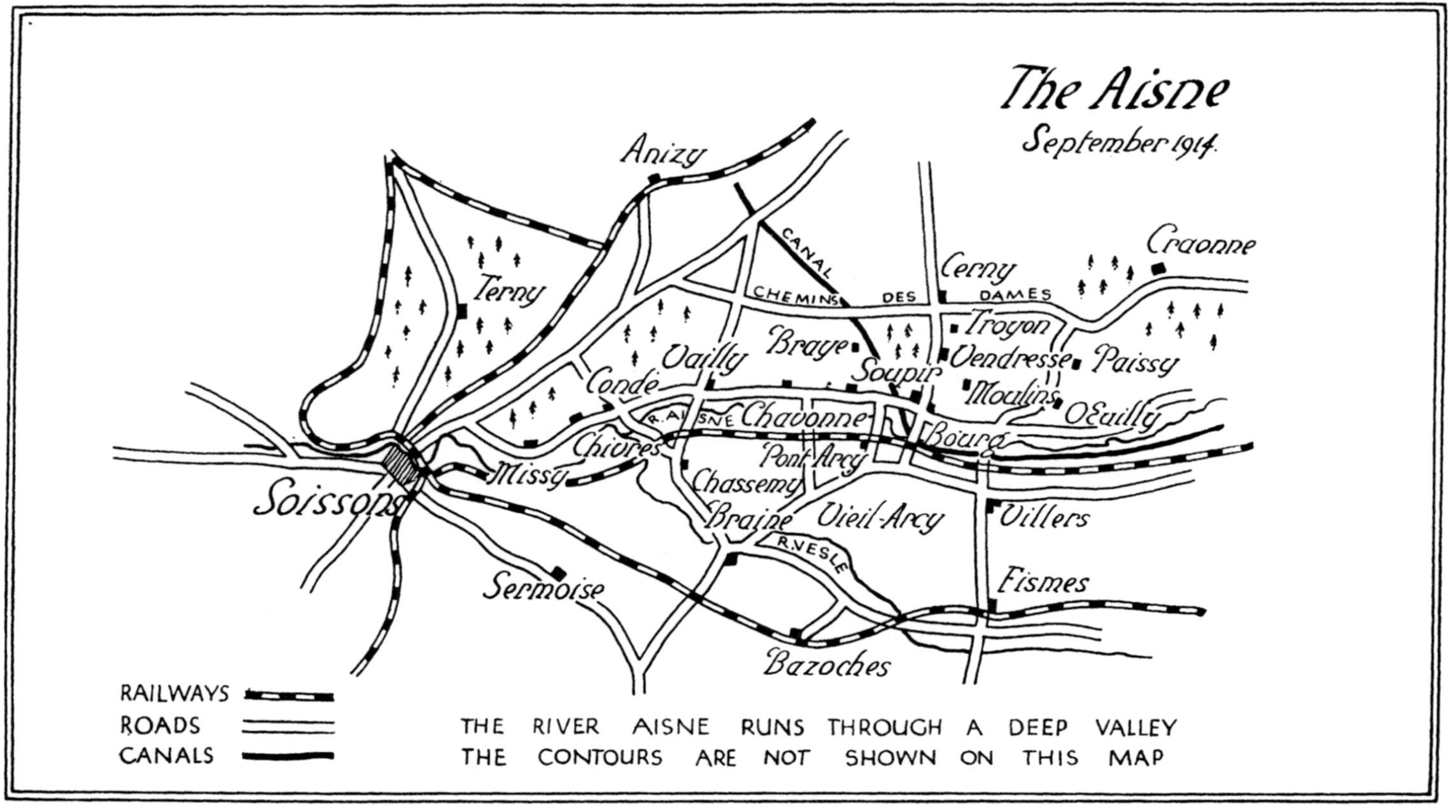
The Aisne
September 1914.
Anizy
Terny
Craonne
Cerny
CANAL
CHEMINS DES DAMES
Troyon
Braye
Vailly
Soupir
Vendresse
Paissy
Condé
Moulins
Œuilly
R. AISNE
Chavonne
Bourg
Chivres
Pont Arcy
Missy
Soissons
Chassemy
Braine
Vieil-Arcy
Villers
R. VESLE
Sermoise
Fismes
Bazoches
RAILWAYS
ROADS
CANALS
THE RIVER AISNE RUNS THROUGH A DEEP VALLEY
THE CONTOURS ARE NOT SHOWN ON THIS MAP

The 1st Division on the right was directed to cross the Aisne at Bourg.

The cavalry patrols sent out to reconnoitre the bridges before the general advance began reported that the bridge over the Aisne at this village was only partially destroyed, whilst the aqueduct which spanned the Aisne canal was still intact. This canal ran parallel to the Aisne along part of the front occupied by the British Army.

The 3rd Cavalry Brigade reached Bourg before C Squadron, and when the advance troops of the squadron entered the town they found this brigade engaged in fighting for this place. Some little time elapsed before the village was completely in our hands, but about 10 a.m. the enemy was driven out and the bridge was captured, the patrols were then enabled to cross the river. The bridge was not destroyed to any very great extent, and the engineers were soon able to repair it.

On crossing the river C Squadron sent detachments to Vendresse, Moulins and Chivy, with orders to reconnoitre towards the Chemin des Dames. These patrols very soon came into contact with the enemy, and reported the presence of the Germans in large numbers north of Vendresse with artillery in position. The passage of the Aisne over a partially destroyed bridge naturally took some time, and the 1st Division was not in a position to push on very far that day. The enemy in reality did not offer any very serious opposition to the 1st Division, except by shelling the bridge and the surrounding country.

Some time after dark the various detachments of C Squadron were recalled and concentrated at Bourg.

The patrols from B Squadron were on the move long before daylight, and reconnoitred towards the Aisne. Their orders were to report on the bridges at Chavonne, Cys and St. Mard. They reported that the enemy appeared to be occupying a strong position on the high ground above Chavonne and Soupir, and that the bridges over the Aisne were all destroyed, but those over the canal were still standing. They had some difficulty in carrying out their mission, for as they descended the slopes leading down to the river they were in full view of the enemy, who shelled them unmercifully.

As it was impossible to cross at Chavonne the squadron was directed to Pont Arcy, but on reaching this latter place the bridge was also found to be destroyed. The destruction was, however, not absolutely complete, as several of the iron girders still spanned the river. Later on in the day the infantry of the 2nd Division managed to creep across the Aisne by means of this frail support. Horses, of course, could not cross, but information arrived that the 1st Division was crossing at Bourg, so B Squadron made the best of their way to this place, passed over the river with the 1st Division and marched along the far bank of the Aisne to rejoin the 2nd Division, which was dribbling over the river at Pont Arcy.

The squadron now attempted to advance towards Soupir, but by this time the hostile fire had become very heavy indeed, and any further advance was almost impossible ; it therefore took cover behind a high bank which gave some protection to men and horses. The rest of the day was most unpleasant for all ranks, for the enemy shells fell crashing all round whilst the men crouched behind the feeble shelter of the bank. The casualties were not heavy, yet the hours seemed very long indeed.

At Chavonne the Guards found a boat, by means of which small parties of men were ferried across ; these were enabled to gain a footing on the far side, and drive away the enemy from the actual river bank. A bridge-head was thus formed which left the broken bridge entirely in our hands. The whole of the 2nd Division was not across the Aisne by dark, but a strong foothold had been secured on the northern bank of the river.

B Squadron was withdrawn to Bourg at dusk, where the night was spent.

To turn now to the adventures of A Squadron on 13th September. At dawn patrols were ordered forward to cross the Aisne at Vailly, but on entering the village of Chassemy they met units of the 5th Cavalry Brigade, who informed them that the bridge at Vailly was destroyed, and that the Germans were entrenched in strength on the opposite bank. Nevertheless patrols from the squadron were pushed down to the river in the endeavour to find some other bridge, and they found that the enemy had here also omitted to destroy the bridges over the canal in front of the 3rd Division.

Whilst this reconnaissance was in progress, the advance guard of the 3rd Division entered Chassemy, whereupon the German artillery opened a very heavy fire upon the village, which began to crumble into ruins and was soon burning fiercely, and for the time being became quite untenable.

Careful searching disclosed a narrow footbridge which spanned the Aisne, and which the enemy had overlooked. Along the solitary plank which formed the bridge and in spite of the hostile fire, the 8th Infantry Brigade managed to cross in single file during the afternoon. As it was impossible for A Squadron to cross by this bridge, they remained halted all day by the side of the river, finding what cover they could and watching the slow defile of the infantry across the Aisne.

After the sun had set the squadron moved into the grounds of La Tuillerie Chateau, situated about two hundred yards from the bridge.

On this evening as the men of the Regiment turned into their various bivouacs, they little thought that upon the following day the advance was to be brought to a complete standstill. The I Corps at any rate had forced the crossing of the Aisne, and it was hoped that the enemy rear guards would withdraw during the night. But many weary years were to pass, and battles would be fought on an infinitely larger scale than any which had so far taken place, before the 15th Hussars were once more to advance in pursuit of a beaten foe.

Throughout the hours of darkness the engineers worked desperately to repair the destroyed bridges, and to build fresh ones across the river. All night long hostile shells burst amongst the working parties, but undeterred by the hostile fire they continued their work without a moment's respite.

The 1st Division marched on 14th September covered by the 1st Guards Brigade ; as the enemy was so close, C Squadron not only covered this advance, but sent out strong detachments to either flank, on the right to Paissy and on the left to Chivy.

By 5 a.m. the advance guard reached Vendresse. The 3rd Cavalry Brigade, operating in front of the 1st Division, reported that the Germans were in strength all along the Chemin des Dames.

Acting upon this information the advance guard deployed and commenced an attack against the Chemin des Dames, which road they eventually occupied, and also captured the Fabrique de Troyon, a conspicuous factory on the top of the ridge.

But the enemy was in great strength, and shortly afterwards by heavy counter-attacks forced the Guards Brigade to evacuate the factory and fall back on to the reverse slopes of the ridge, south of the Chemin des Dames. The battle soon developed into one of fierce attack and counter-attack, and in a short time the other two brigades of the division came up and were forced to deploy. By the afternoon the line extended from about north of Paissy to just south of Courtecon.

The Germans had a considerable preponderance in artillery, and as their guns had been in position for some days, the ranges were accurately known. At the time their fire seemed to be of incredible intensity, for shells of heavy calibre burst far behind our line, whilst in the battle area the fighting troops were pounded unceasingly by the enemy guns.

As soon as the infantry fight became engaged, and the opposing forces were fighting at very close quarters, all reconnaissance became impossible, and as this is the chief duty of divisional cavalry, it was inevitable that the squadron played but a humble rôle in the great battle.

Nevertheless there was plenty of work for the men to do. The patrols on the flanks remained out all day reporting on the operations of the flank formations, for it must be realised that at this period of the war divisional headquarters were forced to rely to a very great extent on their squadron of cavalry for their information as to what was taking place to their front and on their flanks.

Towards the evening the fighting gradually died down, and the squadron was enabled to concentrate in a field near Vendresse, where the horses were fed (there was no opportunity to water them) and here the men rested for a few hours.

Throughout the night, as the men lay out in the open field, the hostile shells passed over them and could be heard bursting on or near the bridges which spanned the Aisne.

As far as the 2nd Division was concerned the situation on 14th September was almost exactly the same as that of the 1st Division. The 6th Infantry Brigade formed the advance guard, and B Squadron not only covered their advance but sent strong detachments to either flank. Direct to the front B Squadron marched by Moussy and Verneuil, with orders to reconnoitre the high ground by the Chemin des Dames. The squadron occupied Courtecon on the right and Froidment on the left. The patrols had not advanced very far, before they encountered the enemy in some strength, they were nevertheless able to obtain some information as to the German positions before they were forced to withdraw. After some fighting the squadron concentrated at Verneuil.

The information obtained was considered so important that Lieutenant Straker[1] was sent direct to Sir Douglas Haig's headquarters with his report.

During this reconnaissance the squadron came under very heavy fire, at times at very close range, and was extremely lucky to escape with few casualties.

It was not long before the 2nd Division deployed for the attack, which met the most obstinate resistance, and in a short time every unit of the division was employed. These attacks did indeed succeed in a few places, but with the inevitable result that those who made them found themselves isolated, and were inevitably forced to retire. The Germans replied to our attacks by strong counter-attacks, heralded by very heavy shell fire.

[1] Lieutenant Straker remained with Sir Douglas Haig as A.D.C. throughout the whole of the war.

B Squadron took very little part in the battle after the infantry fight had begun. Except for constant patrols, they awaited at Verneuil the outcome of the struggle.

By nightfall the 2nd Division was established on a line from Beaulne, through Brale and Les Champs d'Erny, with its left flank about La Court. This left flank was in the air, as communication had not yet been established with the 3rd Division, which was operating on the left.

B Squadron spent the night lying in the open, by the side of their horses.

The 3rd Division, as related, had more difficulty the day before in crossing the Aisne than either of the two divisions of I Corps. Two infantry brigades succeeded in establishing themselves on the far side of the river by dawn on 14th September, and were entrenched on the high ground just north and north-west of Vailly.

At nightfall on the 13th the 5th Cavalry Brigade had been unable to cross the Aisne, but by dawn on 14th the bridge was available for use, and the brigade commenced to cross over at 7 a.m. with the idea of continuing the pursuit.

A Squadron formed up, prepared to follow, but no sooner had the 5th Cavalry Brigade begun to defile across the bridge than it came under the heaviest of fire, and it soon became evident that it was impossible to remain on the northern bank. In consequence the brigade withdrew, but not without heavy casualties.

A brigade of artillery, which had also been sent across the Aisne at dawn, found itself unable to debouch from Vailly and also withdrew to the southern bank.

The 7th Infantry Brigade later in the day succeeded in crossing the bridge, and entrenching about Vailly.

Thus the 3rd Division had all its infantry lightly entrenched on the northern bank, supported by its artillery on the southern bank, but only able to provide cover at fairly long ranges.

A Squadron did not take any very active part in this battle, numerous patrols were galloped across the bridge under heavy fire, but they were forced to withdraw without accomplishing very much. The squadron remained halted about two hundred yards from the river bank, sheltered as far as possible from the heavy shell-fire which continued throughout the day, but the casualties were not heavy, and in spite of the heavy shell-fire and the strong counter-attacks of the enemy, the three infantry brigades of the 3rd Division managed to entrench themselves in a semi-circle round Vailly. When night fell the troops bivouacked where they were on the battlefield.

On the night of 14th September the situation of the British Army was rather precarious and naturally there was a certain amount of anxiety as to what would happen the following day. It is true that the first three divisions had forced the crossings of the Aisne, but in front of them was an enemy, strongly entrenched and in large numbers, with a great superiority in artillery, whilst in rear was an unfordable river, crossed by a few frail bridges, all of which were under the direct fire of the German guns. The fighting throughout the day had been very severe indeed, and all reserves were used up. In the event of the line being broken, retreat was practically impossible. In consequence there were possibilities of a disaster of the first magnitude.

British infantry does not, however, easily abandon a position which has once been occupied, and it is possible that the British who crossed the Aisne on this occasion were the most stubborn troops in the world, and there was in reality little fear that they would be forced to give way before any attack the Germans could launch.

As was anticipated, 15th September proved to be a day of severe fighting. The Germans made the most determined attacks along the whole front of the British Army, and throughout the day our troops sheltering in their shallow trenches were subjected to an intense bombardment. The battle raged from sunrise to sunset, but by nightfall the troops remained approximately on the same ground as they had occupied the previous day.

During this fighting the 15th Hussars sent out numerous patrols, all of which brought back information of the greatest value. The staffs of the first three divisions were unanimous in their praise of the constant flow of accurate information supplied by the 15th Hussars. Darkness found the Regiment saddled up in the same places where they had spent the previous night, and although no one at the time realised the fact trench warfare had already begun.

A type of warfare which was stationary, and in which the opposing sides faced each other in elaborately constructed trenches, was at this period quite a novel idea. In peace, training for a war of this nature had not been very elaborately practised, for the British Army had been trained chiefly for a war of movement. The Battle of the Aisne lasted for some time before anyone realised that on this part of the battle front, at any rate, there had now arisen a situation which precluded all idea of movement.

It was anticipated for some days that at any moment a

move of some sort would take place, and it was hoped a move forward, but the question of a retreat had also to be taken into consideration. The squadrons of the 15th Hussars were therefore kept "standing to" day and night, ready to march forward with the advance guard, or if necessary to form part of a rear guard.

The story of the part played by the 15th Hussars during the long-drawn-out Battle of the Aisne can be related in a few words. For the first few days all three squadrons remained saddled up in the open. As soon, however, as it became evident that for the present at any rate the battle had become stationary, the three divisional headquarters abandoned their bivouacs by the roadside, and moved into more comfortable quarters. The divisional mounted troops moved with the headquarters. On 18th September A and B Squadrons billeted at Braine and Bourg respectively, and on 19th September C Squadron moved into the Ferme de la Fabrique, near Bourg. Thus for the first time since the Battle of Mons both men and horses were in a more or less permanent billet with the prospect of several days' rest.

No doubt the reader of this chronicle of the 15th Hussars will not have failed to realise the very severe strain to which both the men and the horses of the 15th Hussars had been subjected. It is difficult in a short account to elaborate the hardships endured.

Yet the Regiment had been on the move day and night for over three weeks, and there had been little rest for anyone. The horses had perforce to be saddled up for days and nights in succession, and if an opportunity to unsaddle ever did arise it was only for a few hours. The question of watering and feeding had always been a cause of continual anxiety throughout the campaign. The horses had to be fed and watered whenever a chance arose, and at the most irregular hours. Nevertheless, though they were all fit and well, and still capable of any amount of work, naturally many had lost a considerable amount of flesh.

After a few days' rest all began to fill out again, and in a very short time the horses were as fit as they had been when they left Longmoor. There was scarcely a sore back in the Regiment, and not a horse had become a casualty from want of care in shoeing or any similar reason.[1]

It must not be imagined that during this period the squadrons

[1] It is interesting to compare the casualties sustained amongst the horses, other than battle casualties, in 1914, after 28 days continual fighting and marching, with those which the Regiment suffered just over 100 years before, in 1808, during the retreat to Corunna.

On Sunday, 30th October, 1808, the 15th Hussars embarked 560 troop horses at Portsmouth. On 11th January, 1809, on reaching Corunna only 200 men were mounted, and only 30 horses were considered fit and serviceable to embark on 15th January. The remainder were shot.

had nothing to do, for they were fully occupied : the Signal Service was at this time not so thoroughly organised and equipped as it later became, and inter-communication between the various headquarters and the front line was carried out by means of mounted orderlies. It was not until many months later that the use of mounted orderlies for this duty was discontinued ; the Royal Flying Corps was still in its infancy, and the staff had to rely to a very great extent for information as to the ever changing situation on the battle front upon the news brought by the cavalry patrols, consequently the N.C.O.'s and men of the 15th, trained especially for this type of work, were busily employed.

The 3rd Division, as already narrated, had only succeeded in pushing its infantry across the Aisne at Vailly. A Squadron was asked to keep open the communications across the river, between the infantry of the division on the northern bank and the artillery and divisional headquarters on the southern bank. A signal station was formed, dug in and barricaded in the cellar of the Lodge of La Tuillerie Chateau, and extra signallers were attached to the squadron, but for some days, until lines had been constructed and cables buried, the only means of communication were the Hussars. As the only bridge was under the direct view of the enemy and under constant fire, the work of the runners was most difficult and dangerous.

A Squadron in addition had another important duty to perform, namely to protect and watch the left flank of the 3rd Division, which was in the air, owing to the gap which existed between this flank and the right flank of the 5th Division. Later, when the regimental machine-gun detachment arrived from England, it was attached to A Squadron to help it in this task.

When the 15th Hussars left Longmoor, the regimental headquarters remained in England. They embarked, however, with the first reinforcement, and proceeded to Le Mans, where they remained for a short time, until in fact orders arrived for all reinforcements to join their units. Headquarters in consequence were broken up, and the officers, N.C.O.'s and men sent to the different squadrons.

Lieutenant-Colonel H. A. L. Tagart[1] joined the headquarters staff of the Cavalry Corps, then in process of formation ; Major H. D. Bramwell received a command on the lines of communication, where he remained until he assumed the command of the 15th Hussars some months later ; Lieutenant H. F. Brace[2]

[1] The late Major-General Sir Harold Tagart, K.C.M.G., C.B., D.S.O.

[2] Now Lieutenant-Colonel H. F. Brace, D.S.O., M.C. (Commanding 15th Hussars).

joined C Squadron, and Captain the Hon. J. D. Y. Bingham[1] joined A Squadron as second-in-command.

It was not until many months later that headquarters were once again reformed, when the 15th Hussars eventually were assembled together as a regiment.

When it became known at Longmoor that the Regiment had suffered heavy casualties, especially A Squadron, and that there was a shortage of officers, both Captain B. Ritchie[2] and Captain E. Bald, who had been called up from civil life, volunteered to go to the front as troop leaders in their old Regiment, although both were fairly senior officers. Captain Bald was indeed senior to the squadron leader, but both officers loyally waived their rank, and took their places as troop leaders, and the Regiment owes them a debt of gratitude for their action in coming forward at a time of stress. The attached officers with A Squadron left to rejoin their own units, whilst Captain Bradshaw of the Indian Cavalry joined A Squadron to complete numbers.

The whole of the Regiment was thus made up to strength in men, horses and equipment.

The machine-gun detachment under Lieutenant B. Osborne also left England with the first reinforcement, and on its arrival in France was sent up to join A Squadron. Its arrival was most opportune, for as has already been stated, the position on the left of the 3rd Division was always difficult, and the presence of the machine guns on this flank was of the greatest service.

The machine-gunners found the squadron only lightly dug in, for at this time squadrons carried but few entrenching tools. Lieutenant Osborne, however, with his own tools, which were carried on the machine-gun pack, constructed a fairly good position at the edge of Chassemy Wood, facing the Condé bridge and the village of Condé. This village was held by the enemy and strongly entrenched and the position was known as Condé fort. The bridge was intact, but always remained " No Man's Land "—neither side could use it. A strong detachment of the squadron was always kept in readiness to support the machine-guns which remained in this position, exposed to the constant fire of the enemy night and day, until the British Army moved from the Aisne, but by their presence they entirely prohibited the use of the bridge to the enemy.

The Germans in their retreat had inevitably left behind small parties which had become detached from their main bodies, and these were wandering about the country or hiding in the woods behind our lines. It was also asserted that the Germans had left

[1] Now Lieutenant-Colonel the Hon. J. D. Y. Bingham, D.S.O.

[2] Now Major B. Ritchie, O.B.E.

behind spies and artillery observers, carefully concealed in haystacks and such like hiding places. These individuals were supposed to be plentifully supplied with telephones, and it was presumed could watch all our movements and positions and report them at once to the hostile artillery. The Regiment on several occasions was employed in searching for these persons. Elaborate drives were organised, and the woods and very extensive caves behind our lines were searched; but, it must be confessed, without much result.[1]

There is very little to chronicle of the doings of the 15th Hussars during the later stages of the Battle of the Aisne : the usual guards and orderlies were found, besides numerous liaison patrols and working parties, the various bridges over the Aisne were put in charge of the squadrons, and the Hussars and Cyclists were made responsible for traffic control.

It must not be imagined that the situation was peaceful and quiet. Day after day the Germans launched the most powerful attacks against the British trenches, and they continued to bombard our lines and back areas without intermission. But in this history of the 15th Hussars it is hardly possible to go into details of the numerous fruitless efforts the enemy made to break through the British lines.

For a time, even after the Aisne had become a quiet sector, and the focus of the war had moved to other parts, the enemy continued to attack our positions, and it often happened that one or all of the squadrons were hastily turned out and ordered to man the reserve trenches.

Trenches in time became continuous ; communication trenches were dug, cables were laid and as far as actual fighting was concerned the divisional cavalry became practically inactive.

The fighting on the Aisne died down. The days passed in glorious September weather. An occasional aeroplane flew overhead, and now and then a lonely shell burst. The woods took on the most gorgeous autumn tints and for many hours by the Aisne all was peace and quiet.

This rest on the Aisne, which gave a period of recuperation to all, was thoroughly appreciated, but it came as no surprise when it was rumoured that the Army was to leave this quiet sector

[1] The men of B Squadron did make a capture. On 20th September a strong party went out to search the forest about Pont Arcy. On entering a wood, it was noticed that there were people in the wood, for wisps of fresh straw were hanging on the branches of the trees. Following up this trail, the men came upon a small tent hidden in the depths of the wood, in which five Germans were sheltering. They had hidden their little shelter as much as possible by branches and leaves. The terror of these men on their capture was intense, as they had been told it was the invariable custom of the British to cut off the right hands of all their prisoners ; they were relieved to discover that it was not our habit thus to mutilate our enemies.

and march to fresh battlefields, where more important events were taking place, for no one supposed he was destined the spend the rest of the war in this pleasant situation.

The roads and railways behind the British Army had for days been crowded with French troops, all moving to the north and west, and it was clear that the Allies were making the most determined efforts to outflank the German right. As the artillery fire on the Aisne died down, the terrific roar of the guns which sounded towards the west and north told of the efforts of the French to turn the German right flank. At night the men watched the far horizon, flickering with the reflection of the distant artillery duel, and realised, whilst all was more or less quiet on the Aisne, stupendous battles were being fought in other sectors. And so as time went on the noise of the battle faded further and further away for the " Race to the Sea " was taking place, and fresh battles were being fought in areas far removed from the comparative peace of the Aisne.

THE MAIL

Chapter IV

THE FIGHTING IN FLANDERS AND YPRES 1914

SO far in this story of the 15th Hussars it has not been difficult to record the actions of the different squadrons from day to day, as their relative positions never altered to any very great degree. But when the Army moved from the Aisne, the three divisions to which the squadrons were attached fought in different areas, and at times changed places. In fact, towards the end of the Battle of Ypres they almost ceased to be separate units, but all fought together, and in a certain amount of confusion.

It is now no longer possible to keep to the chronological order which has been followed up to date. The records of the three squadrons must more or less be detailed separately, and the narrative may appear in consequence rather confused, but every effort will be made to keep the story of the three squadrons distinct and clear.

A Squadron left the Aisne and moved to the North of France fourteen days before the other two squadrons, whom we will leave quietly on the Aisne whilst the adventures of A Squadron are detailed.

The 3rd Division received orders to move from the Aisne on 1st October, and during the nights of 1st/2nd and 2nd/3rd it was relieved by the 16th Infantry Brigade and the 2nd Cavalry Brigade. The operation was a difficult one, but was completed without let or hindrance. The greater part of the march was carried out by night, owing to the precautions necessary to prevent the enemy obtaining a premature knowledge of the movements of the British Army.

A Squadron marched at 6 p.m. on 1st October and reached Le Meuse on 5th October, where it expected to entrain. But on arrival at this place it was ordered to continue the march to Compiègne, where the squadron did eventually entrain, but with some difficulty, as there were no facilities for boxing horses, and it was not until 9 p.m. that the train finally left the station.

During this move no one was quite certain as to the future destination of the squadron, although it was imagined that it was moving somewhere to the North of France. It was little realised by all ranks that they were on their way to places which were later to become terribly familiar to the British Army, although at this time they meant nothing more to most people than names on a map. But these small and comparatively obscure towns and villages of Northern France were destined to be the scenes of great battles, in which soldiers drawn from every part of the British Empire would eventually take part.

A Squadron detrained at Etaples about midday on 6th October and marched at once to Abbeville. The 3rd Division concentrated about this place during the next day.

The French Army had lent the 3rd Division a number of motor lorries, and in these the majority of the infantry were conveyed. So that by the evening of 11th October the greater part of the 3rd Division was distributed along the Aire Canal.

A Squadron left Abbeville on 8th October and, marching during the night and halting by daylight, reached Busnes on the 11th.

The French cavalry was in considerable numbers about this area, and had already been engaged for some days with the enemy cavalry and Jaegers. But it appeared that so far the enemy had no considerable force of infantry in this part of the field to support his cavalry, and as this was not well trained in dismounted fighting, it was not anticipated that the division would have much difficulty in driving it back.

On the right of the 3rd Division marched the 5th Division, and on the right again was the 21st French Division. Both these divisions had been fighting for some days with the Germans, and were more or less held up, but it was hoped that the advance of the 3rd Division would eventually turn the enemy's right flank, and thus relieve the pressure further south. It was anticipated that the French cavalry, operating further north, would be able to protect the left flank of the 3rd Division whilst it advanced.

By dark on 11th October A Squadron had already exchanged shots with advance parties of the enemy, and it appeared probable that there would be a certain amount of fighting on the following day.

At 4 a.m. on 12th October A Squadron marched from their billets with orders to reconnoitre towards Lestrem.

Progress was, however, extremely slow, for the country was intersected by numerous dykes and canals, and most difficult to work over, and to add further to these difficulties there was a thick fog which made it impossible to see more than a few yards. It would be impossible to imagine worse conditions for an advance guard.

As the patrols from the squadron cautiously approached Fosse they were met by heavy rifle-fire, and were unable to advance. The infantry of the advance guard, which was following close behind, was forced to deploy, and commenced an attack against the village, but the enemy were holding Fosse in strength, and in consequence the advance was very slow.

As time went on the fog lifted, but only to disclose considerable fighting taking place. The British were heavily engaged outside Fosse, whilst the French cavalry was struggling to capture Lestrem. Fighting continued all day, and it was not until just before dark that both these places were captured and the Germans forced to retire ; they fell back on to the line Bout Deville–Croix Barbee–Richebourg St. Vaast. The British troops halted where they were on the battlefield for the night, and A Squadron bivouacked near Paradis.

Early in the morning of 13th October the squadron moved forward and almost immediately came in contact with the enemy cavalry. Captain Bald's troop was leading, and succeeded in driving off the Germans, inflicting losses on them, but the squadron was held up outside Bout Deville, which was held in some strength.

The 1st Gordon Highlanders now advanced to the attack, and in a short time also became heavily engaged. A Squadron, with the regimental machine-guns, was ordered to support the left flank of this attack. Captain Bradshaw's troop was sent to locate the right flank of the enemy and gaily moved off to carry out its mission, but as the day wore on no news was heard of him or his men. The last information received was that they had dismounted and were advancing on foot against a small orchard, evidently held by the enemy. Eventually Captain Courage rode over to the flank in an attempt to get in touch with them.

The sight of loose horses galloping wildly about gave some inkling that all was not well, but the fire of the enemy was by this time so heavy that it was impossible to approach the place where Captain Bradshaw and his men had last been seen.

It was not until some time later that authentic information could be obtained as to what had happened. It appeared that Captain Bradshaw found it impossible to advance mounted, and in consequence had dismounted and advanced on foot against what was taken to be the enemy's right flank. But the Germans were in strength, and the troop, soon pinned to the ground, was unable either to advance or to retire. By this time the whole party only numbered ten rifles, and in a few moments Captain Bradshaw and five of his men were killed and the other five wounded and helpless. The wounded were eventually all taken prisoners, amongst them Corporal Garforth, who, as already narrated,[1] had been awarded the Victoria Cross.

[1] See p. 38.

Just before dark Richebourg St. Vaast was captured, but only after severe fighting. It had been a most unpleasant day, continuous fighting and heavy shelling, and it was not until late at night that the squadron retired to Rue Du Ponch, where the men were able to snatch a hasty meal and a few hours rest.

The 3rd Division again attempted to renew the advance on the 14th, the chief effort being directed against the German right flank, for it was still hoped that they could be outflanked. The opposition which had so far been encountered was from German cavalry supported by Jaegers, but on this day the advance had not continued very far before shells began to burst amongst the advancing troops, which made it quite evident that batteries were in action of a far heavier calibre than those which normally accompany a cavalry division. There was no doubt that the enemy had received strong reinforcements of infantry.

The fighting on the 14th was severe, and the division was unable to make very much progress. Major-General Sir Hubert Hamilton, the divisional commander, was killed about 10 a.m. by a shell whilst superintending the operations on the left flank of his division.

Throughout the whole of these operations the French cavalry advanced on the left of the 3rd Division, and it was the chief duty of A Squadron to maintain touch between the French and British, and to ensure that there was no gap between the two forces.

The French cavalry in this part of the field was composed chiefly of Cuirassiers. The armament of these troops consisted of a short carbine in addition to their swords, and equipped as they were in armour, it was almost impossible for them to carry out their task in face of the German fire. Furthermore, the country was most difficult for mounted troops to operate over. For the most part it was absolutely flat, and the view was restricted by numerous villages, copses and enclosures. The roads were narrow and bordered by deep dykes, most difficult to cross by a heavily loaded cavalryman, and in consequence the Cuirassiers made but slow progress. They nevertheless proceeded with the most dogged determination, and in spite of every obstacle succeeded in keeping up with the advance.

The Germans occupied the village of Riez-Bailleul, and from this position could enfilade the 8th Infantry Brigade. The French cavalry made several gallant but unavailing efforts to capture it and consequently no advance could be made.

As darkness fell the fighting died down and the troops bivouacked on the battlefield. The squadron was alarmed during the night, and formed up, dismounted, for an attack, but it was not required, so the men remained lying by their horses until dawn.

The advance was resumed on the 15th, the squadron moving as usual on the left flank of the division. During the day it passed through the village of Bout Deville, where were found the bodies of Captain Bradshaw and his men. They were buried where they had fallen.

Although the Germans fought stubbornly the 3rd Division managed to capture Croix Barbee, Pont du Hem and Rouge Croix, and by nightfall a line was occupied along the La Bassée –Estaires road.

The enemy on the 16th did not offer a very serious resistance for some reason or other, and the squadron only twice came in touch with the hostile patrols. Towards the evening the Germans were located in some strength in occupation of a factory near Aubers. The whole of A Squadron deployed, but was unable to advance, and at dark was withdrawn to bivouacs near the Rue de Bacquerot, by which time the whole of the division had reached the line Fauquissart–Pietre–Ligny le Petit.

The line reached on this evening was destined to be the high-water mark of the advance of the British Army for many years to come. For although a slight advance was made during the next few days, the 3rd Division was forced to fall back eventually on to the approximate positions occupied on the night of 16th October.

Captain Courage on his arrival at Fauquissart got in touch with the *curé* of the village, who told him that he had lived in the district for many years and knew it well ; that he had often attended the French Army Manœuvres in this area, and that he had also listened to the conferences at the close of the operations.

At these conferences the umpires had always decided that it was impossible to hold the Fauquissart Ridge so long as the Aubers Ridge was in the hands of the enemy. The British proved that this decision was wrong, for under the real test of war they held the ridge for four long years, in spite of the fact that during the whole time the Germans were on the Aubers Ridge.

On 17th October after very severe fighting a short advance was made. Strong reinforcements of German infantry had, however, appeared in line, which offered the most stubborn resistance. In spite of this resistance Herlies was captured after a bayonet fight, and the French cavalry also succeeded in capturing Fromelles.

The successes gained on this day gave a feeling of optimism

to everybody. For it was considered that although the Germans had everywhere made a determined effort to oppose our advance, they had been driven from their positions by the dash and impetuosity of our attacks, and it was hoped that they would be forced to retreat on the following day.

A Squadron bivouacked near Aubers, under heavy shell fire all night.

The orders for A Squadron on the 18th were, in consequence of this optimistic feeling, to advance through Herlies and then push forward as far as they could. The hour of start was a very early one, but as soon as the advance scouts entered the village of Herlies they found that during the night the Germans had reoccupied some of the houses on the eastern outskirts, from which they had been driven the night before.

The squadron made every effort to push through the village, but encountered so heavy a fire that no advance was possible; efforts were made to turn the position and also to advance dismounted, but with no success, for the enemy was in far too strong a position. Although the squadron had been unable to advance, it had been enabled to locate the enemy's positions and to estimate his strength. The Germans were thus found to be strongly entrenched along the line Fournes–La Bassée: they were eventually forced to evacuate Herlies, but not before an infantry brigade had been brought up to turn them out. As no further advance was possible, the 3rd Division entrenched on the ground already gained.

A Squadron had spent the whole day fighting on the outskirts of Herlies, and, when night came, threw out an outpost line to protect the left flank of the division.

On 19th October every effort to advance absolutely failed, the troops therefore continued to dig themselves in as deeply as they could. It now appeared as though the situation was about to change, and that we were no longer to be the attackers, but that the initiative had already passed to the enemy.

The Germans were about to launch their attacks in large numbers, and the British Army was forced to abandon the offensive, and in fact was hard put to it to maintain the ground already gained.

The German drive for the Channel Ports had in fact begun and was to continue for many weeks of desperate fighting.

In front of the 3rd Division the Germans held the village of Le Pilly and as their presence in this place was most embarrassing, it was decided on 19th October that this village had to be captured at all costs. The 2nd Battalion of the Royal Irish Regiment was detailed to commence the assault at midday.

A Squadron received orders to support this attack and rode forward to Le Pluich Farm, where the men dismounted and in extended order marched across the fields to Le Riez. The whole of this movement was carried out under very heavy shell-fire. At Le Riez they joined a battalion of the Middlesex Regiment, which had also been moved forward to assist the Irish in their operation. The machine-gun detachment under Lieutenant Osborne was placed on the left flank of the Royal Irish and co-operated with them in the attack. The enemy offered a most determined resistance and it was not until about midnight that the village was in our hands, and we only succeeded in capturing it after a very hard fight.

When the 15th Hussars received orders to assist in the capture of Le Pilly, they had no illusions whatever as to the tremendous difficulties of the task. The squadron had thoroughly reconnoitred the area, and all knew the ground and the position and strength of the enemy. It was quite apparent that when the village was captured, it would be impossible to hold, for it formed a salient right into the German line and was enfiladed from every side. It seemed to all ranks of the squadron that the task was a forlorn hope.

Captain Courage states that he was astounded at the calmness of all when they realised that they were asked to participate in an attack which seemed foredoomed to failure, and the certain death of a great number of those taking part.

When the squadron leader reported to Lieutenant-Colonel Daniel commanding the Royal Irish, the latter stated that he knew his battalion would take the village but it was a question whether they could hold it. He then asked the squadron to protect his left flank during the operation. The fight at Le Pilly cost the Royal Irish the loss of the greater part of the battalion, but A Squadron on the left flank escaped very lightly indeed, as the severest fighting took place actually in the village itself.

The machine-gun detachment was in action the whole time, and by its covering fire undoubtedly assisted in the final capture of the village. Although the greater part of Le Pilly had been captured, the Germans still held out in a few houses, from where they were never dislodged. But, as already stated, the situation had entirely altered, and it was no longer a question of any further advance.

A Squadron was withdrawn after this fight and joined the divisional reserve, but only for a few hours.

At dawn on the 21st the Germans launched assault after assault against the positions occupied by the 3rd Division, and accompanied these attacks with the heaviest of shell fire. In spite of the gallant efforts of the Royal Irish Regiment, Le Pilly was recaptured, and the enemy even succeeded in breaking our line in some places. Every rifle that could be spared had to be thrown into the fight, for at times the situation looked very serious indeed, and the division was hard put to it to hold its ground.

A Squadron stood to at dawn, and shortly afterwards moved forward dismounted, and occupied some roughly constructed trenches near Le Pluich Farm. In this spot it remained all day, under continual and heavy shell fire, although no infantry attack developed against this part of the line. The squadron was relieved shortly after dark by detachments of the Royal Scots, and withdrew to bivouacs with the horses some little way behind the line.

The Germans continued their attacks on 22nd October, heralded in all cases by the heaviest of artillery preparations, but in spite of all their efforts they were unable to make any substantial advance against the 3rd Division. The French were, however, forced to abandon Fromelles.

The general situation thus became so unfavourable that it was decided to withdraw the whole of the II Corps to a position further back, where it was anticipated the corps would be in a better position to offer a stubborn resistance.

Although A Squadron had not actually become engaged with the enemy, it had spent the whole day under heavy shell-fire; after dark, in accordance with the orders to fall back, the squadron marched off and halted near the Rue de Bacquerot in the same field it had previously occupied. The whole of the 3rd Division eventually retired without much difficulty, and occupied the line Fauquissart–La Quinque Rue. The machine-gun detachment remained in the front line until almost the last, and it was not until 3 a.m. on the 23rd that it also was withdrawn.

For several days now the adventures of A Squadron have alone been chronicled. It will be remembered that both B and C Squadrons were left quietly on the Aisne, where but little fighting was taking place. We will now return to these two squadrons, and bring their story up to date.

The time eventually arrived when the I Corps in its turn was removed from the peaceful Aisne, to be flung into the fresh holocaust which was taking place in Northern France.

C Squadron marched at midnight 14th October to Arcy St. Restitute. From this place it marched by dark to Neuilly St. Front, where, aided by feeble light of lanterns, it entrained for an unknown destination. The squadron passed through Paris, and eventually detraining at St. Omer, marched at once to Cassel. Here the squadron was sumptuously housed and revelled in billets far away from the firing line.

B Squadron left the Aisne at dark on 13th October and marched direct to Fere en Tardenois, where it also entrained. Passing through Paris, it detrained at Hazebrouck, where the men were billeted and remained in peace until 17th October.

This movement of the 15th Hussars from the Aisne to the north of France was destined to be the last occasion on which the Regiment was transported by rail, until it entrained near Cologne on its way to Ireland four years later. It is hardly necessary to elaborate the tremendous events which took place in the history of the whole world between these two simple operations of the Regiment.

Both B and C Squadrons thoroughly appreciated their rest in the pleasant towns of northern France. Their billets on the Aisne had been subjected to continual shell-fire, the inhabitants had fled, and all ranks were forced to depend on their rations alone, which although excellent, became in time rather monotonous. But now everyone could buy what he wished, and all revelled in the pleasure of spending money. By day and night the menacing rumble of the distant guns told of the desperate fighting which was taking place, and all realised that this time of pleasant leisure was only momentary.

Whilst at Cassel C Squadron sent out numerous patrols which wandered far afield. Some reached the coast, and from the shore they watched our ships in action against the Belgian coast. It somehow gave to us all a feeling of comfort to think that we were in touch with the Navy, even if it was only a distant view. For there were our ships, a sign that the Navy was ready to support the troops on land.

C Squadron marched at dawn on 20th October and covered the 2nd Infantry Brigade, which formed the advance guard to the 1st Division. The Flanders country which was later to become so terribly familiar to all, seemed at the time quite strange. It was indeed a very different countryside from the wooded heights of the Aisne. This area had the aspect of a large market garden with its close cultivation and its innumerable small farms and enclosures, but all was in the course of time to be fought over and obliterated. It seemed a pity that a so highly civilised spot was doomed to destruction.

C Squadron reached Poperinghe without any adventures, threw out an outpost line until nightfall, and after dark retired into billets in the town.

B Squadron remained at Hazebrouck until 17th October.

The feeling in this town was most optimistic. Long columns of French cavalry passed through Hazebrouck, and it was confidently reported that the Allies were about to turn the enemy's right flank. Where ignorance is bliss it is, perhaps, folly to be wise.

On 17th October B Squadron marched to Boeschepe and remained in this village until dawn on 20th October, when it formed part of the advance guard to the 2nd Division, marched by Reninghelst, through Ypres, and took up a position north-west of Zonnebeke, linking up with the 7th Division and the cavalry. B Squadron withdrew to Bryke just before nightfall, directly after being relieved by the infantry.

The arrival of the I Corps in the north of France was most opportune, for the situation had rapidly developed in a way which was not at all favourable to the British Armies.

In recounting the movements of A Squadron, it has already been described how the II Corps was by this time acting on the defensive.

The Cavalry Corps about Messines was barely holding its own in face of the numerous powerful assaults launched by the enemy.

The 7th Division and the 6th Cavalry Brigade, which had originally been landed on the coast of Belgium with the intention of relieving Antwerp, had been forced to fall back, and by this time, with every rifle in the firing line, were trying hard to stem the German advance between Menin and Ypres ; their situation was almost desperate.

The French cavalry was operating on the left flank of the British Army, and so far no very strong enemy attacks had developed in this area, and it was still hoped that the enemy might be outflanked on the right. It was not until after the fighting on 21st October that this hope was finally abandoned. For it then became evident that the enemy had brought up entirely new formations in this part of the field, which absolutely precluded any idea of an advance.

A strategical problem of some complexity thus arose, and it became a question for the Commander-in-Chief to decide how he would employ the I Corps fresh from the Aisne. There were two alternatives, they could either be employed to strengthen the line south of Ypres, which was very dangerously weak, or they could be placed on the left of the 7th Division north of Ypres. It was this latter alternative which was decided upon, and, as events were to prove, the presence of the 1st and 2nd Divisions in this position undoubtedly prevented a great disaster.

The future was in consequence full of the most dangerous possibilities, for the safety of the Channel Ports was in grave jeopardy. All ranks realised the terrible strategical disaster which would be inevitable if the enemy should succeed in breaking through the thin line, which now stood between them and the domination of the Channel.

It thus came about that the 2nd Division marched to a position on the left of the 7th Division and the 1st Division continued the line further north on the left of the 2nd Division. Still further north the Belgian Army and French Marine Corps continued the line to the sea and the interval between the Allies and the British was bridged by the French cavalry.

In accordance with these movements C Squadron marched from Poperinghe at 2.30 a.m. on 21st October with the advance guard of the 1st Division.

No opposition was encountered until the advance guard approached Langemarck, when the leading troop (commanded by Lieutenant H. Brace) located the enemy in the occupation of some hurriedly-constructed trenches. The leading infantry brigade was forced to attack with some strength before he could be driven from this position.

Directly the enemy had abandoned these trenches, strong patrols from the squadron were sent forward to keep touch with him. These patrols (commanded by Lieutenant C. Stanhope) were driven out of the villages of Langemarck and Koekuit, but they were enabled to report that the Germans were in force and strongly entrenched. Eventually the whole of the 1st Division was forced to deploy, but was unable to effect any material advance. The left flank of the 1st Division was protected by the French cavalry which was engaged in the Forêt de Houthulst, but it was unable to retard the steady advance of the Germans.

In consequence the left flank of the division was eventually left in the air, and about 4 p.m. the majority of C Squadron and the cyclists were collected together, and sent to reinforce the left flank about Bixschoote. But the day's fighting had been enough for the enemy, and as darkness came on the battle died down.

About 6.30 p.m. C Squadron was withdrawn to Boesinghe, and remained there in reserve during the night.

The French Cuirassier division on the left of the British looked magnificent and displayed the greatest bravery, but they could not seriously interfere with the advance of the German infantry supported by modern artillery.

The Cuirassiers were at this time still dressed in their old uniforms, which gave a touch of the picturesque to the usual grim and drab aspect of a modern battlefield. The sight of these gorgeous horsemen, as they moved backwards and forwards, inevitably brought to mind scenes of Napoleonic warfare, and recalled the pictures by Meissonier. Modern war is not at all picturesque, and the British higher commanders experienced a feeling of anxiety as to their left flank throughout the day, because the French Cavalry were not able to offer any very serious resistance to the enemy.

The 2nd Division had received rather optimistic orders for the operations on 21st October, and B Squadron was told to push forward as far as possible in the direction of Thorout. The advance guard to the 2nd Division was formed by the 4th (Guards) Brigade, and B Squadron joined them just before dawn.

It soon became quite evident that no real advance was possible, for the enemy was encountered in overwhelming strength. The 7th Division on the right of the 2nd Division was barely holding its own against the repeated assaults of the enemy.

In spite of the resistance of the Germans, the 4th (Guards) Brigade by dint of severe fighting gained ground slowly to its front, but in the course of this movement a gap occurred between the right of the Guards and the left of the 22nd Brigade, the left flank unit of the 7th Division. This gap B Squadron was ordered to fill.

By 2 p.m. the Guards had crossed the Haanebeke Stream, north of Zonnebeke Railway Station. Their line, which by this time stretched from St. Julien to the railway, was very extended.

B Squadron had so far been moving forward mounted, but at 2 p.m. the fire became so heavy that they were forced to dismount. Leaving as few men as possible with the led horses, they placed every rifle that could be spared into the firing line, and attempted to continue the advance on foot. The squadron was opposed by considerable rifle- and machine-gun-fire, whilst shells of all calibres burst unceasingly amongst the men. A further advance soon became impossible, and the men lay down in the open fields, without shelter of any kind against the storm of hostile fire.

It must be realised that at this time there were no trenches of any sort, nor was it possible for the men of the Regiment to construct their own trenches, for at this period of the war, the only entrenching tools carried by the cavalry were on the pack horses, and it was seldom that they could be brought anywhere near the firing line.

B Squadron, however, was not required to repel any hostile infantry assault, for the Germans concentrated all their efforts against the 7th Division away on the right. This unfortunate division, already pretty severely handled, was very hard put to it to resist the fury of the hostile attacks, and the situation was on the whole unsatisfactory.

At dark B Squadron was relieved by a detachment of the Coldstream Guards, and retired to bivouacs and the horses at Bryke.

It was very seldom that the squadrons were not relieved about nightfall. But it must be remembered that the squadrons had always to solve the problem of feeding and looking after their horses. Troop horses are not swayed by strong patriotic feelings, which would enable them to endure patiently discomfort and hardship, and if the squadrons were to remain mobile the horses had to be kept in good condition, which entailed care and attention. It was indeed a great strain on the men, when after a long day's fighting, they were forced to return to the horses, and spend much of their hard earned rest in grooming, watering and feeding them.

By nightfall on the 21st the 2nd Division was disposed as follows. The right of the 4th (Guards) Brigade rested on Zonnebeke, the 5th Infantry Brigade was on its left, in touch with the 1st Division. The 6th Infantry Brigade still remained in reserve.

Thursday, the 22nd, proved to be a day of heavy fighting all along the front of the 1st Division ; as far as the British were concerned it was a most successful day, and the enemy can have no very pleasant memories of the Battle of Langemarck.

Shortly after dawn the Germans opened a heavy bombardment, and after considerable artillery preparation attacked all along the line held by the 1st Division. This attack was particularly heavy and determined between Het Sas and Langemarck, where a fresh and picked corps of Germans advanced. This corps was composed of young men from the different German Universities, and they moved forward with the greatest determination and bravery. In spite of the very heavy casualties caused by the rapid and accurate shooting of our infantry, these fanatics succeeded towards evening in breaking our line, and occupying our trenches. After the very severe handling they had received, they were in no position to follow up their success and take advantage of the gap they had succeeded in creating. In the course of their assault they took some prisoners from us ; these prisoners were released by the successful counter-attack launched by us on the following day.

Our men reported that many of these young Germans had never fired their rifles during the attacks, but advanced against us with arms linked, singing patriotic songs, and absolutely intoxicated with military ardour and patriotism. This corps was practically annihilated in its attack and in the course of our counter-attack, a fearful slaughter of the best youth of Germany.

C Squadron with the cyclists had been moved just before dawn to a position of readiness half a mile south of Pilckem; here they remained saddled up and ready to move at a moment's notice. At 4.30 p.m. information was received that our line had been pierced as a result of the attack already recorded; in consequence C Squadron was ordered to a position opposite the spot where the breach had occurred, and occupied a line along the Ypres–Langemarck railway north of Pilckem. Here the squadron remained all night; except for the occasional splutter of machine-gun-fire, and a few lonely shells which burst along the railway line, the squadron passed a quiet night.

The 2nd Division was not really heavily pressed on this day, 22nd October; it was, however, forced to draw back slightly in order to conform to the movements of the troops on the right and left. This withdrawal involved the abandonment of Zonnebeke.

Towards evening it was reported that the enemy had not yet occupied this village, and Lieutenant Liddell was sent forward with a strong patrol to clear up the situation. The patrol found that Zonnebeke was full of Germans, who were fortifying themselves in the village. The men came under heavy fire and were lucky to escape with their lives.

This record of B and C Squadrons is now brought up to date with that of A Squadron. By nightfall on the 22nd the men of C Squadron were lying out in the open on the railway line near Pilckem. B Squadron was bivouacked near Bryke, and A Squadron was lying out in a field further south near the Rue de Bacquerot.

The 23rd October was not a day of very severe fighting for the I Corps. The 1st Division counter-attacked at dawn in order to re-establish the line which had been broken the previous day. The attack was entirely successful, all the lost ground being regained and numbers of prisoners captured. After this successful assault C Squadron was withdrawn from the railway, and retired to Boesinghe. The squadron remained saddled up all day, but except for finding the usual despatch riders and orderlies was not otherwise employed.

The German attacks on the front of the I Corps on the 23rd were not very determined, so that the 2nd Infantry Brigade was withdrawn in corps reserve; to this brigade the 1st Troop of C Squadron was attached and so remained until 30th October.

During the day reinforcements of French troops began to arrive. These belonged to one of the best corps of the French Army. They arrived in the very best of spirits and began to take over the line from the 1st Division. As far as B Squadron was concerned there is not much to chronicle for the 23rd. The 17th French Division relieved the 2nd Division during the day, and the squadron was left in peace until dark, when it marched to Verbranden Molen.

It will probably be simpler and lead to less confusion if the record of A Squadron is now resumed, and its adventures alone chronicled for the next few days, until in fact it joined in the fighting outside Ypres, and the three squadrons of the Regiment were more or less together again.

It will be remembered that the 3rd Division had withdrawn on 23rd October to a more favourable position.

On 24th October the hostile artillery opened on to this new position with unabated fury, and later on in the day the attacks were renewed all along the front held by the 3rd Division. The battle now developed into a fight for trenches, during which the squadron of divisional cavalry did not play a very important rôle, so that this is not the place to describe in detail the struggle which endured throughout the day, but attack and counter-attack followed each other in rapid succession.

About midnight the enemy succeeded in occupying some trenches held by the Gordon Highlanders, and the squadron stood to in order to assist in the counter-attack which was organised to recover these lost trenches. They were not required, as the gallant Highlanders had counter-attacked on their own initiative, and recovered all the lost ground.

There is not much to record of A Squadron in this area during the next few days. What happened on the Aisne took place here, and the battle slowly developed into trench warfare. The trenches at first were not very elaborate, but in the course of time both sides succeeded in digging themselves in. A Squadron remained in reserve, very often the only reserve left to the division ; numerous patrols were sent out to keep in touch with the front line, and to observe the ever-changing situation.

About this time the units from the Indian divisions were arriving in ever-increasing numbers.

A series of fierce battles took place round the little village of Neuve Chapelle, but as A Squadron took no very important part in these battles, this history is not the place in which to record them. The squadron was moved up close behind the assaulting troops, but was never actively engaged. On the whole the fighting in this area slowly died down, for the Germans were now concentrating all their efforts on the great struggle taking place round the city of Ypres.

Towards the end of the month the 3rd Division was relieved

by the Indian divisions. On 31st October A Squadron marched in pouring rain to Meteren, where it was forced to bivouac in the open for the night. The usual optimistic rumours were in circulation, such as are usually current after a relief. It was reported that the 3rd Division were to go into Army Reserve, and everybody was looking forward to a period of ease and quiet.

But at this time there was little leisure for any soldier of the British Army, and at 2 p.m. on 1st November A Squadron was ordered to march into Belgium. They spent the night at a small farm near Locre, and as a matter of fact remained there quietly until 6th November.

It now became apparent that the I Corps had been fought almost to a standstill, and on the 5th and 6th of November the 7th and 9th Infantry Brigades marched east of Ypres to the support of this corps. A Squadron marched at 5 p.m. on 6th November. The roads, however, were so crowded that the squadron could make no progress, and was forced to return to the former bivouacs ; they marched again at dawn on 7th November through the burning city of Ypres to the *halte* on the Menin Road. The led horses were sent away, and the men lay down in the open to snatch what rest they could, in anticipation of the strenuous work which lay before them.

The situation in the Ypres salient was by this time almost desperate, and the British Army had scarcely a soldier left in reserve.

It is now necessary to return to the history of B and C Squadrons.

On 23rd October, as has already been recorded, the French Army commenced to relieve the units of the I Corps.

C Squadron in consequence of this relief marched during the night of 24th/25th through Ypres, and went into billets in a farm about one mile south of the town.

Ypres was at this time untouched. As the troops marched through the streets a bright moon showed up the celebrated Cloth Hall in a most picturesque manner.

The Cafés were crowded, and the inhabitants all about in the streets. They watched with interest the long defile of British troops through the town. In the middle of the square a squadron of French Cuirassiers, still dressed in their old-time uniforms, fitted in completely with the background of old Flemish houses. The whole aspect of Ypres was so attractive that all ranks promised themselves a return visit later. But this, alas ! was never possible, for when the squadrons again marched through the town the greater part of it had ceased to exist.

On the 24th the 2nd Division was ordered to relieve certain units of the 7th Division, who by this time were so exhausted that they were hardly able to offer any very serious opposition to determined hostile attacks. The 2nd Division therefore moved up to a line about Zonnebeke to Poezelhoek.

About 10 a.m. it was reported that the enemy had broken our line, and the 5th Infantry Brigade was in consequence marched to Eksternest ; B Squadron was ordered forward to form a defensive flank on the right of this brigade. The squadron therefore occupied a line south of the Menin Road about Gheluvelt.

The orders were for the 2nd Division to attack, as the higher commanders did not wish to lose the initiative, and it was considered that the best form of defence would be an active one. Owing to the fact that the 2nd Division had only just been relieved by the French and was not all in position, it was decided the postpone the attack until the 25th. B Squadron therefore remained on their extended line during the night, and anticipated that they would receive orders to advance on the next day.

C Squadron spent the 25th quietly in billets. The owner of the farm was lying dangerously ill, and all ranks were requested to keep as quiet as possible so as not to disturb the old lady. In a few days her farm was to become a blazing ruin.

Although the orders for the 2nd Division were to attack at dawn on the 25th, for various reasons this attack was postponed until 3 p.m. No very great advance was made although the 4th (Guards) Brigade were enabled to reach the western slopes of the Reutel spur. In this fight B Squadron did not play a very important part ; patrols were sent out to keep in touch with the ever shifting eddies of the attack, but the majority remained standing to their horses day and night near Hooge.

On the 26th the 1st Division moved forward at 3 a.m. to support the 7th Division. C Squadron covered the advance and moved through Zillebeke on to the Menin Road. The orders were that an attack was to be delivered on either side of this road, in order to relieve the pressure on the 7th Division.

The men of the 1st Division as they marched forward looked the picture of health and fitness, compared to the hollow-eyed men of the 7th Division.

As a patrol from C Squadron moved up the Menin Road it encountered small parties from the 7th Division, whose Officers and N.C.O.'s had all become casualties, and the leaderless men were straggling back to the rear. The corporal in charge of the Hussar patrol (Corporal MacKay) informed these stragglers that his men formed part of the 1st Division advance guard, which was at this moment advancing to their support. This news acted like magic, and the tired men at once turned about and returned to the firing line on their own initiative.

The head of the advance guard had no sooner reached Veldhoek, when it was found that a battle was already taking place in this quarter. The 1st (Guards) Brigade was in consequence forced to deploy, and as it was unable to make very much headway against the enemy, the 3rd Infantry Brigade also deployed. In a short time the whole of the division was heavily engaged. (The reader will remember that the 2nd Infantry Brigade had been drawn into Corps Reserve.)

Battery after battery moved forward into action, and as the intensity of our fire increased so did that of the enemy. The patrols from C Squadron remained out in front as long as they could, until they were eventually driven back on to the infantry firing line; the squadron then collected near Veldhoek and remained there awaiting further orders.

By nightfall the infantry was digging in amongst the beet fields, under an unceasing bombardment from the enemy. After dark C Squadron retired to the shelter of the woods by Hooge, but remained saddled up throughout the night.

The 2nd Division was not heavily engaged on the 26th, but it was unable to carry out any real forward movement as the divisions on its flanks could not advance. In consequence B Squadron had not very much to do, although numerous patrols were sent out. They remained saddled up standing by their horses in a constant state of anxiety, awaiting at any moment the orders to join in a battle which so far was not developing too favourably for us.

It is very difficult in writing the story of the 15th Hussars to describe their movements during the 1st Battle of Ypres.

As the Regiment fought at this period, not as a whole, but broken up into numerous small detachments, to follow the records of small patrols or to record all their movements is manifestly impossible, and all that can be given is a rough outline of the work which was done.

Owing to the flat and wooded nature of the country, it was always very difficult to find out what exactly was taking place. Divisional headquarters therefore sent out a continual succession of mounted patrols from their divisional cavalry to report on the varying phases of the battle. At this time it was quite possible to do this, because the trenches were still only rudimentary, and the fighting was practically in the open. The highly trained patrols from the 15th Hussars were a very reliable and speedy source of information, not only as to what was taking place in the actual firing line, but also what was happening to the flank formations.

As there had been no time to bury the cables deeply, directly the hostile bombardment opened, the wires were at once destroyed, and the roads became death traps ; then the only means of communication was by the mounted orderly, who could gallop across country. At times the whole of this duty devolved on the 15th Hussars.

Although the Regiment never suffered the annihilating casualties of the infantry and the rest of the cavalry, yet there was a steady drain of men and horses, for the squadrons were under ceaseless shell fire both by day and night.

As the war developed and trenches and wire became more elaborate, and highly scientific modes of communication came into use, mounted patrols and orderlies entirely fell into disfavour. But there can be little doubt that, if in the later stages of the war the divisions had been served by highly trained divisional cavalry, their value would have been found incalculable. The Cavalry Corps, which alone had the use of well-trained cavalry patrols in some of the later battles of the war, by Officers' Patrols were always kept in the closest touch with the actual situation of the firing line.

Besides the duties already mentioned, the squadrons provided the personal escort to the divisional commander and were the last reserve of the divisions, only to be used at moments of extreme peril.

The duties performed by the squadrons, although in no way spectacular, were nevertheless very important.

From 27th October to 29th October the I Corps battled desperately to maintain its position, but it is impossible to record in detail the action of either B or C Squadron during this period. They simply carried out the duties which have been described. By this time all hopes of an advance had been entirely abandoned, and it was now only a question as to whether the line would break under the continued assaults of the enemy. The men never off-saddled, but stood to their horses day and night, expecting at any moment to receive the orders that they were to hold out to the last man in some reserve position.

On 30th October the Germans continued their attacks in strong force all along our front. C Squadron was not very heavily engaged, and there is not much to record of its doings on this day. Except for the usual strong patrols which were sen t out, the rest of the squadron spent the day standing to their horses awaiting further orders.

B Squadron on the other hand had a strenuous time. The

attacks against the 2nd Division were pressed with the greatest determination by the enemy, and although the division was able to beat off all these assaults there were periods during the battle when the situation appeared most precarious.

A very large number of patrols were sent out, so that only two weak troops were left with divisional headquarters as escort. Finally these two troops were sent under Captain the Hon. W. A. Nugent to join Lord Cavan's brigade, whose right flank had become exposed owing to the fact that the cavalry on the right, after a very severe fight, had been driven from their positions.

Although the cavalry had been driven from the advanced trenches, it had not fallen back very far, and the squadron was enabled to join up with the 10th Royal Hussars and the Royal Dragoons about Klein Zillebeke. The Royal Scots Greys were also still holding out about this place, so that on the whole the situation was not so desperate as had at first appeared and the line was finally linked up.

After dark the 15th Hussars retired back to the farm they had occupied during the day. On their return, however, they found the farm in flames ; all ranks now worked desperately hard to extinguish the fire, which by this time was burning fiercely. The task was not carried out without danger for the enemy shelled the building the whole time, but eventually the fire was put out. This effort to save the farm was indeed a labour of love in the Ypres salient.

On 31st October one of the hardest fought battles in the Ypres salient took place, and it would not perhaps be an exaggeration to say that this day was one of the most critical in the whole history of the war, and to those who took part in the fighting the memory will always be a very grim one.

At an early hour the enemy commenced a heavy bombardment along the whole front, and shortly afterwards launched a series of assaults, delivered in great strength and carried out with the utmost determination. The main brunt of the attack fell upon the troops on either side of the Menin Road, and the chief focus of the battle centred round the village of Gheluvelt.

Here in the story of the 15th Hussars it is only possible to record the movements of the two squadrons, who owing to their duties played but a minor rôle in the great struggle. Other histories have described the splendid way in which the British Army fought on this day, and have recorded the great bravery displayed by all ranks. The Germans did not break through, and did not reach the Channel Ports, but it was only due to the stubborn British soldier that the enemy's plan did not succeed.

At dawn the usual officers' patrols went out from the two

squadrons, and on the return of these patrols from the front line, and from the flank formations, their information proved to be most depressing, for they reported the fierce attacks all along our front and serious loss of ground in many places. About 9 a.m. the cyclists attached to C Squadron were sent north of Gheluvelt to strengthen the line there. A few hours later, about 12.30 p.m. the enemy succeeded in breaking our line in some places, and down the Menin Road streamed the scattered remnants from different units of all divisions.

The last few days' fighting had been of such a desperate and fierce character that the infantry had almost reached the limit of human endurance ; in some cases the men, left without officers and N.C.O.'s and half dazed from want of sleep, fell back towards Ypres. Both B and C Squadrons called in their patrols, and collected together as quickly as they could ; C Squadron marched to near Veldhoek and B Squadron to Westhoek. Their orders were to hold on to these positions to the very last, and also to collect all stragglers, re-form them and send them back to the front.

In spite of the heavy fire, the Corps Commander[1] rode forward with his staff and a small escort as though it was a field day. He dismounted, planted his flag by the roadside, and personally helped to re-form and rally the men. Rifles were collected, and those who were unarmed were re-equipped, the men were formed up into small parties, and placed under the command of officers and N.C.O.'s, who had hastily been gathered together from every direction. Arrangements were made for each man to have something to eat and a cup of tea, and after a short rest they all gallantly marched back to the inferno from which they had just come.

Throughout the whole of the battle the mounted despatch riders from the Regiment were continually employed, carrying messages backwards and forwards from the front line. They never failed, although their duties were carried out under conditions of the very greatest danger and difficulty.

During the crisis of the battle, a disaster of the first magnitude occurred to the I Corps. A conference of the staffs of the 1st and 2nd Divisions was taking place in Hooge Chateau, when a shell burst in the room where the conference was being held, and the greater part of the two staffs were killed or wounded. Major-General S. H. Lomax, who commanded the 1st Division, received wounds from which he subsequently died.

This meant that during the crisis of the fight the greater part of the directing staff was obliterated. Brigadier-General H. J. Landon, who commanded the 3rd Infantry Brigade, assumed

[1] The late Field-Marshal the Earl Haig of Bemersyde, K.T., etc., etc.

the command of the 1st Division and collected a staff from where he could.

Towards evening the German attack died away, for they had failed in their object. Although the British had received a stunning blow, they were not knocked out. Throughout the day numerous small detachments had grimly held to their positions, and refused to budge, and units which had been driven from their trenches, with dogged determination, attempted to regain them, and thus the British line held firm. Although shaken and shattered, the Army continued to fight.

As soon as it was dark, the tired men dug themselves in on the ground they occupied. The 15th watered their horses, and stood by them all night, awaiting whatever fate should hold in store for them the next day.

The shell-fire continued if anything with increased intensity during 1st November. The men of C Squadron were employed in digging trenches just east of Hooge ; during this operation they were heavily shelled, and many men and horses were killed and wounded. It was with the greatest difficulty that a place could be found for the led horses ; it was possible for the men to find or dig a little cover for themselves, but the horses were perforce in the open, and as the salient round Ypres was now in the process of formation, the shells seemed to come from every direction.

B Squadron had exactly the same difficulty with its horses, and it was impossible to protect them.

It would be difficult to record in detail the movements of B and C Squadrons during the next ten days ; they carried out their usual duties and eventually found themselves the only reserves left to the divisions. They therefore dug strong positions near divisional headquarters, where they were ordered to hold out to the last in the event of the enemy breaking through the line, a contingency which appeared extremely likely. Their casualties slowly mounted up, for every part of the salient came under fire, and it was almost impossible to find shelter.[1]

The I Corps had now been fighting for some time, and the casualties had been fearful. There was also a certain amount of confusion ; battalions, brigades, and even divisions, were all mingled together, and efforts were made to reorganise, but as the battle never ceased for a minute, the harassed troops had little time to re-form. The reserves were all exhausted, the Germans were in superior numbers, with very much stronger artillery, and apparently unlimited ammunition. Night and day their

[1] On 3rd November Lieutenant P. P. Curtis and Second Lieutenant A. Cubitt with a draft joined B Squadron.

bombardment had been unceasing and attack had followed upon attack. There was no respite for the men in the trenches, nor even the prospect of relief.

At this time there were none of those amenities which later made trench life bearable. There were no duck-boards, communication trenches, or dug-outs. The trenches were merely connected shell holes ; communication was almost impossible, and it was with the greatest difficulty that food supplies could be taken to the front line. And yet the men held on.

Later on in the war there were many fierce battles, but probably the First Battle of Ypres was the most desperately contested of all. The faces of the men showed what they were enduring, all had in their eyes a look of tremendous strain, all were unshaven, caked in mud and in the last stages of exhaustion. But all ranks realised that behind the thin khaki line, which was so grimly and fiercely clinging to its shell holes, lay the Channel Ports ; and once the line was broken there was nothing to stop the German Army marching straight to Calais, and so these men clung on.

In this manner B and C Squadrons passed the time until the night of 10th November.

The story of A Squadron was brought up to 7th November, and the narrative left the squadron lying in the open near the *halte* on the Menin Road. The three squadrons of the 15th Hussars were now fighting on the same battlefield, and for the first time since the commencement of the war the men of the Regiment met together. This meeting cheered everybody up, the men needed cheering as the outlook was rather gloomy.

At dawn on 8th November A Squadron marched on foot to support a battalion of the Bedfordshire Regiment, which owing to very heavy casualties was extremely weak in numbers. The squadron occupied trenches south of the Menin Road, which were scarcely more than scratches marked on the ground. A few shelters of sorts were found and in these the men took cover. Throughout the day A Squadron was bombarded in its miserable shelters, but no infantry attacks actually developed against that part of the line which it was holding, although on the right and left the enemy attacked with vigour, and in some places succeeded in entering our trenches. It appeared just about nightfall that the situation was most serious and that the British line was broken. A Squadron therefore fixed bayonets, moved to the Menin Road and lay down, prepared to resist to the last man. In this spot they lay all night, expecting at any moment to see the German infantry advancing against them. Nothing of the sort, however, occurred. The squadron nevertheless remained lying in the open all the next day, the men were unable to move and were cruelly shelled. Towards dark the Germans opened with machine-gun-fire and attempted to advance. They were met by the steady fire of the men and easily driven back. Captain Bald was wounded during this attack, but on the whole the casualties were not heavy. At 7.30 p.m. A Squadron was relieved and withdrew to its bivouacs near the *halte*.

Here it remained during 10th November under continuous shell-fire, but it was not employed. Late in the evening, Lieutenant B. Osborne, with the machine-guns and one troop of A Squadron, were sent forward to the trenches south of the Menin Road, near Veldhoek, where they occupied a defensive post under the orders of the 9th Infantry Brigade.

At dawn on 11th November the enemy opened a very heavy bombardment along the whole front east of Ypres. This was the heaviest fire that anyone had so far experienced ; drum-fire the Germans called it, and it obliterated many of the primitive trenches in which the men were crouching. So far every attempt of the enemy to reach the Channel Ports had failed, but this was to be one last and desperate effort to batter a way through our lines to the longed-for goal. For this battle they brought up fresh and picked troops, the flower of the German Army, the Prussian Guard, who, under the eyes of the German Emperor, now attacked with the greatest valour and determination on either side of the Menin Road. The adventures of the three squadrons during this battle will be described in detail.

At an early hour C Squadron stood to its horses, as directly the hostile bombardment started it was anticipated that a serious situation was impending. At 9.30 a.m. reports came back that the line had been broken and that the situation was desperate.

The squadron and the cyclists were immediately ordered forward and thus at this early hour the final reserves of the 1st Division were employed. As C Squadron moved forward on foot to the front line the situation appeared very obscure, and it was very difficult to discover how our line ran or how far the Germans had penetrated. The squadron therefore took up a position in a sunken road east of Veldhoek, and from there sent out numerous patrols to find out what had actually taken place.

The enemy appeared to be on all sides, and as bullets were coming from the left flank the squadron was forced to withdraw the left troop and face it north.

Our own infantry could be seen advancing to an attack against the enemy behind the position occupied by the squadron, and the patrols reported small parties of enemy lying in the fields in the rear. A single British gun was in action in front, and heavy rifle-fire from the trenches well in advance could also be heard.

The Black Watch had a redoubt somewhere to the left front, which evidently was still holding out, as their wounded trickled back through the squadron.

It can thus easily be realised how very difficult it was to elucidate the situation, nor did anyone really discover what was actually taking place ; bullets were flying in all directions and Germans appeared to be everywhere.

As a matter of fact, writing years after the event, it appears that the enemy had broken our line in places, but isolated detachments of British soldiers still held on, whilst a few Germans who had advanced right forward, lost and bewildered, were lying low, only occasionally firing a shot ; the majority of attackers never advanced beyond the line they originally captured from us.

About midday C Squadron was recalled to Hooge, but at 4 p.m. was again ordered forward, as it had been decided to make a counter-attack to regain the lost positions.

Brigadier-General FitzClarence, V.C. (commanding the 1st Guards Brigade) was to command and organise this attack, for which details had somehow been collected from all divisions and reported to the general in the evening.

The scene which took place in the ruined farm which was the general's headquarters was perhaps a memorable one. The shattered room was lit by candles stuck in bottles ; outside the rain fell in torrents, and one by one the different unit commanders came in to report the arrival of their commands. Unshaven, soaked to the skin, and dead tired, they stood round the table to give their reports and the number of men they had with them. It was sad hearing. Most of the battalions were commanded by subalterns, and few numbered more than a score or so of tired men. Outside in the pouring rain, caked in mud, the unfortunate men detailed for this attack lay down under what cover they could find, and prayed only for rest and peace.

The counter-attack did not succeed, and the general himself was killed at the head of his men. This effort although unsuccessful, probably prevented the enemy from realising the alarming breach he had battered through our lines. Before this counter-attack was launched, the Germans had only between them and the Channel Ports a few handfuls of exhausted men whose resistance could have been brushed aside without much difficulty.

Directly the counter-attack had been launched, C Squadron

was ordered to return to Hooge for the protection of divisional headquarters.

To turn now to the adventures of B Squadron on 11th November. Early in the morning the reports arrived that all along the front there was very heavy shelling. Later on information was received from the French on the left that an attack was developing about Langemark, and the patrols reported that heavy attacks had developed against both the 1st and 3rd Division.

At about 9.17 a.m. therefore the few remaining reserves of the 2nd Division moved forward to about Polygon and Nonne Boschen Woods ; at the same time B Squadron was sent to Westhoek, with orders to defend that place to the last.

By the time that the squadron arrived at this position the enemy had already overrun our line, and was approaching Westhoek.

As a result of this attack, two British batteries—the 9th and 16th—were left in the open. The battery commanders, with great gallantry, collected the stragglers who were passing through the guns, and dismounting the drivers, managed somehow to beat off the enemy, and by hard fighting were enabled to retire out of action, without the loss of a single gun. As they fell back they unlimbered at Westhoek on the line already occupied by B Squadron, and once again came into action. B Squadron thereupon supplied an escort to the guns, with orders to protect them at all costs. The fire from these two batteries in their new positions proved most effective, for they fired at point-blank range against the advancing enemy.

Meanwhile the rest of the squadron extended dismounted through Nonne Boschen Wood, where the men lay down in the open, prepared to put up as good a fight as possible. The Germans did not, however, press through this wood, and the 2nd Division was enabled to collect units for a counter-attack. At 3.30 p.m. the 2nd Battalion Oxfordshire and Buckinghamshire Light Infantry began an advance through Nonne Boschen Wood. In spite of the heavy fire B Squadron had kept a few mounted patrols with the front line, and as soon as the counter-attack developed, these advanced on either flank, and did not retire until the infantry commenced to dig themselves in. Throughout the whole of the battle B Squadron was largely responsible for keeping up the communications of the 2nd Division and in the evening the commander personally congratulated the men on the way they had kept him informed of the situation in the front line.

After dark the majority of the squadron was withdrawn to

Hooge. Lieutenant P. P. Curtis[1] and his troop were left in Nonne Boschen Wood during the night, for the purposes of communication.

A Squadron was also roused very early in the morning of 11th November by the German bombardment, and the first orders received were to send a troop forward to the front line to act as gallopers to the various headquarters, for every cable had been destroyed by the bombardment.

At 10 a.m. the remaining two troops of the squadron reported to the 9th Infantry Brigade, and occupied the trenches near Herenthage Chateau, just south of Veldhoek. The reader will remember that the machine-gun detachment and one troop had already been sent forward the night before.

Shortly after the squadron had occupied its position, two men belonging to the regimental machine-gun detachment tumbled into the squadron's trenches with the information that the machine-guns had been rushed by the Germans, but in spite of this news it was evident that at least one of the guns was still in action, for all could plainly hear the sound of its firing. Eventually after a few short bursts this also ceased, and it became evident that the detachments must have been overwhelmed.

The actual facts will of course never be known. Lieutenant Osborne and his men were brave and determined, and fought to the last man, for no prisoners were taken. It is a certainty that they accounted for many of the enemy before they in their turn were overwhelmed.

As has already been narrated a troop (commanded by Sergeant Scarterfield) had been sent forward the night before with the machine-guns, and occupied the stables of Herenthage Chateau. When the first rush of the attack by the Prussian Guard took place, Sergeant Scarterfield and his men found themselves surrounded; their position was, however, never captured, and they stoutly held out during the whole day. From their position they were able to enfilade the enemy and caused them the heaviest of casualties, the men had the most wonderful targets, of which they took the fullest advantage.

Towards evening a counter-attack was launched by the Royal Scots, who suffered very heavily, but succeeded in driving back the enemy at the point of the bayonet, and thus eventually the small detachment of Hussars was relieved.

Throughout the day the remainder of A Squadron crouched in their miserable trenches, under a continuous and heavy fire. Rain fell the whole time, and the trenches became absolutely

[1] Now Major P. P. Curtis, M.C.

water-logged, therefore as soon as it became dark, the squadron lay out in the open, and here under a pitiless rain, cold, miserable and wet, the men spent the night.

The counter-attacks which the British launched during the night were not on the whole successful, yet the line was perhaps slightly improved. The cold and cheerless dawn of 12th November followed this miserable night, and as the sun rose the heavy-eyed and exhausted troops looked anxiously towards the enemy, anticipating further attacks. But no serious infantry assaults took place, although the intense hostile artillery fire continued all day.

There is not very much more to record of the doings of B and C Squadrons at Ypres. The casualties continued to mount up, for the hostile guns searched every corner of the dread salient, and there was no cover to be found except by digging.

The weather by this time had become abominable, and pouring rain turned the trenches into rivers of mud, which added greatly to the other miseries endured by the troops in the Ypres salient.

At last the much-needed relief for the I Corps arrived and the French troops began to take over the line on 15th November.[1]

At 5 a.m. on the 16th C Squadron marched to Westoutre, where the transport joined for the first time since 26th October.

The horses had never been unsaddled since that date, for the situation throughout the battle had always been so precarious that divisional headquarters never allowed the squadrons to off-saddle. Although the horses had had their saddles on their backs continuously for twenty-one days, there was not a single case of a sore back amongst them.

On the 17th C Squadron marched to a farm near Merris, where orders were received for a rest and refit.

B Squadron left the Ypres salient during the 16th and marched to Poperinghe, continuing the march next day to billets in Hazebrouck.

The 3rd Division was not relieved until some time later. As already recorded A Squadron had spent the night of 11th/12th November, the men lying out in the open on the Menin Road, but at daylight they were forced to re-occupy the sodden trenches they had abandoned during the night, and two troops under Captain B Ritchie were sent to hold the ruins of Herenthage Chateau. Chilled to the bone, the men of A Squadron crouched in the mud and slime of their trench and endured a heavy German bombardment, but luckily the enemy made no attempt to attack. They remained in this extremely uncomfortable position until

[1] Whilst this relief was taking place Lieutenant de B. Hodge and a draft straight from England joined C Squadron.

3 a.m. on the 14th, when they were relieved and retired to a farm near the *halte*.

The rest, however, was destined to be of short duration, for later on in the day the Germans launched an attack against Herenthage Chateau, which they captured. A Squadron was alarmed in billets and was again sent forward to assist in the counter-attack, which was being organised to recapture this place.

After severe fighting the infantry recaptured the stables of the Chateau, but the house itself remained in the hands of the enemy. A Squadron was not employed, and later returned to its ruined farm near the *halte*, which was now shared with C Squadron.

A Squadron was again sent forward to Hooge, about 1.30 p.m. on the 15th, but returned to the farm after dark.

On 17th November the enemy opened a heavy bombardment all along the front, and shortly afterwards launched attacks in considerable strength ; these attacks were only repulsed by our counter-attack, and A Squadron was again ordered forward to about Hooge, to support the 9th Infantry Brigade ; its services were not required and it returned at dusk to its farm.

The First Battle of Ypres was now in reality at an end, although the enemy continued to shell our trenches with considerable fierceness, and some of them were so utterly obliterated that they had to be abandoned.

A hard frost now succeeded the heavy rain, but this was rather an advantage, as it made the trenches far more habitable, and a hard dry frost is never so trying as cold and continuous rain.

At 10 a.m. on the 19th A Squadron again marched to the front line, where they relieved part of the Northumberland Fusiliers south of the Menin Road. During the day the enemy by heavy gun-fire had blown the troops occupying the stables of Herenthage Chateau from their position, but as the place had by this time been reduced to a mere handful of bricks, it was of no tactical importance whatsoever, it was therefore decided not to occupy the ruins.

The tour of A Squadron in the trenches was on the whole uneventful, enemy trench mortars and snipers made movement during the day quite impossible, but no serious attack developed against that part of the line.

At 10 p.m. on 20th November the squadron was relieved without incident by the French, and retired once again to the farm. At 6.15 a.m. the next day the led horses were brought up and the squadron marched through the shattered town of Ypres to a farm near Westoutre, where they remained until the 24th, when they moved to Berthen, and on the 25th the squadron went into billets in a farm near Mont Noir, where it was destined to remain for some considerable time.

So the battle came to an end, perhaps one of the fiercest ever fought. The men composing the Armies who fought and died in this battle were the picked troops of all the belligerents on the Western front: highly trained and disciplined, they comprised the finest manhood of Europe.

The Germans attacked day after day with the greatest determination and valour, but they were opposed by men who were braver and still more determined—for whom there was no question of further retreat—who were prepared to die where they stood.

Thus for the 15th Hussars ended the First Battle of Ypres.

BOOT AND SADDLE

Chapter V

THE WINTER OF 1914–1915; THE REGIMENT REASSEMBLED; THE BATTLE OF YPRES 1915

EVERYTHING is comparative, and to the men of the 15th Hussars the little Flemish farms seemed to be the acme of comfort and luxury, after the trials and discomforts of the Battle of Ypres. Here at any rate was peace and quiet, a warm fire and hot food, with the possibilities of a bath and a shave.

At this time the British Army at the front was such a small unit that the people at home could concentrate all their benevolence upon it. In consequence parcels and presents of all sorts were showered upon the squadrons; many of the parcels contained kindly messages from the donors, the men were almost overwhelmed with their presents, and the postal authorities must have been severely taxed to deal with them all.

When it was announced that leave would be granted, it can well be imagined with what great delight this news was received; at first the officers and later N.C.O.'s and men were enabled to spend a few days at home, and enjoy a period of well-earned leisure.

The days passed rapidly, everybody hard at work looking after the horses, and getting them fit again after the strenuous time they had gone through in the Ypres salient.

It can no doubt be realised that during the progress of the battle no one had much time or opportunity to devote to the horses, and the squadrons always found it most difficult to water and feed them at the proper hours; watering facilities in the Ypres salient did not exist, and there was always the greatest difficulty in bringing up the forage, but in spite of all these hardships the condition of the horses was on the whole good, and they very soon picked up all the condition they had lost during the battle.

All ranks were rapidly re-equipped, and the Regiment brought up to strength in men and horses, and in a very short time the Battle of Ypres became only a memory, and the 15th Hussars were once again ready to take the field.

During December 1914 His Majesty the King visited France, and on 3rd December the three squadrons of the 15th Hussars were drawn up near their respective billets, where His Majesty inspected them. Those N.C.O.'s and men who had received

IN BILLETS

decorations for distinguished conduct in the field had the great honour of being decorated personally by the King.

During the latter part of November, and the greater part of December the I Corps remained in reserve, and therefore except for a few guards B and C Squadrons did not have very much to do.

The 3rd Division on the other hand shortly after being relieved from Ypres took over the trenches opposite Wytschaete. The line here was fairly quiet, and the division was enabled to keep plenty of reserves in hand. A Squadron found the usual guards, examining posts, traffic control posts, orderlies and gallopers to the various headquarters.

All the troops spent some time in improving the accommodation and sanitation of the billets, as well as constructing stables, cook-houses, and so on, for no large body of troops had been billeted in this area for at least a century.

The 3rd Division had the usual amount of fighting which is inseparable from trench warfare, but A Squadron was never engaged and the year 1914 ended quietly as far as it was concerned.

On 5th February, 1915, whilst a relief between the 3rd and 5th Divisions was taking place A Squadron was ordered to take over a small section of trenches just south of Wytschaete. These trenches were rather primitive, and during daylight all movement was impossible. The enemy snipers were very active indeed, and the artillery bombarded intermittently throughout the day and night, for at this period the German supply of ammunition appeared to be unlimited, whereas the British guns did not have a single round to spare. The men of A Squadron replied as best they could, but on the whole there is not much to record of this their tour of duty in the front-line trenches.

When relieved the squadron returned to its old billets and remained quietly there for some weeks, carrying out the usual routine duties.

The I Corps was not destined to remain for a very long period in Army Reserve, for just before Christmas events occurred near Bethune which caused the I Corps to leave its rest billets and march south, once again to take its place in the front line.

The enemy had attacked the Indian troops holding the trenches east of Bethune, and after severe fighting had captured the two important positions of Festubert and Givenchy, which places the enemy continued to hold in spite of our counter-attacks. The Indian troops felt the cold and damp of their first winter in Europe very acutely indeed, and were in no condition to renew their attacks on the lost villages. In consequence the task of recapturing Festubert and Givenchy was allotted to I Corps.

During the late afternoon of 20th December C Squadron was suddenly alarmed, and two troops were ordered at once to march as advance guard to the 3rd Infantry Brigade. The march was through Merville to Bethune. Just as daylight was breaking the advance guard entered the market square of the latter town, where the 8th Hussars were found drawn up. This regiment was still mounted on the Arab horses which the 15th Hussars on leaving India had handed over to them at Lucknow five years before. No one in their wildest dreams could have imagined at that time that they were again destined to meet the Arab horses in a town of Northern France.

The fighting to recover the lost trenches was very severe, but by 23rd December Givenchy and Festubert were once again in our hands, but at terrible cost to the 1st Division, for those few gallant men who had escaped the inferno at Ypres escaped only to fall at Festubert.

On 23rd December the remaining two troops of C Squadron marched from Merris, and the whole squadron collected at Bethune.

The 24th December was spent by C Squadron clearing the battlefield. Many Indian soldiers were found sheltering under what cover they could find, and all quite benumbed and helpless with cold. The weather at this time was very severe indeed, and the men in the trenches really suffered great hardships.

B Squadron, in accordance with the move of I Corps, marched from Hazebrouck on 22nd December to Bethune, where they billeted.

The three squadrons were enabled to indulge in mild forms of festivities for their first Christmas in France ; the dinners were quite adequate, every officer, N.C.O. and man received a present from their Majesties the King and Queen, and from H.R.H. Princess Mary.

At 4.15 p.m. on 31st December the Germans attacked that part of the line held by the King's Royal Rifle Corps of the 1st Division, and succeeded in capturing a small post. C Squadron was in consequence sent up to Cambrin, and remained there saddled up all night. A strong post was placed behind the barrier which had been built across the Cambrin road. Except for an occasional shell and a certain amount of sniping, the night passed quietly. In this manner the New Year was ushered in for C Squadron ; they returned during the evening of 1st January to Bethune.

B Squadron had moved from Bethune on 27th December to

about Locon, whilst A Squadron remained quietly in the farm near Mont Noir.

Thus for the 15th Hussars ended the year 1914.[1]

The British Army had by this time settled down to trench warfare, and all divisions began to make all kinds of arrangements to improve the conditions, not only in the trenches, but also in the back areas. Small experiments for improving the amenities of life were started in a tentative way, and these later became universal and far more elaborate. Divisional baths and laundries were inaugurated, and entertainments and sports organised for the resting battalions.

The town of Bethune, which was still almost untouched by gun-fire, became quite gay, the streets were crowded, the shops all did a roaring trade, and the cafés were always full. The mining country, where both C and B Squadrons now found themselves, with its predominant *pilons* and *fosses* and the acres of miners' cottages, seemed at first very strange after the Aisne and Ypres country, but this area became later on very familiar to everyone in the Regiment, as it did indeed to the whole British Army.

During the ordinary period of trench warfare the squadrons of divisional cavalry did not as a rule have very much fighting to do, but they were by no means idle, as there were many different duties upon which they were employed. There were examining posts to be found on bridges and cross roads, guards over headquarters and important buildings. The various brigade and divisional headquarters had to be supplied with mounted orderlies. The Provost Marshal also required his share of men for traffic control and various other duties. The remainder of the men had to be ready at a moment's notice, for they acted as a mobile reserve in the event of anything serious taking place. At this period of the war the supply of maps was nothing like what it became later on, many of the maps also which were issued were inaccurate, for they were taken from an old survey which dated from the time of Napoleon III, and could not in consequence be entirely relied upon. The officers of the Regiment were therefore employed in correcting these maps, and in reconnoitring all the country and roads in rear of our lines, in order to discover the best routes for the movements of reliefs, supplies and communication.

The 1st Division was subjected to continual attacks by the enemy, which although not delivered in very great strength,

[1] The following officers joined during December. A Squadron: Captain E. E. Clive-Coates (now Captain Sir Edward Clive-Coates, Bart., O.B.E.), Lieutenant A. Smith, Second Lieutenant Sir John Grey, Bart. C Squadron: Lieutenant C. Shaw.

caused considerable casualties and continual irritation. On 25th January and on 29th January the Germans delivered numerous assaults on the position occupied by the division. C Squadron stood to their horses at Beuvry during the day and night, but were not otherwise employed.

The 1st Division was by this time very weak in numbers, and urgently required a rest, it was therefore relieved by the 2nd Division, and in consequence of this relief C Squadron marched on 2nd February to the mining village of Auchel, where all the men were most comfortably billeted, and B Squadron took over their billets in Bethune.

At the end of February the 1st Division returned to the front line, and C Squadron moved from Auchel to Hinges.

On 10th March and the following days was fought the Battle of Neuve Chapelle. The 15th Hussars played but a small part in this fight : A Squadron was not employed at all, B and C Squadrons moved forward to the various advanced report centres, where they stood to until the end of the battle, awaiting further orders. From these places they sent forward the usual liaison patrols ; a few patrols were also pushed forward with the firing line. It soon, however, became quite evident that the battle would never develop into one which would justify the employment of cavalry, and as soon as the fighting died down, the squadrons returned to their former billets and resumed the normal routine.

Meanwhile there had been many rumours that a new cavalry brigade was to be formed, of which the 15th Hussars were to be one of the units. On 9th April definite orders finally arrived for the three squadrons to leave their respective divisions. On 13th April they bade farewell to their old comrades and marched to the vicinity of Hazebrouck, where once again the Regiment formed up as a unit.

It was for all ranks rather a wrench to part from the divisions with which they had been associated since 1913, and with which they had taken part in so many important events. Nevertheless everyone felt considerable satisfaction in the thought that in the future the 15th Hussars would all be together, and would go into battle as a Regiment.

Now that the 15th Hussars were once again formed together as a unit, the work of the squadrons entirely changed in character. No longer were they little independent commands working on their own, but each now formed part of the Regiment, and the Regiment formed part of the 9th Cavalry Brigade, commanded by Brigadier-General W. H. Greenly.[1]

[1] Now Major-General W. H. Greenly, C.B., C.M.G., D.S.O.

This brigade had just been formed, and the other units of the brigade were the 19th Hussars and the Warwickshire Battery R.H.A. Some time later in June the Bedfordshire Yeomanry joined, and thus brought the brigade up to full strength.

Lieutenant-Colonel H. A. L. Tagart, who had commanded the Regiment at Longmoor before the war, was now D.A.A. and Q.M.G. Cavalry Corps. Major H. D. Bramwell therefore took command of the 15th Hussars. The officers actually serving with the Regiment at the time were : Lieutenant-Colonel H. D. Bramwell, Major F. C. Pilkington, D.S.O., Captains the Honourable W. A. Nugent, A Courage, M.C., C. Nelson, D.S.O., E. C. Coates (Reserve of Officers) ; Lieutenant and Adjutant J. Arnott ; Lieutenants C. J. L. Stanhope, A. G. Cubitt, C. H. Shaw ; 2nd Lieutenants Sir John Grey, A. B. Smith.

Attached officers were : Lieutenants W. A. Bagnell, the Maclaine of Lochbuie (Special Reserve), R. B. de B. Hodge (14th Reserve Cavalry Regiment), E. R. Manning (14th Reserve Cavalry Regiment), A. M. Gaselee (Special Reserve), Lieutenant and Quartermaster F. C. Marsh.

The headquarters of the Regiment were at Hondeghem, with the squadrons in the farms round about.

The Regiment ever since the return from South Africa in 1912 had been employed as divisional cavalry, and in consequence the squadrons had not worked together for some considerable time, a certain amount of work therefore had to be done in resorting and reorganising. The 9th Cavalry Brigade was one of the units of the 1st Cavalry Division, and on 19th April Major-General H. de B. de Lisle,[1] who commanded the 1st Cavalry Division, inspected the 15th Hussars, and expressed himself very pleased with the appearance of the Regiment. The next few days passed quietly and uneventfully, but this peace was to be rudely and suddenly interrupted.

At 7.45 a.m. on 23rd April, without any previous warning, orders suddenly arrived for the Regiment to saddle up and turn out at once, and to proceed to the rendezvous as soon as possible at the St. Sylvestre cross roads.

There were many sinister rumours regarding this sudden move ; at first it was stated that the enemy had broken through the French, and that the German cavalry were at Poperinghe. Later it was rumoured that they were using some new and deadly type of shell, but it was not until late in the afternoon that more reliable news began to circulate, and the troops first heard of

[1] Now General Sir Beauvoir de Lisle, K.C.B., K.C.M.G., C.B., D.S.O.

the German poison gas. It was with a certain amount of misgiving that all ranks now learnt that an additional horror had been added to modern warfare, which already appeared to be unpleasant enough, and no one relished being asked to face a new and very unpleasant form of death.

The 9th Cavalry Brigade began its march towards Ypres shortly after 9.30 a.m. On arrival at Poperinghe it was found that the town had been shelled. The crowds of refugees tramping along the roads, the constant thunder of the guns, the long convoys of ambulances making their way towards Hazebrouck, all told of the fierce battle once again raging around Ypres. The 15th Hussars marched through Poperinghe, and reaching the 4th kilometre stone on the Poperinghe–Elverdinghe road, bivouacked there for the night. It was not until the evening that anything reliable could be gathered as to what had taken place during the day. It appeared that the Germans had attacked the French north-east of Ypres, and before their infantry assault they had covered their advance by clouds of poison gas.

The French had given way in face of this new terror, and by their retreat had placed the Canadian Corps in a position of great difficulty. It was further reported that both Hetsas and Lizerne were in the hands of the Germans and that they had crossed the canal, but that counter-attacks were being organised by the French, which it was hoped would restore the situation.

The next morning, 24th April, the 1st Cavalry Division was placed under the orders of the French, commanded by General Putz, and was moved into reserve trenches, the horses being kept in the woods some way in the rear.

The 1st Cavalry Brigade was in trenches just east of Woesten, with the 9th Cavalry Brigade in reserve. At 9.15 a.m. the 15th Hussars marched to a wood about one kilometre west of Woesten. They spent the whole day and the following night in this wood, the whole time in pouring rain.

The next day, 25th April, at 8.30 a.m., orders were issued to the Regiment to march to a position about two kilometres south of the village of Oostvleteren, in order to support the Belgians if trouble should arise. The Belgian trenches were reconnoitred in case it became necessary to occupy them. The day, however, passed quite quietly, and at 7.30 p.m. the 15th Hussars moved to Eykhoek, where they remained during the night. Throughout the whole of the 25th and 26th of April the noise of the gun-fire was tremendous and continuous, and told of the heavy counter-attacks taking place about Ypres. The Regiment remained undisturbed until 6 o'clock in the evening of 26th April, when C Squadron relieved a squadron of the 19th Hussars in the reserve trenches north-east of Woesten, and later on at 8 p.m. both A and B Squadrons were sent up in support of C Squadron. The horses were all left at Eykhoek. On 27th April A and B Squadrons returned to this village at daylight, and C Squadron returned at 7 p.m., after having been relieved by A Squadron of the 9th Lancers.

The French counter-attacks, although not so successful as had at first been hoped, had nevertheless much improved their position, and except for a small post at Hetsas, they had succeeded in driving the Germans to the east of the canal. The first German gas attack, which came as such a terrible surprise to everyone, and which (if it had been pressed home) might have altered the whole course of the war, had by this time definitely failed, General Putz therefore no longer required the support of the British cavalry.

At 9.30 a.m. on 28th April the 15th Hussars marched to Herzeele, but owing to the congestion of traffic on the road did not reach their billets until 11 p.m. They remained in this village until 2nd May, when they moved to Esquelbecq, and on the following day to Hondeghem, where they remained quietly until 6th May.

At midday on 6th May an order was received for a digging party to proceed to Ypres. The orders were for a very strong party, and in consequence the greater part of the Regiment had to turn out. By 3 p.m. they were on the march, and by 7 p.m. were bivouacked in a farm about one mile west of Ypres.

As soon as the horses were fed and watered, the working party of eight officers and two hundred men marched to the canal north of Ypres, where under the direction of the Royal Engineers a defensive line of trenches was dug, on completion of which, about 2.30 a.m., the working party returned to the farm and spent the day there. The next night work was continued, and at 2 a.m. on the 8th it was finished, the party returned to their horses, and after breakfast rode back to Hondeghem, but their sojourn there was of very short duration, and a few hours after they had settled in, orders were received to return at once to the Ypres salient, where the situation at the moment was critical.

The original gas attack and the subsequent retreat of the French had placed our troops holding the salient in a very awkward predicament. The position was in fact a long narrow tongue pushed out into the enemy's lines. It was therefore decided by G.H.Q. to withdraw from this unfavourable situation; on 4th May this was successfully accomplished, and a new line occupied nearer Ypres. The enemy did not take long to move up to our fresh trenches, and in a few days renewed the bombardments and attacks against our new positions.

The situation continued very unfavourable, everywhere the enemy could overlook the trenches and back areas, and the troops holding the salient still suffered severely. It was therefore decided to move the cavalry to Ypres, to share in the defence of the town.

The Regiment received its orders at 2.15 a.m. on 9th May, and by 4.15 a.m. the whole brigade was on the march. Without any incident they reached a farm just south of Vlamertinghe, where the rest of the day was spent.

At 8 p.m. orders were received for the 15th Hussars to proceed to the battle zone, and twelve officers and two hundred and sixty men marched through Ypres to Wieltje, where they proceeded to dig themselves in about this place as well as they could.

The 10th May was passed in these trenches, and the men had to endure with what patience they could the continuous shelling by the enemy. About 5 p.m. this shelling increased, Lieutenant-Colonel H. D. Bramwell was severely wounded, and the command of the Regiment passed to Major F. C. Pilkington. 2nd Lieutenant Sir John Grey was also wounded.

During the night of the 10th/11th May a new line of trenches was dug east of the former line. By 2 a.m. this fresh line was finished and occupied by B Squadron, with A Squadron in support, and C Squadron in reserve. The 19th Hussars were on the right, and the London Rifles on the left.

At this period of the war the British Army in France was very short of gun ammunition, and the troops had to undergo what is perhaps the most nerve-shattering and trying of all ordeals, a heavy bombardment to which there can be no reply. The 11th May was no exception to this rule, and all day long the 15th Hussars crouched in the miserable trenches they had dug during the night, and endured the heavy shelling of the enemy, to which our guns were perforce silent. About 2 p.m. as the situation looked unpromising, A Squadron was moved up on the left of B Squadron.

Towards evening the 1st Cavalry Division was ordered to relieve the 83rd Infantry Brigade about the Verlorenhoek road, and thus in accordance with these orders at 1 a.m. on 12th May, the 15th relieved a battalion of the York and Lancaster Regiment, and took over a line of trenches north of the Ypres–Zonnebeke

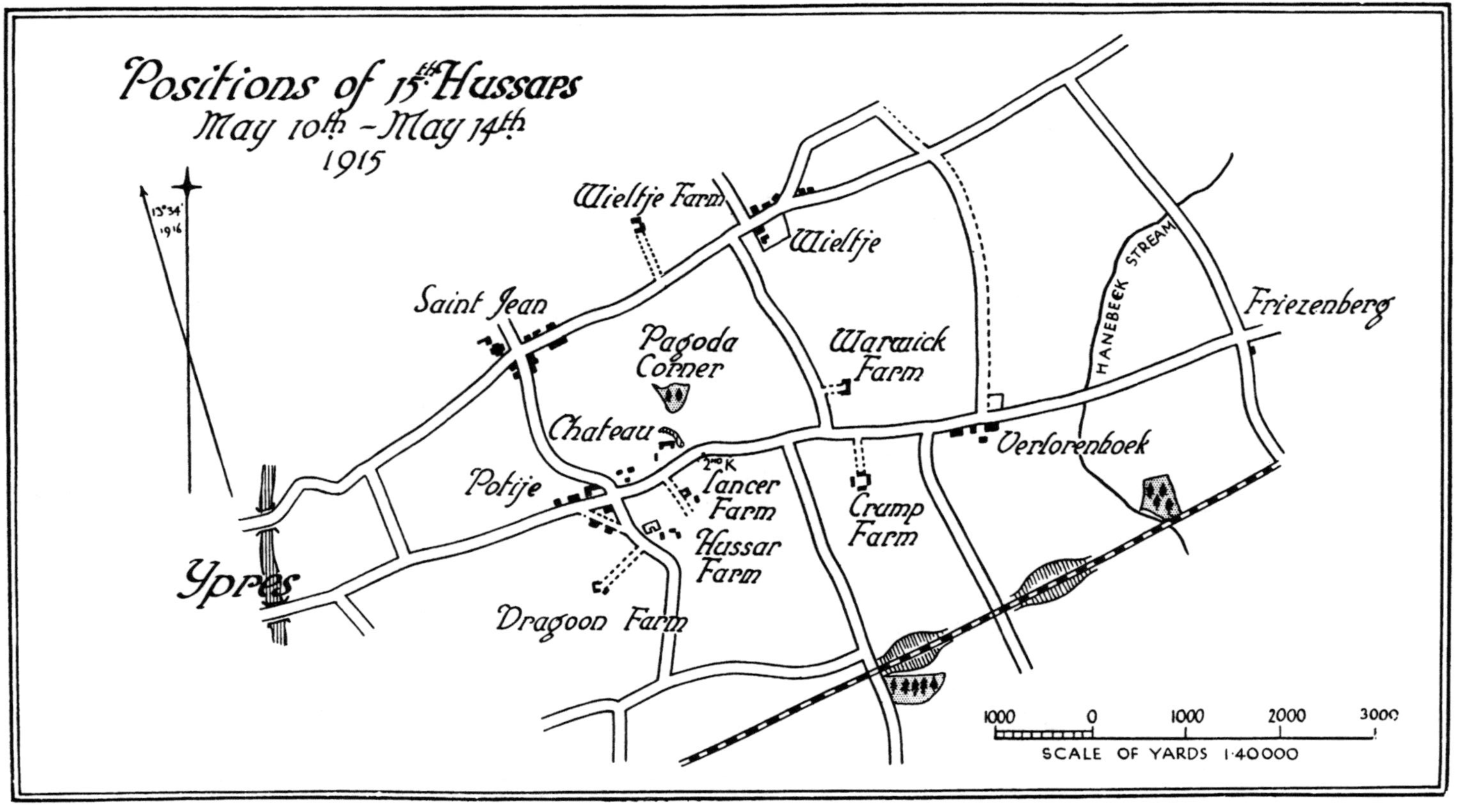
Positions of 15th Hussars
May 10th – May 14th
1915
13°34'
1916
Wieltje Farm
Wieltje
Saint Jean
Pagoda Corner
Warwick Farm
Friezenberg
HANEBEEK STREAM
Chateau
Verlorenhoek
Potije
2nd K
Lancer Farm
Crump Farm
Hussar Farm
Ypres
Dragoon Farm
1000 0 1000 2000 3000
SCALE OF YARDS 1:40000

road (about Warwick Farm). These trenches were in a deplorable condition, they had been almost destroyed by the enemy bombardments, and required a considerable amount of work to make them even bullet-proof. The day passed fairly quietly, with little shelling, in spite of which the 15th suffered some casualties, for the enemy snipers were very active, and the trenches afforded but feeble protection.

At 9 p.m. the 15th Hussars were relieved by the 5th Dragoon Guards, and returned to the reserve trenches they had occupied the previous day, just north of Potije.

The next day, 13th May, was to prove a day of grim memory to all ranks of the 1st Cavalry Division.

At 5 a.m. the heaviest bombardment that anyone had so far experienced came crashing down on the area occupied by the division. All communications were instantly cut, and the different units were isolated.

Directly it was realised that something really serious was taking place, patrols from the Regiment were sent out to get in touch with the front line. These patrols reported that in some places our troops had been blown out of their trenches by the bombardment, but that the part of the line occupied by the 9th Lancers still held firm. The terrific bombardment, and the consequent fog of war, made it impossible to obtain accurate information, but by midday the situation appeared critical, although so far no very heavy infantry attack had been directed against that part of the line held by the 1st Cavalry Division. The bombardment had been most severe and the trenches were becoming almost untenable.

Sometime during the morning, the squadron leaders were discussing the situation with the commanding officer, when a shrapnel shell burst over the trench, very severely wounding Captain the Honourable W. A. Nugent and Captain A. Courage. The former died a few days later from the effect of this wound. Thus at the crisis of the battle the Regiment lost the services of two experienced and able squadron leaders.

About midday information was sent back by the 4th Dragoon Guards that they had put their last reserves into the line, and needed help, C Squadron was therefore sent up to support them. In spite of a very heavy barrage, C Squadron moved forward across the open, and occupied the front line just south of Wieltje.

Meanwhile in other parts of the battle front the outlook was not at all promising. On the right and to the south of the 1st Cavalry Division, the 3rd Cavalry Division had been driven from its trenches, and it was decided to launch a counter-attack to re-establish the situation. In consequence the 9th Cavalry Brigade was ordered to take over that part of the line still held by the 3rd Cavalry Division, in order that the troops thus relieved would be available for the counter-attack. At 3 p.m. therefore A and B Squadrons moved up into trenches with their right on the Potije–Ypres road, near the 2nd kilometre stone, where they were in touch with the 19th Hussars, who had relieved the 10th Hussars,

The counter-attack launched by the 3rd Cavalry Division was at first most successful, and the troops made considerable progress, but they encountered very heavy machine-gun-fire and were finally brought to a standstill. The 8th Cavalry Brigade which made the attack suffered such heavy casualties that eventually the men were forced to fall back to their original starting point.

While this fight was raging on the right of the 9th Calvary Brigade, units of the 1st Cavalry Brigade were driven from their positions, and retired through C Squadron into the trenches occupied by A and B Squadrons.

When this retirement became manifest, the men of C Squadron immediately moved into the abandoned trenches, which they continued to occupy in spite of the very heavy bombardment.

It was whilst this retirement through C Squadron was taking place a newly-arrived officer with the advanced two troops of the squadron shouted in his excitement, "What do the 15th do now?" A very gallant N.C.O., Sergeant E. E. Everest (who was later killed at the Battle of Bourlon Wood) replied: "The 15th never retire, they stay where they are," and the order was given that no one was to budge. Shortly after these two troops moved forward and occupied the vacated trenches, and thus filled the gap. Towards evening the fighting on both sides slowly died down.

As soon as it was dark the 9th Cavalry Brigade received orders to retake the northern part of the trenches, from which the 3rd Cavalry Division had been driven, and also to get in touch with that division, which was about to retake the southern portion of the lost line.

At midnight, in pitch darkness and in pouring rain, the 15th Hussars formed up, and with fixed bayonets advanced to the assault of the German trenches, the position of which was only vaguely known. The reader can well imagine how very difficult and hazardous was this task. Luckily an officer who had been through the First Battle of Ypres remembered a track which led to the ruins of a farm near which the German trenches were supposed to run. The Regiment was thus enabled to keep its direction, and to the relief of everybody the trenches were found abandoned by the enemy. They were, however, badly knocked about, and almost untenable, consisting for the most part of shell holes filled with liquid mud. Our dead, our dying and our wounded were lying in all directions, mostly from the 8th Cavalry Brigade, and the first thing to be done was to evacuate the wounded.

As this line was quite untenable orders were received at 2 a.m. to dig a new line a little further back, to the west of Crump Farm, about half a mile west of Verlorenhoek. The task seemed almost hopeless, there were only about three hours before dawn, there were no tools, and the men were very tired. Fortunately some tools were obtained from an engineer working party, and by 3 a.m. work began. In spite of very great fatigue, everyone worked with feverish energy, in a desperate endeavour to construct some sort of cover; it was a case of everyone for himself if he did not wish to be found lying in the open when dawn broke. Throughout the night rain fell heavily, which added to the other miseries. It was indeed fortunate that the dawn broke dull and foggy, obscuring everything, and the mist did not clear until about 8 a.m., by which time a fairly good line had been dug. These fresh trenches had one great advantage, they were screened from the direct observation of the enemy, so that a certain amount of work could be carried on during the day.

The 14th May passed fairly quietly; no doubt the enemy required time to reorganise, in the same way as we did, after the fierce fighting of the day before. In consequence the 15th Hussars were more or less left in peace, and were enabled to construct an adequate trench line.[1]

At 9 p.m. the Royal Scots Greys relieved the 15th Hussars who retired into reserve to huts south of Vlamertinghe, where they remained peacefully until 17th May.

[1] During the day Captain R. H. Tribe, R.A.M.C., who served with the Regiment throughout the war (now Father R. Tribe, Director of the Society of the Sacred Mission) heard that there were wounded men lying in front of our trenches. Although it was broad daylight he walked out across the open towards the German trenches to see what could be done; there were very many wounded, both our own and the enemy. Captain Tribe thereupon organised parties to bring in these wounded men. Whilst employed on this, parties of the enemy were encountered, engaged on a similar task. Although no actual truce was arranged, the enemy respected the Red Cross armlets, and Captain Tribe was enabled to exchange some wounded Germans for Englishmen (chiefly Essex Yeomen and Life Guards). On the same day a patrol led by the Maclaine of Lochbuie obtained the most valuable information. This patrol pushed out well into the enemy's lines, found that they had been abandoned, and that the Germans had fallen back to the Hanebecke stream. A machine-gun was brought in, and from the equipment of the numerous enemy dead most important identifications were secured. Both Captain Tribe and Lieutenant the Maclaine of Lochbuie were awarded the Military Cross.

Major-General H. de B. de Lisle, commanding the 1st Cavalry Division, inspected the Regiment on 16th May and congratulated all ranks on their fine work during the recent operations. In addressing the 15th Hussars the divisional commander said : " I have striven to get the Regiment under my command, and you have now fully justified my hopes ; you have well maintained the high traditions the Regiment has gained in the past. The British cavalry are the best in the world, and the 15th Hussars stand out as one of the finest regiments of our cavalry."

On 17th May the 1st Cavalry Division relieved the 80th Infantry Brigade in the trenches ; the 9th Cavalry Brigade formed the reserve and the Regiment therefore remained in its huts at Vlamertinghe. On the 18th, the 9th Cavalry Brigade received orders to relieve the 81st Infantry Brigade about Hooge. A battalion of infantry, the 5th Duke of Cornwall's Light Infantry, was put under the command of the G.O.C. 9th Cavalry Brigade, to assist the two cavalry regiments in their task.

The 15th Hussars left their huts at 6.45 p.m. on 18th May and marched to the *halte*, one and a half miles east of Ypres. Here the inevitable delay took place, for the guides as usual had lost their way. But at last, well on into the night, the Regiment, moving by half squadrons, began to make their way up to Hooge.

The relief which commenced about midnight was not completed until about 4 a.m. the following morning. The units relieved were the Argyll and Sutherland Highlanders and the Cameron Highlanders.

The line which the Regiment now occupied was from the stables of Hooge Chateau, just north of the Menin road, to Sanctuary Wood, a frontage of about five hundred yards. Two companies and two machine-guns of the 5th Battalion Duke of Cornwall's Light Infantry, much reduced in numbers, came under the orders of Major F. C. Pilkington, now commanding the 15th Hussars, to assist in the defence of this place. The 19th Hussars were on the right and the Queen's Bays on the left.

The condition of the trenches was very bad, there were many gaps in the parapet, and the southern sector near Sanctuary Wood was almost untenable, as the mud and water was over two feet deep. There was very little wire, and no communication trenches of any sort whatever. Movement during the day was in consequence almost impossible. During 19th May the Regiment remained in these trenches. The enemy snipers were very active indeed, and until the parapets were rendered bullet-proof the casualties were fairly heavy.

As soon as darkness fell all ranks set to and worked hard to improve the trenches, rebuild the parapets, dig communication trenches, and put up wire. The work was much hampered by snipers, and the hostile machine-guns occasionally swept the ground. Every now and then star shells lit up the working parties, who had to fling themselves down and remain motionless until the light died away. In spite of these difficulties a considerable amount of work was done.

The ration parties also had very great difficulty in delivering their supplies, as the enemy kept the Menin road under shell fire, and everything had to be carried into the trenches across the open.

THE ROAD OF ILL-OMEN—YPRES TO MENIN, MAY 1915

As the position of the enemy trenches was not known to any degree of certainty, an endeavour was made to locate exactly where they were. Two patrols crawled out through the wire, and remained out all night, returning just before daylight with an accurate report of the German positions.

The 20th May passed fairly quietly, and directly it became dark, work was resumed with the same activity as the night before. 21st May was passed in the trenches, and on the whole the enemy did not show much activity although his snipers were very assertive. Captain C. Nelson and Lieutenant R. de B. Hodge were both wounded.

The 15th Hussars remained in the front-line trenches during 22nd and 23rd of May, and the days passed as uneventfully as any days could in the front-line trenches of the Ypres salient. Nevertheless they were anxious days, for the fear of another gas attack agitated everyone, and hourly the direction of the wind was closely watched. The 23rd was a particularly quiet day, with hardly a sign of activity on the part of the Germans, although, during the night before the sound of heavy traffic had been heard behind their lines.

Orders were received that the 9th Lancers would relieve the 15th Hussars in the front line the night of the 23rd/24th May, and in accordance with these orders, this relief commenced after dark on the 23rd, but it was a very slow process. The original orders were for the 9th Cavalry Brigade to go back to the huts at Vlamertinghe, but as the wind was most favourable for a German gas attack, it was thought wiser to cancel these orders, and the Regiment was placed in reserve. The relief was not completed until 2 a.m. on the 24th, when the 15th Hussars, tired out after the long tour of duty in the front-line trenches, were disposed as follows: C Squadron in G.H.Q. reserve trenches just south of the Menin road, near where the railway crosses it, the remaining two squadrons and regimental headquarters were in the Ecole de Bienfaissance.

Hardly had this relief been effected and the troops settled in their new positions, when the enemy released heavy clouds of poison gas over a wide front, which swept the area held by the cavalry, and in a short time a very serious battle began, as the Germans attacked all along the line, advancing behind their gas clouds, accompanied by a heavy artillery bombardment. The 15th Hussars were undoubtedly most fortunate. The heaviest gas cloud passed over the trenches from which they had just been relieved by the 9th Lancers, and this gallant regiment suffered heavily. By the time the gas had reached G.H.Q. line the cloud was much thinner, nevertheless C Squadron suffered considerably. Some men, scattered along the trench and in dug-outs, overcome by fatigue, were badly affected, owing to the difficulty of rousing them. The delay in the relief proved a blessing in disguise to the two squadrons and headquarters in the Ecole, as the attack began before the last arrivals had settled down, hence there was no delay in arousing the men and adjusting mouthpieces; the casualties in consequence were very light.

The gas-masks issued at this time were but primitive affairs, consisting only of a cotton wool pad, but the German gas was not then as deadly as it later became, and except for sore eyes and headaches, most of the men who had been in the Ecole were not much affected by it.

Captain Stanhope, who was in command of C Squadron, seeing numerous wounded and stragglers coming back, realised that the situation was serious, and at once decided to reinforce the 9th Lancers. As the squadron moved forward it collected the stragglers, and reoccupied the trenches astride the Menin road near Bellewaarde.

Captain F. Grenfell, V.C., who commanded the squadron of 9th Lancers in this part of the line, had barely twelve men fit to fight, and could not have held on much longer. He was therefore overjoyed at this timely reinforcement.

Captain Stanhope and his men remained in this spot all day, in spite of every effort of the enemy to dislodge them, and although at times they were quite isolated. Later when the troops holding the line north of C Squadron had been driven from their trenches by the enemy, the squadron found its left flank in the air ; Captain Stanhope in consequence drew back his left flank, and faced north, and thus C Squadron fought facing north and east.

Meanwhile the two squadrons in the Ecole were ordered into the G.H.Q. line, where C Squadron had been ; whilst moving forward Captain Brace was wounded. As soon as the G.H.Q. line had been occupied, patrols were sent forward to elucidate the situation, as it was not known whether the Germans had broken through the front line or not. The first reports which came through from these patrols established the fact that the enemy was not within two thousand yards of the G.H.Q. line, and later the patrols reported the front line intact, although hard pressed.

At 5 a.m. orders were issued for A and B Squadrons to reinforce the front line and support the 9th Lancers. Some men of the York and Lancaster and East Yorkshire regiments went forward with these two squadrons.

This move forward was a hazardous undertaking, for to all appearances the ground was an open sloping plain, in full view of the enemy, and there were no communication trenches, and at the same time the enemy was vigorously shelling every part of the salient. It was lucky that nearly everybody in the two squadrons was intimately acquainted with the ground, and by making use of a sunken ditch and other cover of which they knew, the men succeeded in reaching the front line without any casualties. Later on in the day a counter-attack delivered by an infantry brigade over this piece of ground was brought to a complete standstill by the hostile artillery.

B Squadron reported to the officer commanding 9th Lancers, and was at first posted, with about two hundred York and Lancasters, in support, at the western edge of Zouave Wood. They had not been very long in that position when the situation became critical, and they were ordered to line the northern edge

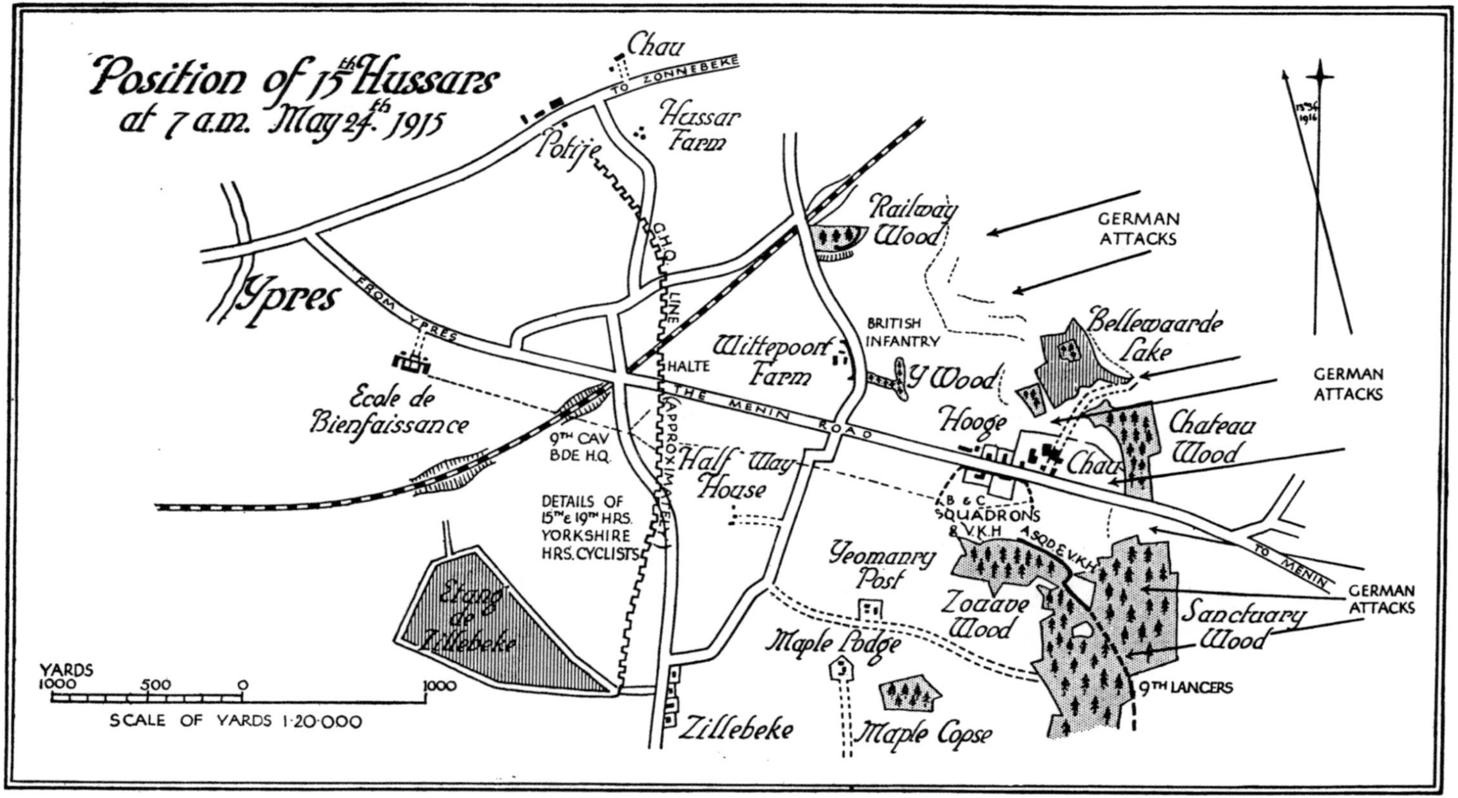

Position of 15th Hussars
at 7 a.m. May 24th 1915
Chau
TO ZONNEBEKE
Hussar Farm
Potije
Ypres
FROM YPRES
G.H.Q. LINE (APPROXIMATELY)
HALTE
THE MENIN ROAD
Ecole de Bienfaisance
9TH CAV BDE H.Q.
DETAILS OF 15TH & 19TH HRS. YORKSHIRE HRS. CYCLISTS
Etang de Zillebeke
Railway Wood
GERMAN ATTACKS
BRITISH INFANTRY
Wittepoort Farm
Y Wood
Bellewaarde Lake
Hooge
Chateau Wood
Chau
Half Way House
B & C SQUADRONS & V.K.H
A SQD E.V.K.H
Yeomanry Post
Zouave Wood
Sanctuary Wood
TO MENIN
9TH LANCERS
Maple Lodge
Maple Copse
Zillebeke
YARDS
1000
500
0
1000
SCALE OF YARDS 1·20·000

of the wood. From this position, which they occupied throughout the day, they were enabled to bring fire to bear on the Germans advancing across their front, north of the Menin road. An abandoned machine-gun which was salved and brought into action proved of the greatest value. Unfortunately, there were no trenches facing north in Zouave Wood and the squadron had perforce to lie out in the open, and in consequence suffered somewhat severely.

A Squadron reported to Captain Grenfell on the left of the line, but as C Squadron had already reinforced him, the men were not immediately required and were kept in support, they occupied a communication trench just south of the Menin road, which they themselves had dug during their previous tour in the trenches.

About 6.20 a.m. the line to the north gave way, and Captain Grenfell ordered A Squadron to counter-attack, to try and restore the situation. This order was soon countermanded, as it was realised that the German break through was on too great a front, and that an attack with small numbers was doomed to failure. Unfortunately Lieutenant Gaselee did not hear the second order, and lost his life in starting out to lead his troop against the enemy.

Orders were then issued to hold this trench and face north. C Squadron, as already narrated, conformed to this movement. The three squadrons were thus more or less together, but the situation was very critical ; as it appeared that they were about to be surrounded another flank had to be formed facing west, in fact, facing the town of Ypres.

North of the Menin road the Germans could be seen advancing towards Railway Wood and Birr cross roads, but British troops were still holding Witteport Farm. The heavy fire opened by the three squadrons caught the enemy in flank, prevented any advance in a south-westerly direction, and finally brought this attack to a standstill.

Throughout the day the battle raged about Bellewaarde, and after repeated bombardments the Germans renewed their attacks, but wherever they found they had determined and resolute men against them, who quite refused to budge and were prepared to die where they stood, their onslaught melted away.

Meanwhile Major Pilkington with the machine guns, a few men of the 15th Hussars and details from the 19th Hussars, Cyclists, Yorkshire Hussars, and several other units, was ordered to organise the defence of the G.H.Q. line, from south of the Menin road to the south-east corner of Zillebeke Lake. This line was not particularly good, everywhere it was overlooked by the enemy, but its defence was most urgent, as it was all that stood between the sorely-tried front line, and the town of Ypres.

The weather had been glorious, an ideal spring day. Towards the evening, when the Germans realised that their great attack had failed, the battle slowly quieted down ; one by one the guns ceased their roaring, and by the time darkness had fallen, all sounds of fighting died away, and both combatants had leisure to lick their wounds.

During the night the sorely-tried troops in the front line were relieved ; B and C Squadrons between 9 and 10 o'clock at night. The orders were, however, that the troops were not to leave the G.H.Q. line until the front line reliefs had been completed ; these two squadrons therefore remained in this line until 2 a.m., 25th May, when they marched back to the huts by Vlamertinghe. A Squadron was relieved independently and reached the huts about 5 a.m.

The men, although very tired after their long tour of the trenches and the heavy fighting, were full of spirit, as one sergeant said on his way back to Vlamertinghe, when he was asked how he had got on : " It was the best Bank Holiday shoot I have ever had." (It happened to be Whit-Monday.)

The 15th Hussars had not allowed the Germans to take one inch of ground from them, and had inflicted very heavy casualties on the enemy ; all ranks felt that they had played an important part in the historical battle of Ypres, and considering the heavy fighting the casualties had not been very severe. From 10th May to 24th May the 15th Hussars lost in killed and wounded nine officers and one hundred and thirty-eight other ranks.

General Greenly, the brigade commander, addressed the officers at 8 p.m. on 25th May as follows : " I should like to have seen the whole Regiment on parade, but it is now late, the men are very tired, and I do not wish to disturb them. Nevertheless I do not wish to delay longer in coming to tell you what I think of the great performance of yesterday. Every officer and man from top to bottom could not have done more. By your magnificent work you not only saved the situation in that part of the line, but by holding on were instrumental in saving thousands of lives, which must have been lost if the salient to the south had been cut off. The corps commander, General Byng,[1] knows and fully realises all you did. I cannot put into words half I would like to say or the praise due to you. All I can say is—you behaved as the 15th always do and that is the

[1] Now Viscount Byng of Vimy, G.C.B., G.C.M.G., K.C.B., M.V.O.

highest praise I can give. I thank you from the bottom of my heart for all you did, and I thank you on behalf of the Army also. I wish you to tell the men what I have said."

From 26th to the 28th of May were passed in the huts at Vlamertinghe, the men washing and resting; a working party was found the night of 27th/28th, but otherwise nothing much happened.

At 3.30 p.m. on the 28th the 15th Hussars embussed on the Vlamertinghe-Poperinghe road and travelled to Wormhoudt, where the horses and transport were found; they had moved there from Hondeghem. This march had been carried out with the greatest difficulty, owing to the fact that every available man had been sent up to reinforce the Regiment in the trenches, leaving only one man to six horses, including officers and sergeant-majors.

Throughout the war the cavalry had one great advantage over the infantry. After a hard fight and heavy casualties, they had ample time to reorganise and train the reinforcements. The billets about Wormhoudt were comfortable, and the weather during the whole of June was beautiful, and this quiet peaceful spot in Flanders seemed very far from war and all its attendant horrors.

On 11th June the Bedfordshire Yeomanry joined the 9th Cavalry Brigade, thus bringing it up to full establishment.

The 15th Hussars soon fell into the ordinary routine of life behind the lines. Training was carried out continuously, the horses were got into proper condition, and the Regiment was soon ready for anything.

On 15th June the 9th Cavalry Brigade was inspected by the Commander-in-Chief,[1] who in addressing the Brigade said: "I have come before you to-day to say a few words to express my appreciation and thanks for the magnificent work you have done in the past few weeks. I want to congratulate you all most heartily on your splendid conduct and personal gallantry, and upon your wonderful performance in the trenches at Ypres, where you showed that cavalry can fight as well in the trenches as on horseback. Trench warfare is not the work of cavalry, nor are you trained for it, yet you have shown that you are as capable in one branch of the Service as in the other. The conditions under which you have held on to the trenches assigned to you were of a most trying and arduous nature, yet not one had wavered, and all had done their duty without flinching. The brigade was placed in a very hot corner, where owing to the continuous shelling of the enemy it was impossible to obtain adequate cover, but by your steadfast bearing in the terrible

[1] The late Field-Marshal the Earl of Ypres, K.P., etc., etc.

position you have added fresh lustre and still greater honour to the magnificent honours you already possess ; this is what I want you to remember when you think of the losses you have suffered. You had some terrible experiences up there, but every regiment has covered itself with glory. This record I am sure you will maintain throughout the campaign, in whatever sphere of action you may be engaged."

AT THE END OF A TREK

CHAPTER VI

THE PERIOD OF TRENCH WARFARE

THE end of the Battle of Ypres 1915 marked the close of a distinct phase of the war, especially so far as the cavalry was concerned. The British Army had up to then been acting almost entirely on the defensive, and with very few reserves in hand. The cavalry had therefore been used as a mobile reserve, ready to move at the shortest notice to any threatened point. The regiments in consequence were always in a state of tension, for the order to saddle up and turn out might arrive at any moment. The infantry divisions all appreciated the fact that they were supported by a mobile reserve, composed of the very best material.

But after this Battle of Ypres (except for the Battle of Verdun which was not an attack against the British) the German Army was forced to act on the defensive, and the initiative passed to the Allied Armies. New forces were arriving daily from England in ever-increasing numbers, and strong reserves began to accumulate. In consequence, the cavalry was no longer required as a mobile reserve and was assigned a new rôle.

In the course of time, it was the intention of the British commanders to deliver powerful assaults against the German positions, and it was hoped that when the German trenches had been captured, a gap would thus be created through which the cavalry could be launched to seize important strategical points in rear of the German lines. But the cavalry was destined to suffer many grievous disappointments before it was enabled to achieve any real success—until in fact, the Battle of Amiens in August, 1918.

It is not necessary to describe the story of the next few years in great detail.[1] It is chiefly a story of life in billets behind the lines, of working parties, an occasional tour in the trenches, and the constant repetition of the "gap" failure. Here in these pages the story will be told as briefly as possible, for it was not until the Battle of Cambrai in 1917 that the 15th Hussars were engaged in fighting of any great importance.

It is curious to realise that exactly one hundred years before this date, in 1816, after the Waterloo campaign, the 15th Hussars had been billeted in the same area. Sir Coloquhen Grant, commanding the Hussar Brigade (he had commanded the

[1] The details of marches, billets and working parties will be found in Appendix A.

Regiment during the retreat to Corunna) took up his residence at the Chateau of Esquelbecq, where the headquarters of the 1st Cavalry Division were in 1915. An account of this appeared in the *Daily Mail* of 14th June, from their special correspondent, Mr. G. Valentine Williams, and reads as follows :—

Daily Mail—June 14th, 1915.

"THE CHATEAU OF THE 15TH HUSSARS.

"I have to-day encountered one of those strange coincidences which are bound to occur when the British Army is fighting over ground which is soaked deep in the blood of its ancestors. The whole of the zone of the British Army in France and Belgium has, since the Middle Ages, known the British fighting man. The armies of Edward III and Henry V, of Marlborough and Wellington, fought over the ground where to-day the khaki of the British Empire is seen.

"Not so long ago Indian troopers might have been encountered on the field of Agincourt in the shadow of the great crucifix raised to the pious memory of the gallant French nobles who fell when 'la journée fatale d'Azincourt,' as the inscription on the Calvary runs. Aire and Saint Venant were besieged by Marlborough, Béthune and Arras were all-important points in the famous 'Ne Plus Ultra' lines which he forced. To-day by the purest hazard, I ran across another link with our great military past—a link between the picturesque 15th Hussars who fought at Waterloo and the more soberly clad regiment which bears that number in the Army List to-day.

"Some of the 15th Hussars are to-day quartered in billets round a beautiful old chateau which is so perfectly preserved that one may trace the marks which successive centuries have scored upon its ancient red brick walls. On one of the slender round towers are still to be seen the holes made during a siege by a gun which the besiegers set up in the village market place across the moat, two hundred yards away, and the iron bars of the castle gateway are bent here and there by the shot which the defenders poured out against the assailants.

"In and about this chateau General Grant's Fifth Cavalry Brigade that fought at Waterloo, consisting, I believe of the 11th and 15th Hussars and a regiment of Dragoons, lived for two years after the battle. The 15th Hussars were quartered in the chateau itself, and this morning I saw and handled for myself the thick iron rings which they drove into the walls of the outbuildings in order to hitch up their horses. Now a thick screen of beeches stands between the former horse lines of the 15th and the chateau, but, according to the proprietor, who supplied these facts to my informant, the trees have been planted since, and it was to these rings, stout iron rings of English manufacture, that the 15th Hussars tethered their horses a hundred years ago."

During the greater part of the summer of 1915 the 1st Cavalry Division supplied very strong working parties, employed in the construction of a reserve defensive system of trenches west of Ypres, about Elverdinghe. The officers and men were relieved periodically, and replaced by fresh parties from those with the horses in the back areas. On 6th September all working parties rejoined their units, and the most strenuous training began, for the " gap."

The men, after their two months' digging, were fit enough, but their riding muscles were soft and the horses required steady work to prepare them for the very strenuous task they would have to perform if the " gap " was successful.

It was quite evident to everybody that the British Army was about to take the offensive, but where or when remained a dead secret. On 23rd September orders were received for the 9th Cavalry Brigade to march at once to the concentration area.

Two night marches brought the 15th Hussars to Estrée Blanche, where they stood to their horses at dawn on 25th September, and awaited the opening of the Battle of Loos.

It appeared at first that everything was going very well indeed, and orders were issued for the cavalry to move up close to the battle. By 2 p.m. long columns of cavalry were on the move along all the roads, and the sight of these large masses of horsemen moving forward gave to all the impression that the enemy must be on the run. Everyone was to learn in course of time, and after many disappointments, the mistake of excessive optimism.

The Regiment marched slowly forward, along the crowded roads, and by 8.30 p.m. reached Vaudricourt, where all ranks went into bivouacs in the chateau grounds. Throughout the night it poured with rain, so everyone had a very uncomfortable time. The very optimistic hopes held by nearly everybody on the 25th, that the cavalry would be enabled to go through the gap, rather changed on the 26th, when the Germans began their heavy counter-attacks, and it seemed indeed at times that our infantry would have great difficulty in holding the ground they had already gained. Thus the likelihood of the advance by large bodies of mounted cavalry did not seem very evident.

The Battle of Loos continued for several days, but the 1st Cavalry Division took no part in it. The 3rd Cavalry Division

TRENCHES NEAR LOOS
(Converted German trenches.)

had indeed taken its share in the fight, but dismounted and in the trenches.

After remaining in the open for three nights, most of the time in pouring rain, the Regiment withdrew to billets at Marles les Mines. From this place the cavalry sent a large working party up to the battlefield, where the men remained for several days working at the very depressing occupation of burying the dead, who were lying out in large numbers. They also refaced the German trenches, collected all the abandoned material, and tidied up the whole battlefield. As the work was done under shell-fire, there were the inevitable casualties.

Meanwhile the rest of the Regiment moved to Febvin-Palfart, where it remained for just over a fortnight. On 19th October the 15th Hussars marched farther back to billets about Glomenghen, with the squadrons billeted in the villages round about. The stay of the 15th Hussars in this area was not of very long duration, as it was decided to move the cavalry right back to the coast. In consequence, on 17th November, the 15th Hussars marched over snow-covered roads to their new billets : headquarters and C Squadron at Doudeauville, A Squadron at Bezingham, B Squadron at Zotteau, and the machine-guns at Crandal. These little villages buried in the heart of the country were destined to be the homes of the Regiment for some considerable time to come. They offered few or no attractions, but Boulogne was easy to reach.

On 10th October Lieutenant-Colonel H. A. L. Tagart completed his period of command of the Regiment, and sent the following farewell order :

"To-day I completed my four years command, and after twenty-five years service my name will cease to appear on the list of the 15th Hussars. I shall never forget the happy years spent with you, and still less shall I forget the personal debt I am under to all my old friends, officers, N.C.O.'s and men alike, who have invariably given me their loyal help and assistance. In bidding you all farewell, God-speed, and a happy return to the Old Country, when our work here is well done, I need express no anxiety that the future records of the Regiment may equal that of its glorious past. The work you have done out here has already shown conclusively that the name of the 15th Hussars will always stand unsullied in the highest ranks of His Majesty's Service. Good Luck and Au Revoir."

On 15th November Brigadier-General R. Greenly relinquished the command of the 9th Cavalry Brigade on promotion to B.G.G.S. of a Corps Staff. On leaving, he expressed himself highly satisfied with the work of the 15th Hussars, and thanked all ranks for their loyalty and co-operation whilst he was in command of the brigade. Brigadier-General S. R. Kirby, C.M.G., took over the command of the brigade the same day.

Directly the cavalry was settled in its new billets, orders were received to take over a section of the trenches. It was thought that confusion might be caused by the very different strengths of a cavalry division and an infantry division. Therefore each cavalry division formed a brigade, each brigade formed a battalion, and each regiment formed a company. The strengths then more or less corresponded with those of similar infantry formations and a dismounted brigade of cavalry could relieve an infantry brigade without too much confusion. The 15th Hussars Company, therefore, consisted of : an officer commanding, his second-in-command, six subalterns, one S.S.M., twelve sergeants, four signallers, one trumpeter, six batmen, sixteen corporals, and two hundred and sixty-four privates. Each regiment in the brigade found a similar company, the whole forming a strong battalion known as the 9th Battalion.

This system was not carried on throughout the war, as on the whole it was found more convenient to occupy the trenches in the cavalry formations. It was soon realised by infantry staffs that a dismounted cavalry brigade was only slightly stronger than an infantry battalion.

Sahagun[1] and Xmas Day of 1915 were passed in these billets, the Xmas dinners were more than ample, the district was a great centre for turkey breeding, and turkeys were in consequence abundant, and fairly cheap. In addition General Sir George Luck, G.C.B., and the old comrades of the Regiment sent out a liberal supply of plum puddings, tobacco and sweets.

On 30th December the company of the 15th Hussars entrained at Devres. It will be realised that the so-called company was in fact the 15th Hussars dismounted. Enough men were left behind to keep the led horses mobile, so that they could march if necessary. Reliefs were carried out periodically, but on the whole the majority of the men preferred a tour in the trenches to remaining behind with the horses. In the back areas they had hard work and were thoroughly bored ; they also had no chance to distinguish themselves, whilst those in the trenches had the satisfaction of feeling that they were helping to win the war.

The section of trenches which the cavalry occupied was east of Vermelles, part of the battlefield of Loos. When the battle had ended after attack and counter-attack, both German and

[1] Battle of Sahagun fought 21st December, 1808, in Spain. The anniversary of this battle is always celebrated by all 15th Hussars both past and present.

British in many cases occupied the same trench, separated only by barricades of sandbags.

There was one particular part of the line, north of Loos, where the fighting had been very heavy indeed. The Germans here had a strong and intricate system of trenches, known as the Hohenzollern Redoubt. This strong point had been captured by us after desperate fighting, and was only held with difficulty, and troops occupying this part of the line were subjected to continuous attacks. It was therefore decided that the cavalry should take over this section.

At this period of the war mining was carried out to a very large extent by both sides along the whole front held by the British armies. The part of the line now taken over by the cavalry, owing to the chalky nature of the soil and the proximity of the enemy, lent itself particularly well to this form of warfare. The exploding of large mines by either side was of almost daily occurrence, and the subsequent struggle for the lip of the crater was often of a very determined and sanguinary character. It is particularly trying for troops holding a line of trenches to know that they are mined, and to anticipate that any minute the ground may be exploded from under their feet. Thus whilst the troops were fighting in the trenches, the Royal Air Force continued to battle overhead in the air, and deep down in the bowels of the earth the struggle was maintained by the various mining companies.

The infantry who had been holding this part of the line before it was taken over by the cavalry had suffered very severely from this form of warfare, and the enemy felt that here at any rate he had the upper hand, and was in consequence full of aggression. The cavalry coming fresh from the back areas and full of fighting spirit were ordered to do all they could to reduce this supremacy of the Germans, a task which was eventually accomplished.

The lucky star of the Regiment was in the ascendant during the tour of the trenches, for on the whole the 15th Hussars suffered comparatively few casualties. The mining district round Vermelles afforded excellent billets, and the chalky nature of the soil made it possible to construct good dug-outs, while Béthune was only a few miles away, and still not much knocked about, there was every facility in that town for obtaining luxuries and even amusements for those not actually in the trenches, so taking it on the whole, the situation of the Regiment was not too bad.

From Devres the 15th Hussars proceeded by train to Fouquereuill, where they remained for a few days. On the fifth of January, the 9th Dismounted Cavalry Brigade (9th

Battalion) relieved the 1st Dismounted Cavalry Brigade (1st Battalion). The men marched to the trenches at 7 a.m. carrying forty-eight hours' rations on them. A cavalryman's equipment is not designed for trench warfare, and many expedients had to be devised to enable the men to carry up all they required, along the many miles of narrow communication trenches, but nothing really convenient was ever evolved, and the cavalryman was undoubtedly much hampered by his unwieldy equipment when fighting as an infantry soldier.

From 5th January until 9th January the Regiment remained in the front-line trenches. The artillery on both sides were active, and there was a considerable amount of retaliation on the trenches, which seriously inconvenienced the unfortunate individuals holding them.

At this time the enemy was still superior to us in all the weapons of trench warfare, and his rifle grenades were a great nuisance and caused casualties ; he was very energetic also with his trench mortars. It was most exasperating to all ranks when, having worked hard all night to improve the trenches and to construct good defences, their whole labour was destroyed by German trench mortars in a few minutes the next morning.

On 9th January the Regiment was relieved by units of the 3rd Cavalry Division, and at midnight returned to Sailly. Whilst in reserve, the Regiment found large working parties every night. The day time was passed in cleaning up, bathing and sleeping. One of the greatest causes of anxiety was the prevalence of trench feet, which at this time of the year was a real danger, and the very greatest care had to be taken to prevent it ; luckily, owing to the precautions taken, the cavalry did not suffer very severely.

The next tour of the front-line trenches lasted from 17th January to 21st January, but nothing happened important enough to record.

On 26th January, owing to reports that the enemy intended to attack, the 15th Hussars were suddenly moved up at about 7.15 p.m. from the reserve position, and occupied Railway Trench, where they remained all night. There was a very heavy bombardment by both sides, but no infantry attack developed, and by midnight the situation had calmed down. The 15th Hussars remained in Railway Trench until 9 a.m. in the morning, when they occupied the cellars underneath the ruins of the houses in Vermelles. Here they remained until the 29th, when they returned to the front line. Once again the tour was without incident, and on 2nd February the 15th

TRENCHES, MIDNIGHT

Hussars were relieved, and retired to billets in the town of Béthune.

In this town they remained until 8th February, when they moved up to the reserve trenches. On the 10th February they again went into the front line.

At. 6.30 a.m. on 11th February the enemy exploded a mine near the Hog's Back, a name for part of the trench system. The explosion caused an immense crater. This crater, which connected with several other craters, the result of former explosions, utterly demolished this part of the line. The 15th Hussars immediately seized the lip of the crater and also occupied Hog's Back Trench, which was not usually held, as it was known that underneath was another mine ready to be sprung at any moment. Owing to the resolute attitude of the Regiment no hostile infantry attack followed, neither did the enemy attempt to occupy the crater. The troops therefore withdrew at 7.30 a.m., leaving behind listening posts, and by 8 a.m. everything was once again normal.

The day was not destined, however, to pass without further excitement, for at 4 p.m. bugles sounded from the German lines, and a very heavy bombardment was opened on the trenches occupied by the cavalry. Every conceivable missile was thrown at the trenches ; shells of all calibres, aerial torpedoes, trench-mortar bombs and rifle grenades. The enemy also put down a heavy machine-gun barrage. This bombardment lasted for about an hour, but no enemy attack followed, and the cause of the trouble remained a mystery. Although the trenches were much knocked about, the casualties luckily were slight. All ranks worked hard throughout the night in order to repair the shattered trenches, as it was known that the cavalry was to be relieved by infantry the next morning, and everyone naturally desired to hand over his section in as good a condition as possible.

The following morning, 12th February, two battalions, the 8th Royal Fusiliers and the 7th Royal Sussex, relieved the 9th Cavalry Brigade in the trenches. On the completion of this relief the 15th Hussars marched to La Bourse. On 13th February the cavalry entrained and returned to the back areas and the horses.[1]

[1] The following is an extract from a letter of the G.O.C. I Corps, to which the cavalry had been attached during its time in the trenches :—" The Dismounted Cavalry Division having gone, I would like them to know how much I appreciate all they did in the line. They showed a most gallant and cheerful spirit, kept the Bosch under control, and did an immense amount of work in the trenches. They set a fine example and have handed over their part of the line greatly improved and in good order. We are all most grateful for their work."

Shortly after the return of the cavalry to billets, the Machine-Gun Corps was formed, and each cavalry brigade formed a machine-gun squadron from the trained personnel in the regiments. In consequence on 24th February the regimental machine-gun sections were transferred to the 9th Machine-Gun Squadron. To replace these machine-guns, and to increase the fire power of the cavalry, the Hotchkiss rifle was issued, one to each troop, and during the whole of March and the following months all ranks were busily employed in learning its mechanism. This new weapon was not supposed to be the arm of a few specialists, but everyone was expected to understand its use.

In March, 1916, the organisation of the cavalry was altered, the Cavalry Corps was disbanded, and the 1st Cavalry Division came under the direct orders of the First Army. This did not much affect the Regiment, which remained in the vicinity of Doudeauville.

A QUIET DAY ON THE FLANDERS FRONT

It now appeared to many that the war would never change its character, and that this stationary trench warfare would endure to the end and never again would armies be on the move and in the open. Some felt that the day of the cavalry was over. For very many months the cavalry, as cavalry, was to remain the least important and useful branch of the Service. This was a galling and distressing thought to all, and life in the little villages miles away from all activity was dull and monotonous to a degree.

Nevertheless all ranks continued their training strenuously, keeping themselves and horses fit for their opportunity if it should ever come.

There was, however, one way in which the cavalry could be of the greatest service to the armies. The new divisions were arriving in France in ever-increasing numbers, and their supply of officers had become a very serious question. In the cavalry there were still N.C.O.'s of the old army. These men, imbued with the spirit of discipline, and filled with the high traditions of the old Regular Army, were the very best material from which to draw a supply of officers. The 15th Hussars sent a large number of N.C.O.'s with commissions to infantry battalions. Everyone of them in their new positions upheld the highest traditions of the 15th Hussars, and earned the praise and gratitude of all those with whom they served.

On 17th April the 1st Cavalry Division was inspected by Sir Charles Monro,[1] commanding the First Army. The 15th Hussars marched to Hardelot for this parade, which was carried out with all the old-time ceremony of a Review, and the division presented a fine spectacle as it marched past on the sands.

The long stay of the 15th Hussars in this area was about to come to an end. Everyone anticipated that the Army was to attack, and to attack not with the small forces which had hitherto been employed, but with the whole might of the British Empire.

The long and terrible struggle round Verdun had at length ended in favour of the French, and during the whole time the British Army, although preparing for the Somme, had remained more or less inactive. But all this was about to change, and everyone felt we were to enter a new phase in this long and bitter war.

The Regiment spent a few days' intensive training by the sea, drilling on the sands, and preparing once again for the "gap." The expected orders were at last received and on 24th June the 15th Hussars left their familiar billets and marched at night to an unknown destination. Four night marches brought them to Querrieu, near Amiens, where bivouacs were found in a field close to the village.[2]

The Regiment was now in a part of France entirely new to all ranks, but a part of the country with which they were later to become very familiar indeed. Many places which at this time were scarcely more than names on a map were destined to become closely connected with the history of the British Army in France, and to become the scenes of some of the most strenuous fighting of the war.

At this time the Somme was one of the quietest parts of the line and seldom figured in the communiqués. The whole aspect

[1] The late General Sir Charles Monro, Bart., G.C.B., G.C.S.I., G.C.M.G.
[2] It was here each man was issued with a steel helmet.

of the countryside was also quite different from that over which the battles had so far been fought. The rolling plains of this part of agricultural France, with the scattered villages, woods and farms, were very different from the highly cultivated and very densely populated parts of Flanders, or the mining country round Loos, or even the wooded heights of the Aisne.

The Battle of the Somme was destined to last for several weeks and was fought with the greatest determination and bitterness on both sides. Many thousands of lives were sacrificed, a whole drama of courage and heroism was enacted—tremendous bombardment and counter-bombardment, attack and counter-attack, days of great exultation and days of great depression.

But the 15th Hussars took no real part in this great battle. This history can only record a story of march and counter-march, of working parties, of bivouacs and billets, a dull and uninteresting record of dry facts. But behind this uninteresting catalogue it must be remembered lie hopes and fears, anxiety and disappointment. The bare statement of fact that the Regiment received sudden orders to march at a certain hour means little to the reader years after the event, but to those who received the order it was all very different. It meant great anxiety, hope for success, fear of disaster, and deep questionings as to what the future held in store.

As day slowly dawned, and the 15th Hussars stood to their horses awaiting the order to advance, to all came the question : " What do the next few hours hold in store for me ? " For at any moment the orders might arrive, and in the next few minutes the Regiment might once again be asked to endure to the utmost. Nor perhaps, after the lapse of time, is it possible to realise the hardships endured. The long night marches, the weary hours in the saddle, the cold wet bivouacs, and all the discomforts of protracted operations.

Furthermore, throughout the battle there was for the cavalry the terrible sense of disappointment, they never had the satisfaction of feeling that they had achieved any success. For them it was always disappointment. But in spite of hopes deferred their morale was never lessened, and after repeated failures the 15th Hussars remained in good heart and ready for another effort.

It is impossible in a regimental history to discuss the reasons for the failure of the cavalry on the Somme. But new weapons of warfare, bad weather and bad luck, and a combination of unfavourable circumstances over which the cavalry had no control, all led to a situation which culminated in failure to realise the high hopes that had been entertained.

The British attack on the Somme was launched on 1st July

and as it was hoped that a situation would be created which would allow of the cavalry being successfully employed, the 1st Cavalry Division concentrated about Bresle. The 15th Hussars marched at 3.20 a.m. to La Houssaye.

As is now a matter of history, this great British attack succeeded in some places beyond the highest expectations, but in other parts the results were not so encouraging, and in certain places the attack was only a costly failure. But nowhere were the successes gained of such a nature as to justify the employment of cavalry on a large scale, in consequence at 5 p.m. orders were received for the return of the 1st Cavalry Division to Querrieu, which place the Regiment reached at 7 p.m.

Although the initial attack had not produced a situation which allowed the employment of cavalry, yet the authorities were hopeful that later on the opportunity might arise which would give the cavalry their chance. But a cavalry division, owing to its large number of horses, takes up a considerable amount of room and requires a quantity of transport. As the congestion at rail-heads was very great it was decided to move the cavalry further back. In consequence the 15th Hussars retired through Amiens to billets at Bettencourt Riviere, where they remained for a few days.

Meanwhile those divisions which had taken part in the attack of 1st July were replaced by fresh ones, and another attack on a grand scale was organised for 14th July. The Fourth Army was to attack with the objective the enemy's second line between Longueval and Bazentin le Petit. This attack was to be made in conjunction with a French attack south of Guillemont, and an attack by the Reserve Army north of La Boisselle. The cavalry in anticipation of this battle moved up towards the front on the evening of 11th July.

The 15th Hussars marched by night to their former bivouacs at Querrieu, arriving there early on the 12th. The next night they marched to Buire sur Ancre, where the whole of the 1st Cavalry Division was concentrated by the 13th.

The cavalry were ordered to be ready to move at 4 a.m. the next day. In the event of the attack being successful all along the line it was hoped that the cavalry would be able to advance. The 2nd Indian Cavalry Division was to lead, followed by the 1st Cavalry Division, with objectives Leuze Wood, Morval and Les Boeufs.

The 15th Hussars stood to their horses at dawn on 14th July, but awaited in vain the orders to advance, for the situation never developed into one which would justify the employment of cavalry.

A NIGHT MARCH IN FRANCE

The Regiment remained in the field at Buire sur Ancre for ten days, standing to at two hours' notice. There was, however, no opportunity for the cavalry, and once again they retired to Querrieu on 24th July.

At Querrieu they remained until 9th August, when the 1st Cavalry Division was ordered to retire to the back areas. The 15th Hussars made two marches to the village of Gamaches, where they billeted. About the end of August the 1st Cavalry Division came under the direct orders of the Cavalry Corps, which had been re-formed and consisted at this time of five Cavalry divisions. As it was known that the enemy were feeling the strain of the battle, it was still hoped that the cavalry would soon have their longed-for opportunity.

During the evening of 5th September orders were received for the cavalry to march next morning. Two days marching brought the 15th Hussars to bivouacs about the village of Daours, near Amiens, where they remained for a few days. During this time officers carefully reconnoitred the trenches and cavalry tracks, and every possible preparation was made to ensure that the " gap " would be a success.

On 14th September the 15th Hussars marched to the Carnoy valley, where they bivouacked for the night.

At dawn on 15th September the Fourth Army attacked between the line Combles Ravine and Martinpuich with the objective of seizing the line Morval–les Boeufs–Flers. The Reserve Army and the French also attacked this day.

For some time it had been whispered that the British Army was in possession of some new weapon of war which would produce a tremendous effect on the battlefield. Cavalry officers had been withdrawn to train with a new branch of the service. Although the secret had been well kept, trains had been seen carrying what appeared to be curious kinds of tractors, and rumours as to the existence of Tanks were prevalent, certain individuals had even seen them manœuvring, so that their appearance was not altogether a surprise. But on the whole the secret had been very well kept, in a way perhaps too well kept, as nobody knew how to co-operate with this new and strange implement of war. In this attack Tanks were wonderfully effective, and perhaps the fullest advantage of their strangeness was not taken into consideration, as they were quite unexpected by either side. After all, in this battle they were only an experiment, and it could hardly be expected that anybody would understand the full use of Tanks in their first battle, an arm that was so utterly revolutionary.

It was hoped that when the infantry had captured their objectives the cavalry would be enabled to advance and seize

Rocquigny, Villers au Flos and Bapaume. The actual objectives detailed to the 1st Cavalry Division were Rocquigny and Barastre. The 9th Cavalry Brigade were to be divisional reserve.

By dawn 15th September the 15th Hussars were ready and awaiting the order to advance. These orders were never given, and once again there was no opportunity for the cavalry. The infantry attacks had gone well, but they had been held up in places, and nowhere had enough elbow room been gained to allow the cavalry to deploy. In consequence at 6 p.m. orders were received for the cavalry regiments to bivouac where they were.

The 15th Hussars remained in the Carnoy valley the next day ready to move forward at any moment as it was hoped that there might still be a chance, but there was none ; they were therefore withdrawn on 17th September to Daours, where they remained until the 23rd when they retired further back, a three days' march to billets in Wail. In this village the 15th Hussars remained for about three weeks.

Meanwhile the battle still raged on the Somme and further attacks on a large scale were contemplated. The cavalry in consequence once again found itself marching to the sound of the guns. The Regiment marched on 19th October and a two days' march brought the 15th Hussars to Naours, where they awaited orders to move up to the battlefield. But in the meantime the weather had become so abominable as seriously to hinder the operations, all the tracks and roads leading to the front line became practically impassable and the mud was in places literally several feet thick, horses and mules were daily engulfed in this mud ; there were even reports of the same thing happening to men going up to or returning from the front line.

It now became apparent that even if the enemy retired voluntarily, the cavalry could hardly follow him up, such was the state of the country. The attacks were constantly postponed owing to the weather ; it was hoped a frost would harden the ground and allow of proper movement. The weather did not improve for some time, and it was finally decided that the operations as far as the cavalry was concerned were over for the time being. Orders were therefore issued for the cavalry once again to march away to the back areas, where they were to billet for the winter.

On 8th November the 15th Hussars marched away from the Somme. Three days' march took them to near Boulogne, where they were billeted as follows : Headquarters, Isques ; A Squadron, Hesdin l'Abbe ; B Squadron, Hesdigneul ; C Squadron, Montaigu Farm, Ecames ; Transport, Hesdigneul.

The Regiment was destined to pass the winter in these villages, not very far from where they had spent the previous winter.

Although the 15th Hussars never actually fought at the Battle of the Somme they nevertheless did play a humble part, for throughout the whole of the battle the Regiment found large working parties, as did all the cavalry. These were employed by the various corps close up behind the trenches, and as the work was always done under shell-fire there were the inevitable casualties.

Whenever an attack was about to take place cavalry working parties were also engaged in preparing cavalry tracks. This was a work of great difficulty and considerable danger. For some days before the infantry assault the men toiled at preparing a route up to the point of the assault, a task carried out under continuous shell fire. On the day of the infantry attack these tracks had to be continued over our own trenches and over the captured German trenches, right on to the final objective of the infantry. The trenches had to be filled in or bridges built over them, shell holes filled in and a road made, and all this work had to be carried out directly behind the infantry assault. It can therefore be well imagined that the digging parties were no picnic and the casualties were heavy. It speaks well of the work done that whenever the cavalry did advance over the tracks they always found them well made and admirably adapted for the purpose for which they had been constructed.

During October, whilst the 9th Cavalry Brigade was on the Somme, Brigadier-General S. R. Kirby relinquished the command of the brigade, and on 31st October Brigadier-General D'Arcy Legard[1] assumed the command.

It did not take very long for the 15th Hussars to settle down to life in billets. Schools of instruction were formed by the cavalry divisions for officers and N.C.O.'s. Leave was opened once again and strenuous training continued. There was perhaps a slight feeling of depression at the prospects of another winter behind the line, and there is no doubt that the failure of the cavalry on the Somme did not add to the gaiety of the winter billets.

Thus ended the third year the 15th Hussars had spent in France, back in billets near where they had spent so many months the previous winter, and still nothing really accomplished.

The year 1917 was ushered in with very bad weather, as snow and sleet fell almost daily. A new anxiety also arose, owing to the strenuous U-boat campaign carried out by the Germans, the question of the supplies for the Armies in France became

[1] Now Brigadier-General D'Arcy Legard, C.M.G., D.S.O.

one of some difficulty, and the authorities were forced to cut down the forage supplies for the cavalry horses to a minimum.

As the stabling was not too good and the weather throughout the winter was exceptionally cold, it became a matter of some difficulty to keep the horses in proper condition. As the winter drew to a close it was anticipated by all that the time was approaching when the cavalry would once again be on the move, and the horses would be severely tested. Unfortunately they were not as fit as could be desired, and it was only owing to the incessant care and attention of all ranks that at the end of March the horses were in good enough condition to endure the strain of active operations.

The contact aeroplanes which had kept touch with the infantry during an attack had proved so successful on the Somme that it was decided to employ them with the cavalry. Schemes and lectures therefore took place in conjunction with the Royal Air Force, and cavalry officers were attached to the Royal Air Force, to ensure that there would be the closest co-operation between the two services in the forthcoming battles.

On 5th April, 1917, the 15th Hussars left their winter billets. The roads were all in a very bad state indeed, the hard frosts of the winter followed by a sudden thaw, as well as the heavy traffic, had utterly destroyed their surface, and it was only with considerable difficulty that the regimental transport could proceed. The 15th Hussars reached bivouacs near Le Moulin Rouge, south-east of Aubigny, on 8th April.

The great British attack about Arras was now on the eve of being launched, and although the numerous bitter disappointments on the Somme had inclined everyone to be slightly pessimistic as to the chance of a real cavalry success, yet on the whole amongst all ranks there was a feeling of hope. The retreat of the Germans on to the Hindenburg Line during the winter, had for a short time brought about a condition of open warfare, and although the 1st Cavalry Division had not been employed, other cavalry divisions had once again found themselves fighting in the open for which they had been trained in times of peace. It was felt that trench warfare was not the inevitable conclusion of modern war. The German retreat during the winter was the result of the "Battle of the Somme."

It is true that the enemy withdrew at his own convenience and more or less unhampered by our pursuit. But it was now possible to imagine a situation when the Germans would again be forced to retreat, but this time with our armies in pursuit, and thus the employment of large bodies of cavalry would once again enter into the sphere of practical politics.

The inconclusive finish to the Battle of the Somme had been chiefly due to the terrible weather conditions which prevailed during the latter stages of the battle, owing to the advent of winter. It was now early spring and several months of fairly settled weather could be counted on.

The general-plan for the Battle of Arras was as follows : the First Army was to attack and capture the Vimy Ridge ; the Third Army was to attack the German defences which ran from Arras to Cambrai (the Hindenburg Line) by attacking this line from flank and rear ; later the Fifth Army was to deliver an attack on the Hindenburg Line from the direction of Queant, with the object of breaking the line opposite that place. These attacks would have the further purpose of drawing the enemy reserves away from the French, who intended to attack later with large effectives, with the idea of finally crumpling up the whole of the enemy trench system.

The Cavalry Corps less the 1st and 5th Cavalry Divisions came under the orders of the Third Army. The 1st Cavalry Division was at the commencement of the battle under the orders of the First Army. It was intended that if the operations were successful, and the enemy were forced to abandon either the villages of Vimy and Baillel, or the Gavrelle–Oppy–Arleux en Gohelle line, to push forward the 1st Cavalry Division to secure the railway at Henin Letard, and the locks and bridges on the Sensee and Haute Deule Canal ; this operation was to be supported by the XIII Corps, the Canadian Corps would also form a flank by facing north.

The commander of the Canadian Corps did not think that there was scope for the employment of a whole cavalry division on his front, as the greater part of the ground was impracticable for cavalry, but he hoped he might use a brigade if all the objectives were captured up to time.

The 9th Cavalry Brigade was detailed for this duty under the Canadian Corps, and the first objective was to be Willerval ; the brigade was then to work northwards with the object of destroying the knot of railways between Avion and Lens, and capturing a quantity of German guns dug into the houses at Lievin.

The British armies attacked on 9th April, and the 15th Hussars stood to their horses at dawn, awaiting the orders to advance. But again, alas, these orders never came. At dark the Regiment unsaddled, but remained in the open field. The 9th Cavalry Brigade was transferred to the XIII Corps on the 14th, but remained where it was until the 16th. At 8 a.m. on that date the brigade marched away from the battle, having accomplished nothing.

The 15th Hussars retired to billets at Boubers, and again found themselves inactive, some way behind the battle front. Although the 1st Cavalry Division had not been in action, yet a brigade of the 3rd Cavalry Division had succeeded in galloping the village of Monchy le Preux, and holding it in spite of the enemy attacks, and in other parts of the battle line small parties of cavalry had succeeded in penetrating the enemy's positions.

Throughout the whole of the operations snow and sleet had fallen almost continuously, and it would be difficult to imagine worse weather conditions. Men and horses were in the open the whole time, and all felt the strain of this exposure. The horses suffered real hardship and the Cavalry Corps lost a number, falling dead where they stood, unable to withstand this tax on their endurance and the severe cold. It must be remembered that for many months the forage ration had been cut down to a minimum, and many of the horses were not really fit enough to undergo the hardships of protracted operations during such inclement weather. The Regiment escaped lightly, losing few horses and only fifty-five had to be evacuated to the base.

During the month of May, the Cavalry Corps, less the 1st Cavalry Division, marched south and took over a line of trenches in the devastated areas north of St. Quentin.

The 1st Cavalry Division did not go into the trenches, but was transferred from the Third Army to the First Army. In accordance with this transference, the 15th Hussars marched on 13th May to La Beuvriere, which place they reached in the evening of 14th May, and where they bivouacked.

During their stay with the First Army, practically the whole of the 1st Cavalry Division were used as working parties and formed pioneer battalions employed about Ecoivre and Roclincourt, and only enough men were left at La Beuvriere to look after the horses.

On 7th June the Second Army attacked the Messines Ridge.

Although it was never anticipated that the situation would develop in such a way as to permit the employment of the cavalry in any force, nevertheless it was decided to concentrate the 1st Cavalry Division in case anything unexpected should happen. This division therefore came under the orders of the Second Army. All working parties rejoined and at full strength the division marched into the Second Army area.

The 15th Hussars marched on 4th June to bivouacs at Estaires, where they remained prepared to turn out at the shortest notice. On 11th June they returned to La Beuvriere, as the Second Army no longer required the cavalry.

Directly the Regiment was back in its old bivouacs, the

majority of the officers and men were again formed into a pioneer battalion and left for Ecurie to work under the XIII Corps.

About this time the enemy intensified his aeroplane bombing raids over the back areas, and raided with remarkable thoroughness. It now became a certainty that if the weather was fine a hostile air raid could be expected during the night. Horses in the open are particularly vulnerable to hostile aircraft attack, but although bombs fell about the 15th Hussars nearly every night, not much damage was inflicted on them.

The pioneer battalion rejoined the Regiment on 9th July. On 11th July a dismounted guard of four officers and two hundred other ranks lined the road near La Buissiere during the visit of His Majesty the King to the First Army area.

The British were about to launch another great attack near Ypres, a third battle of Ypres, which developed into one of the severest struggles of the war. The Cavalry Corps was in consequence relieved from the trenches and the 1st Cavalry Division came under the orders of this corps at midnight 17th/18th July.

It was never anticipated that the cavalry would be employed during the early stages of the battle, as the country was quite unsuited for the movement of mounted troops until a very considerable advance had been made.

On 16th July the 15th Hussars marched to Estaires. The move of the 1st Cavalry Division to this area was in order to support the Portuguese troops in the event of an attack. The approaches to the trenches were reconnoitred and all officers made themselves acquainted with the positions to be occupied in the event of any weakening of the Portuguese line. The Regiment remained at Estaires until 27th August, and during this time also supplied large working parties for the XVIII Corps.

Meanwhile the British attack at Ypres commenced on 31st July. In this great battle the 15th Hussars took no part. Practically throughout the long drawn contest the weather was appalling, and the state of the country was so bad that the use of the cavalry mounted was never remotely possible.

On 27th August the 15th Hussars again marched away to the back areas to billets about Frencq, which place they reached on the 29th.

Lieutenant-Colonel H. D. Bramwell, who it will be remembered had been badly wounded at Ypres in 1915, returned to France on 4th September and once again took command of the Regiment.

On 11th September the 15th Hussars were suddenly ordered to turn out and concentrate at Le Faux. A serious outbreak had occurred amongst the troops in the base camps at Etaples, and the lines of communication had asked for a cavalry regiment to suppress these disorders. The cause of the trouble was the same as led to the Trojan War. The use of cavalry to repress this riot would have been most unfortunate and would have inevitably led to bad blood between the cavalry and other branches of the service. It was with feelings of considerable relief that in the evening the 15th Hussars received orders to return to billets. The 9th Cavalry Brigade had, however, to stand to until 14th September, ready to turn out at any moment. It was finally decided not to employ the cavalry on this unpleasant duty. The trouble very soon subsided and in a few days everything was again normal at Etaples.

The battle raging round Ypres was going in our favour and it was decided to move the cavalry nearer to the scene of the battle. The 15th Hussars marched on 6th October to Serques, which they reached on 7th October, but their stay was of short duration, for on 11th October they marched back to their old billets about Frencq.

The time was now approaching when the Regiment was to give up its quiet and peaceful existence behind the lines. The 15th Hussars had not really been heavily engaged since Ypres 1915; it is true that the pioneer companies had been constantly at work under fire, and in consequence there had been casualties, but these had not been incurred during actual fighting.

But all this was about to change, and in a short time the Regiment was to find itself engaged in battle with the enemy. The 15th Hussars were about to pass through many vicissitudes, through defeat and victory, deep depression and high elation, until finally they were to cross the Rhine as the advance guard of a victorious army.

THE GENERAL

Chapter VII

THE BATTLE OF CAMBRAI
THE WINTER OF 1917–1918
THE GERMAN OFFENSIVE

THE British higher commanders were secretly preparing a new form of attack. The bitter experience of the former battles had shown how difficult and costly it was to try and batter a path through the enemy trench system. It had been amply demonstrated that after days of desperate fighting, when the assaulting troops eventually reached the final objectives, they found themselves confronted with a fresh line of entrenchments, and the assault had to be begun all over again.

The terrific pounding of a modern artillery preparation always created a broad belt of ground which was absolutely impassable by mounted troops, who were thus confined to the narrow tracks that had been prepared with so much toil and labour. A cavalry division was compelled to march along these tracks in column of half sections, and the fighting troops were stretched out to a length of twelve miles ; it therefore took nearly all day to deploy the rear regiments for action, as it was impossible to move along these tracks except at a slow pace.

G.H.Q. decided to do away with the preliminary bombardment, and attempt to surprise the enemy and rush his defences. Through the gap thus created the cavalry would pour and, it was hoped, would be well behind the hostile lines before the enemy had realised what had happened.

The place selected for this onslaught was a quiet part of the line held by the Germans south-west of Cambrai, about Havrincourt.

The Regiment received orders on 9th November to march the following day, and although everyone expected that it was towards a battle, when or where it was to be fought was a mystery, as the secret was very well kept.

At 10 a.m. on 10th November the 15th Hussars marched to Beaurain Chateau, two more days' marching took them to Frenchecourt, from this place the marches were continued by night.

The route lay across the old battlefields of the Somme, through a region which had been so inconceivably shattered by the heavy fighting that it appeared almost fantastic, such was the utter desolation and destruction. After passing through

Battle of Cambrai Nov 1917

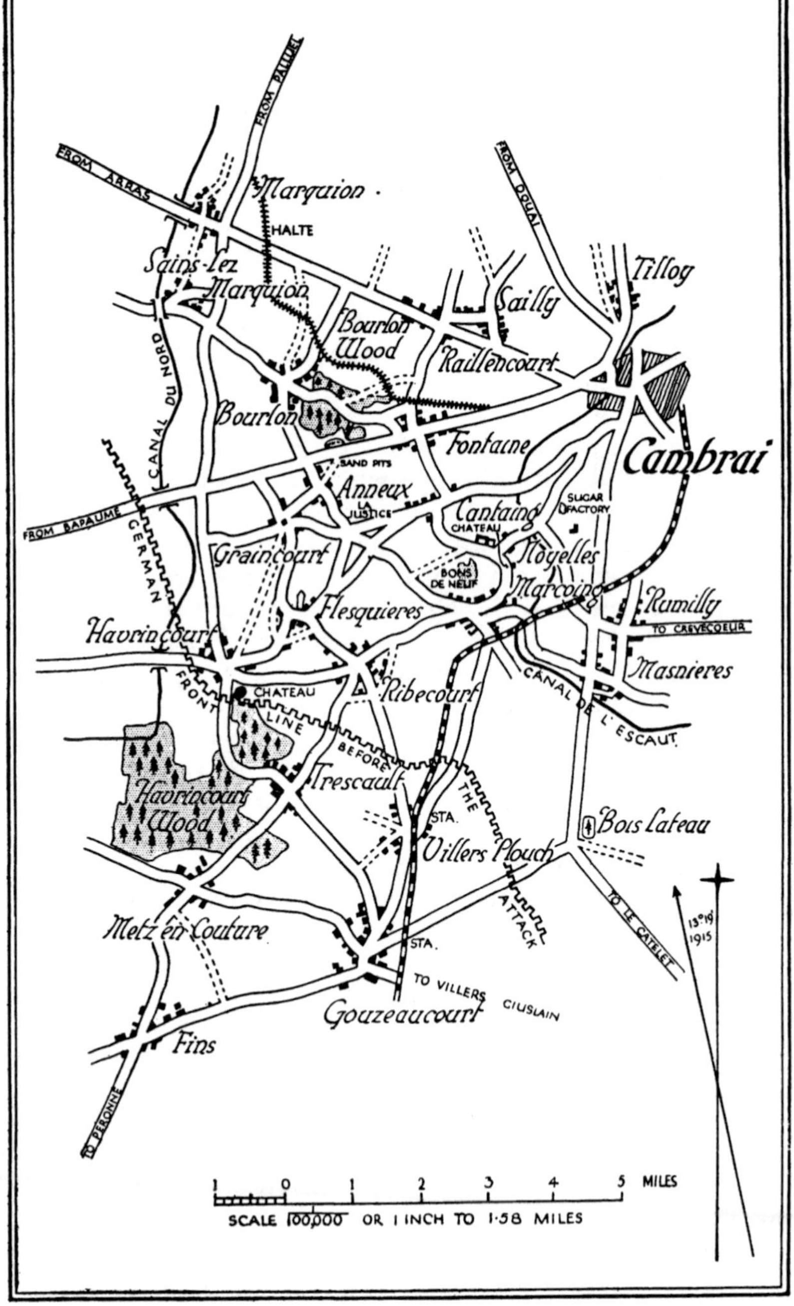

the battle area, the Regiment reached the devastated area, over which the Germans had retired the previous March, and which they had destroyed with Teutonic thoroughness.

In late autumn this obliterated countryside, now seen by the 15th Hussars for the first time, was a most melancholy spectacle. At dawn on 15th November the Regiment bivouacked in an unfinished camp of Nisson huts, at Le Mesnil Bruntel.

A divisional conference was held on 18th, where the secret of the forthcoming operations was disclosed. The conference was attended by senior officers, and was addressed by Lieutenant-General the Honourable Sir Julian Byng, commanding the Third Army.

The object of the forthcoming operation was to break the enemy's trench system by a *coup de main* chiefly by means of tanks, which were to be employed in large number, and to pass the cavalry through the gap thus created.

The objectives of the Cavalry Corps were Cambrai, Bourlon Wood, and the passages over the Sensee River, and to cut off the troops holding the German front line between Havrincourt and that river.

The III Corps was to secure the passages across the Canal de l'Escaut at Masnieres and Marcoing, and also the Masnieres–Beaurevoir line in order to open a gap for the cavalry to pass through. The IV Corps was to seize the Bourlon position as rapidly as possible, stress being laid on the fact that this position should be captured on the first day. The 5th Cavalry Division was given the objective of passing through Marcoing and Masnieres and surrounding the city of Cambrai. It was also to secure the crossings over the river Sensee and cut the railways into Cambrai. The 2nd Cavalry Division was to follow hard after the 5th Division and support it ; the 3rd and 4th Cavalry Divisions were kept in reserve.

The orders for the 1st Cavalry Division were as follows : As soon as they could get through they were to march on Ribecourt, then to move north on both sides of the Canal de l'Escaut east of the Bois de Neufs, the object being to turn the fortified villages of Noyelles, Cantaing and Fontaine, and to assist the 51st Division to capture them. Meanwhile a detachment was to proceed to Sailly and Tilloy, north-west of Cambrai, and there to join hands with the 5th Cavalry Division, and thus isolate Cambrai. The main body of the 1st Cavalry Division was then to move on Bourlon from the north-east and capture it, leaving sufficient troops to hold it until the arrival of the infantry. The division was then to march north-west and seize the crossings over the Canal du Nord between Sains les Marquion and Palleu.

Although this scheme was an ambitious one, it was anticipated that it could be carried out, and all ranks hoped that this time at last something might be achieved.

On 19th November Major F. C. Pilkington took command of the Bedfordshire Yeomanry, which regiment he commanded throughout the forthcoming operations.

With the greatest secrecy the assaulting troops had been collected, hidden and camouflaged in every possible way. Zero hour was to be at 6.15 a.m. on the 20th. About midnight on the 19th the 15th Hussars saddled up in the cold and wet by their huts at Le Mesnil, and marched to near Fins, the concentration point of the 1st Cavalry Division. Just before dawn the horses were watered and fed, and every man was given a good hot meal. As day slowly dawned the division awaited in mass the order to advance. At 6.15 a.m. the bombardment opened, and where before hardly a shot had been fired, there was suddenly let loose all the fury of a very heavy bombardment, and the German trenches were in a moment smothered by an overwhelming artillery fire, and through the smoke loomed line after line of British tanks, advancing to the attack.

The surprise was complete and everywhere the hostile trenches were overrun. It appeared at first that the cavalry had only to advance to certain victory, but it was concentrated some way behind the fighting line, and had a long and difficult march before it could reach the zone of active operations.

It was not until some hours later that information was received by the 1st Cavalry Division as to the progress of the battle.

The 2nd Cavalry Brigade formed the advance guard to the 1st Cavalry Division, then came the 1st Cavalry Brigade, the 9th Cavalry Brigade was in reserve. At 9.15 a.m. the advance guard brigade was ordered to move forward to Havricourt Wood, and the 1st Cavalry Brigade to Metz.

At 11.29 a.m. the 2nd Cavalry Brigade was ordered to push forward to the Flesquieres Ridge. The leading regiment of this brigade, the 4th Dragoon Guards, found that the Germans were still holding out at Flesquieres and Ribecourt. Information however came in that the attack on the Bois de Neves by the 86th Infantry Brigade was making good progress. The 4th Dragoon Guards were therefore ordered to turn Ribecourt from the south and to proceed to the Bois de Neufs. Owing to the heavy machine-gun-fire on the cross roads south of Ribecourt, which was coming from Flesquieres and the ridge to the east of it, this move was considerably delayed, and it was not until 3 p.m. that the advance guard regiment reached the Bois de Neufs, but as the enemy was found to be still holding this wood, the remainder of the brigade halted just south of it. It was found impossible to cross the canal at Marcoing, because the enemy machine-guns were still in position.

As the afternoon wore on, and the attacks made such slow progress, it became evident that the full scheme of operations, as originally intended, could not be carried out, but there was still a hope that a situation might arise which would enable the cavalry to obtain some rapid decision.

About 4 p.m. the 4th Dragoon Guards were enabled to advance through Noyelles to La Folie, and on to the ridge by Cantaing, but here they were heavily counter-attacked and forced to fall back on Noyelles. At 8.30 p.m. orders were issued for the 2nd Cavalry Brigade to hold a line from the north-east corner of the Bois de Neufs round Noyelles on to the canal, and for the rest of the 1st Cavalry Division to bivouac where they were.

During the march of the division through the enemy trench line system, the 9th Cavalry Brigade marching in rear of the division was very far away from the fighting which was taking place at the head of the division and slowly moved forward as the advance guard was able to gain ground to the front. In consequence the 15th Hussars first moved to Metz and then on to Havrincourt Wood, where they were halted, when the orders to bivouac arrived. It poured with rain throughout the night, and the trees of the wood offered but little shelter to the men and horses.

Early on 21st November the attack was resumed, and the IV Corps once again returned to the assault of the Bourlon and Fontaine positions. At 9.30 a.m. the 1st Cavalry Brigade (less the 11th Hussars, who had been attached to the infantry attacking Bourlon Wood) was ordered to move forward from Frescault to assist in the capture of Cantaing. Eventually this was done, one squadron galloping the village mounted, whilst our infantry entered from the other side.

The 15th Hussars had saddled up early in the morning, and stood by their horses awaiting the orders to advance. These orders arrived about 10.30 a.m. when the Regiment marched to Trescault and from there to Ribecourt.

Meanwhile the 2nd Cavalry Brigade had been heavily attacked round Noyelles, the last reserves had been put into the fight, and the situation appeared critical. The 9th Lancers fighting in the chateau grounds east of Noyelles were very hard pressed and needed support.

At 1.30 p.m. the 15th Hussars, having received orders to join the 2nd Cavalry Brigade, marched to Marcoing. By this time the situation had much improved, but A Squadron was sent to join the 9th Lancers and was ordered to clear up the situation on the east bank of the Canal de l'Escaut, between the right of the 9th Lancers and the left of the infantry. The squadron did not become heavily engaged, as the enemy had retired and the patrols were able to reach the wood by the sugar factory which was found abandoned and full of dead Germans.

At 7 p.m. the Regiment received orders to relieve the 9th Lancers, and to take up a position dismounted north-east of Marcoing, between the Bois de Neufs and the Canal de l'Escaut. The relief was carried out without incident, and the enemy made no attempt to attack during the night.

During the morning of the 22nd the 1st Cavalry Division was ordered to reassemble in the Metz area. In accordance with these orders the 9th Cavalry Brigade was to withdraw, but this was not to be done unless the G.O.C. 6th Division was satisfied with the situation ; as everything appeared fairly quiet, units of the 16th Infantry Brigade replaced the 9th Cavalry Brigade. At 1.10 p.m. the 15th Hussars marched to the led horses at Marcoing and from there rode back to Metz.

The attacks were continued on the 23rd, and at dawn the 9th Cavalry Brigade received orders to saddle up and prepare to act mounted. The 51st and 40th Divisions were about to attack the enemy in the Fontaine and Bourlon positions respectively, and the 9th Cavalry Brigade was attached to them. When they had gained their objectives, it was hoped the 9th Cavalry Brigade would be able to pass between them, ride north-west and threaten Marquion, and also protect itself by forming a defensive flank to the north-east, on the hill north of Fontaine.

The brigade marched at 8.30 a.m. The 15th Hussars moved across country to Flesquieres. The march was very difficult, the roads were all congested with traffic, and movement across country could only be carried out very slowly, owing to the old trenches, wire and other obstacles. The 19th Hussars were the advance guard regiment to the brigade, and marched straight to La Justice, the rest of the brigade concentrated behind Flesquieres, which was reached at 11 a.m. By 12.30 p.m. the most optimistic accounts were received as to the progress of the fight in Bourlon Wood, the Bedfordshire Yeomanry in consequence moved up to where the 19th Hussars were halted, in anticipation of an advance forward. Meanwhile the 15th Hussars remained at Flesquieres standing by their horses, and expecting that at any moment the orders would arrive for them to mount and move forward to their objectives.

But the time passed and no orders came, for as the information slowly trickled back from the firing line, it became manifest that the situation was not at all so promising as had at first appeared. Although Bourlon Wood was in our hands, the Germans were still holding the village of Bourlon in strength, and our infantry was also held up south of Fontaine, where the hostile machine-guns were located in large numbers.

The 152nd Infantry Brigade intended, however, to deliver a further assault on Fontaine, and had called for the assistance of tanks, but the tanks could not be concentrated for another two hours, and at least an hour would be required for the assault. It was quite evident that the village could not be taken before dark, and in consequence the 9th Cavalry Brigade would be unable to carry out its original orders. The horses were therefore off-saddled, and with considerable difficulty and delay were watered in the village pond, and the nose-bags were put on. Meanwhile matters had not been going too well in Bourlon Wood. The enemy, who had no attention of relinquishing this important position without a struggle, vigorously attacked the 40th Division, and this division soon became hard pressed.

At 6.30 p.m. the 9th Cavalry Brigade was placed at the disposal of the 40th Division. As there was at this time no possibility of using the mounted troops, they were to be used dismounted.

Enough men were left behind to keep the led horses mobile, and the rest of the Regiment marched on foot to Graincourt. From this place regimental headquarters and the surplus officers returned to Flesquieres. The dismounted Regiment under Captain Brace marched to Anneux, and there came under the orders of the 119th Infantry Brigade. Regimental headquarters and the led horses returned to Metz on the 24th and remained there until joined by the dismounted party some few days later. The operations of the dismounted party during the fighting in Bourlon Wood will now be described.[1]

At 2 a.m. on 24th November the Regiment reported to battalion headquarters of the 12th South Wales Borderers at Anneux, and was ordered to remain in reserve in the sand pits south of the Bourlon Wood, where all ranks tried to get what sleep they could until daylight. At 9 a.m. the 15th Hussars were ordered to reinforce the 19th Royal Welsh Fusiliers, which was holding a line of roughly-dug trenches running east and west, on the high ground about the centre of the wood.

[1] The following officers took part in the fight in Bourlon Wood:—Captain H. F. Brace (wounded); Lieutenants the Hon. A. G. Cubitt (killed), L. G. Souchon, W. J. Lowe, W. P. Alcock, L. N. Kindersley (killed), D. H. M. Clerke; Captain R. Tribe, R.A.M.C.

This position dominated the countryside, and was of great tactical and strategical importance.

Throughout the whole of the day there was constant fighting, and for many hours the battle line swayed backwards and forwards. Captain Brace was wounded during the early stages, but remained at duty until he had to be evacuated to the dressing station. Lieutenant the Honourable A. G. Cubitt having been killed, the command passed to Lieutenant L. G. Souchon. During the fighting the 15th Hussars became split up into a number of small detachments, the adventures of which will now be related in detail. It must be realised that throughout the battle the 15th Hussars fought with the infantry, and that units became very much mixed up, which makes it very difficult to follow accurately the doings of the men of the Regiment.

The defences of the enemy in Bourlon Wood consisted of a series of strong posts strung out through the wood, each one liberally supplied with machine-guns.

At 10 a.m. A Squadron, under Lieutenant W. P. Alcock, and a troop of C Squadron, under Lieutenant W. J. Lowe, were ordered to advance and clear the wood as far as its northern edge. Advancing in extended order through the trees, they succeeded in reaching within one hundred and fifty yards of their objective, but were unable to advance further—the fire of the enemy was too heavy. The men began to dig themselves in, so as to hold the position they had reached. They were not able to remain where they were for very long, the troops on their right were forced to fall back owing to the pressure of the enemy, and the detachment of the 15th Hussars had to retire in order to conform to this movement.

A counter-attack was ordered, with the object of recovering the lost position, and shortly afterwards the line again moved through the wood towards the enemy. The 15th Hussars moved forward by short rushes, supported by covering fire, and eventually succeeded in getting close up to an enemy strong post in the north-east edge of the wood, but at this spot they were brought to a standstill, and had great difficulty in maintaining their position.

Towards evening the Germans launched a counter-attack against the British positions in Bourlon Wood. The attack was prepared by a severe artillery bombardment, and covered by a heavy barrage of machine-gun-fire ; the German infantry advanced to the attack in successive lines. The men of A Squadron fired steadily and the attack made little progress in front of them.

Unfortunately the enemy succeeded in some places elsewhere,

and advanced to some depth. The detachment of the 15th Hussars was soon isolated, and it became necessary to retire in order to avoid complete envelopment.

The retirement was successfully carried out under most difficult conditions, as the enemy fire was extremely intense; the men succeeded in falling back about two hundred and fifty yards, when they turned at bay, and opened upon the advancing Germans a heavy and accurate fire from their rifles and Hotchkiss guns. This at once checked the Germans, who wavered for a short time and then rapidly retreated to their original starting point. The 15th followed them up, and having reached a point within about one hundred and fifty yards of one of the enemy strong points, dug themselves in. In this position they remained all night, and to the relief of all they were unmolested until the next day.

To return now to the doings of the remaining three troops of C Squadron. At 11 a.m. they were ordered to attack a strong point in the centre of the wood. This attack was made in conjunction with a platoon of the 17th Welsh Regiment. They advanced in the usual battle formations towards the enemy position, and worked up to within twenty yards of the German post, but here they found themselves faced in front by very heavy fire and enfiladed on both flanks. An effort was made to hold on to the position gained, but the casualties were so heavy that it became quite evident that to remain where they were meant annihilation. Owing to the very heavy fire, it was with the greatest difficulty that the men withdrew to their original positions.

About 2 p.m. another attack was launched against this strong post of the enemy, and two platoons of the Argyll and Sutherland Highlanders advanced through the position held by C Squadron, but once again the attack failed, and the remnants fell back on to the 15th Hussars.

Later on in the afternoon the German attack developed. The men kept quite cool and fired steadily, with the inevitable result that the attack was brought to a standstill, and the enemy finally withdrew to his original position.

C Squadron, together with the two platoons of the Argyll and Sutherland Highlanders, once again advanced through the wood, and took up a position facing north-east. Here they dug themselves in for the night.

We must now follow the adventures of the men of B Squadron, who had been kept in reserve about the centre of the wood. About midday they received orders to take up a position in the north-west corner of the wood. Passing through the Argyll and

Sutherland Highlanders, they reached a track which ran east and west through the wood, just below the crest of the hill; on the crest of the hill was a strong post of the enemy. The squadron deployed and advanced to the attack in extended order, and covered the advance by a concentrated fire of rifles and Hotchkiss guns. This fire was very accurate and well sustained, and the enemy, unable to face it, abandoned their positions and fell back over the crest of the hill, and the 15th Hussars were then able to advance and occupy the abandoned enemy post. The squadron was soon isolated, and a defensive flank had to be formed on the right, and shortly afterwards the left of the squadron had also to be thrown back to form a flank facing Bourlon village, the squadron was almost surrounded. This small detachment of the 15th Hussars held on to the post they had captured throughout the day, and their casualties were in consequence heavy, and by the evening they could only muster eighteen rifles.

About 6 p.m. the German attack developed, which was intended to recapture Bourlon Wood. Preceded by a heavy artillery preparation, large forces of the enemy attempted to advance through the shattered tree-trunks of the wood. But the eighteen men from B Squadron resisted with grim determination, and opposite them the enemy were unable to make any headway, the men fired very steadily and carefully and checked every effort of the enemy to advance.

Eventually the German assault died down, and the British troops in Bourlon Wood proceeded to dig themselves in on the positions they held, and prepared for what might happen during the night.

As darkness fell, the situation of the 15th Hussars was roughly as follows. In the west edge of the wood were the men of B Squadron, very few in numbers. A Squadron was in the centre with some men of C Squadron, and on the eastern edge of the wood the remainder of C Squadron, with the Hotchkiss rifles more or less evenly divided amongst the squadrons. As the day wore on units became all mixed up, and infantry and cavalry were fighting side by side. By nightfall, however, a very strong line composed of all units had been formed through the wood. Both sides were now exhausted after the strenuous fighting which had taken place, and the noise of the battle which throughout the day had been echoing through the wood, slowly died down, to be succeeded by a silence which seemed almost uncanny, broken occasionally by the report of a sniper's rifle.

At 10 p.m. the enemy attempted to rush the position held by

B Squadron, covering his advance by a heavy machine-gun barrage. For a short time there was a fierce fight, but the enemy was unable to face the steady shooting of the men, and was forced to fall back. The rest of the night was undisturbed.

At dawn on the 25th B Squadron was withdrawn to the centre of the wood, where later the remains of A Squadron were also collected. The whole party was then sent up to the positions occupied by C Squadron, so that the Regiment was once again together. They formed up with the 18th Royal Welsh Fusiliers and details of other Welsh regiments, and then took up a position in the north-west edge of the wood.

At 8 a.m. the enemy once again attacked. The Regiment still maintained an unbroken front, and the Germans were unable to face its fire. Although in a few places some of our troops were forced to retire, the enemy did not gain any success opposite the 15th Hussars. The fighting continued all morning with considerable bitterness. Towards midday the 15th Hussars had expended all their ammunition ; they were then withdrawn to the centre of the wood, where they drew fresh ammunition and remained in reserve. In this action Lieutenant L. N. Kindersley was killed.

At 2 p.m. the 2nd Battalion of the Scots Guards attacked, and succeeded in driving the enemy from Bourlon Wood, and consolidating it.

At 6.30 p.m. the 15th Hussars were relieved, and marched back to Flesquieres, where the night was spent. The horses were sent up the next day the 26th, and the men rode back to Metz.

The Battle of Bourlon Wood had been of a most desperate character, the position was so important that both sides were determined to hold it. The casualties of the Regiment had been severe, and the 15th had to deplore the loss of many brave men left behind in Bourlon Wood. But at any rate the Regiment knew that it had upheld its old traditions and had earned the thanks and praise of its commanders.

The Commander-in-Chief specially mentioned the Regiment by name in his dispatches. The following letter was sent by Major-General J. Ponsonby, commanding the 40th Division, to the Cavalry Corps :

" To Lieutenant-General Commanding
Cavalry Corps.

" I wish to express on behalf of my division, my sincere thanks for the valuable support given by the dismounted Cavalry regiments placed under my orders on 23rd November near Bourlon Wood.

" I wish particularly to bring to your notice the gallant conduct of the 15th Hussars, who on several occasions charged the enemy, and when our right flank was thrown back, assisted in repulsing the enemy and restoring the situation. I enclose extracts from the brigadier-general commanding the 119th Infantry Brigade.

" 'The 15th Hussars came under my command about 4.30 a.m. on the 24th instant, when they were at once rushed up to the hill top and remained in action till late at night the 25th/26th instant. They fought hard the whole time in the ebb and flow of the battle, and assisted to repel repeated counter-attacks, and themselves counter-attacked to re-establish our broken line. Commanding officers speak in the highest terms of the all-round standard of gallantry displayed. To the above-mentioned unit I wish to express my gratitude.'

" J. PONSONBY, Major-General commanding 40th Division.
" 29th November, 1917."

A further mark of the appreciation of the work done by the 15th Hussars was the fact that on the disbandment of the 40th Division at the end of the war a silver bugle and a silver cup, the property of the division, were presented to the Regiment in recognition of its services in Bourlon Wood.

At 7.30 a.m. on 27th November the 15th Hussars marched to the shattered village of La Neuville, where shelter of a sort was found.

During the whole course of the battle the horses and saddlery had been out in the open, exposed to almost continuous rain and sleet, it was therefore urgent to overhaul all the saddlery and harness and to clean up everything thoroughly. The wagons were all unloaded, their contents cleaned and dried, and the saddlery and harness were stripped and everything prepared for careful inspection. All ranks were busily engaged on this overhaul during 28th and 29th. On the 29th the G.O.C. 1st Cavalry Division assembled the Regiment and congratulated all ranks on their behaviour in the recent action.

Meanwhile a new situation had arisen on the battle front. The Germans delivered a counter-attack with considerable force, and had achieved some success, penetrating to a certain depth our defensive positions. As the situation appeared distinctly dangerous, the cavalry was ordered to proceed at once to the scene of the battle.

The orders to saddle up and march at once, reached the 15th Hussars at 1.30 p.m. on 30th November. It may well be imagined that it was with considerable difficulty that this order was carried out, as all the saddlery had to be put together again and the wagons reloaded. After strenuous efforts the Regiment was once again on the march towards the front, to act under the orders of the VII Corps.

The march was by Herbecourt and Peronne, and was carried out with great difficulty owing to the frost which made the roads very slippery. Buire was reached soon after dark, and in the cold and sleet the Regiment proceeded to bivouac. Hardly were the men and horses settled for the night, when orders arrived for the 15th Hussars to turn out again, and once more the Regiment was on the march in the darkness and cold. Roisel was reached about 10 p.m., where an uncomfortable night was spent in the open.

During 1st December the 15th Hussars remained in their bivouacs at Roisel, ready to move at half an hour's notice. The VII Corps, however, did not require them.

The next day, 2nd December, the 15th Hussars were ordered to furnish a dismounted party for duty in the trenches, as the 1st Cavalry Division was to relieve the 4th and 5th Cavalry Divisions. In accordance with these orders seven officers and two hundred other ranks from the 15th Hussars marched at 5 p.m. to Revelon Farm.

The 9th Cavalry Brigade was kept in support during the night just behind the front line, which they occupied the following morning. The section of the line they took over ran from Vaucelette Farm to Gauche Wood.

The time in the trenches passed on the whole very quietly. The enemy after his initial effort had exhausted himself, and was engaged in reorganising, and consequently did not give much trouble. But there was an immense amount of work to be done. Owing to the German advance the position taken up did not form part of the regular trench system, and all the defences had to be constructed anew. The men were very hard worked, digging trenches, putting up wire, and constructing, as rapidly as possible, a regular trench system.

They remained in these trenches until 4th December, when they were relieved by a dismounted party from the 2nd Cavalry Division.

On the conclusion of the relief the men marched back to Roisel. The horses of the Regiment had returned to the former bivouac at La Neuville on 3rd December, a move which had been carried out with some difficulty, for with so many men in the trenches the number of led horses was very great.

The 15th Hussars did not go into the trenches again, but were employed in digging the Guyencourt–Railton line. By

16th December a very fair system had been constructed, and the men returned by rail to the horses at La Neuville.

The 15th Hussars were now ordered to proceed to Le Mesnil Bruntel, but as heavy snow had fallen and there had also been a hard frost, movement across country or along the roads was impossible. It was not until 21st December (Sahagun Day) that the Regiment could move, and once again as in 1808 they marched " O'er rivers of ice and o'er mountains of snow " to their new destination.

It would be difficult to imagine a more desolate place than Le Mesnil Bruntel : situated in a district utterly laid waste by the enemy, what had once been a village was now a pile of broken bricks and rubbish, and the whole area looked at this time of the year more dreary than the northern plains of Alaska. There were a few sheds and huts, but there was a certain amount of material available, all ranks worked hard, and in a short time the place became more habitable, quarters and stables were built, water laid on, and an officers' mess constructed. Thus for the first time in the war, all the officers of the Regiment lived together.

The rest of the year passed without incident. Christmas was kept as gaily as possible under the circumstances. Thus the 15th Hussars saw out their fourth year of the war.

Numerous divisional and corps schools were opened, and there was a continuous stream of officers and N.C.O.'s going backwards and forwards to the various schools and courses of instruction in all parts of the country. On 16th January a party of nine officers and two hundred and twenty-five other ranks proceeded to the trenches near Vadencourt ; they remained in the ruins of the village until 21st January, when they went into the front line, and occupied the left sub-section of the trenches.

The reader will remember that during the winter of 1917 the Germans had retired from the Somme battlefields, destroying all the country behind them, and had fallen back to their carefully prepared trench system, the Hindenburg Line. They had thrown out a strong outpost line in front of this position which they held in some force. The British troops had advanced to within about three miles of the Hindenburg Line, and had thrown out a similar outpost line. The British system of trenches consisted of a series of strong posts, which in places were connected by communication trenches, but in no case were the trenches such an elaborate continuous system as in other parts of the front. The position had however many advantages ; movement during daylight was practicable nearly everywhere,

ON THE WAY TO THE TRENCHES

neither was there any need to worry about hostile mining, rifle grenades or such-like weapons of warfare, which can only be employed when the opposing troops are in close touch. The wide expanse of no-man's-land, in some places as much as two miles, gave ample scope for the conduct of patrols, and made a sudden surprise of the trenches by an enemy raid very unlikely.

On 21st January the 15th Hussars went into the front line, occupying the left sub-section of the trenches. The enemy were fairly quiet on this front, and only indulged in occasional heavy shelling. During the night strong patrols wandered about no-man's-land, and at dawn all ranks stood at their battle stations. On the whole there is little to relate about this period in the trenches.

On 28th January the 15th Hussars were relieved by units of the Canadian Cavalry Brigade, and the men returned by motor bus to their camp at Le Mesnil.

The return of the trench party to Le Mesnil did not indicate a rest, for the Regiment had now to find a very large number of working parties. Ever since the Battle of Ypres, 1915, the British armies had been acting on the offensive, and all training as well as all preparations were directed to that end.

It now became apparent that the armies would be asked to stand on the defensive and resist the whole force of a strong German offensive.

The area in which the Regiment now found itself was particularly weak in prepared defensive positions, and everyone had to set to and work as hard as possible to dig a series of trenches in the back areas, capable of being occupied in the event of an enemy break-through, and all realised that there was not much time for the preparation of these positions.

The 15th Hussars found two strong working parties. These parties were conveyed daily by motor lorry to work on what was known as the Red Line, at Le Verguier and Jeancourt.

On 15th February a strong trench party proceeded to Vermand, and at once went into the front-line trenches.

By this time there was a certain amount of anxiety as to the enemy's intentions, and every effort was made to secure identifications. The large extent of no-man's-land was swept every night by strong patrols, without much success it must be admitted, as the area was a large one to work over in the darkness, nevertheless we were the masters of no-man's-land. On 27th February, by a sudden order of the Cavalry Corps, all battle stations were manned, both in the front line and the back areas, for by this time an attack by the enemy on a large scale was expected.

On 4th March the men in the trenches were relieved and moved to Vendelles, where they remained in reserve until 12th March, when they were finally relieved by the 17th Infantry Brigade, and returned in motor lorries to Le Mesnil. On 17th a large working party marched mounted to Vendelles, and was employed in burying cables.

An important reorganisation of the cavalry had meanwhile taken place: all the Indian cavalry regiments left France for service in Egypt, and the Household Cavalry together with the greater number of Yeomanry regiments, were sent back to the base. The intention was to transfer the officers and men to other branches of the service. To the regret of all, the Bedfordshire Yeomanry left the 9th Cavalry Brigade, with which it had been so long associated. Its place was taken by the 8th Hussars, who joined the brigade on 10th March.

By this time the higher military authorities anticipated an attack by the enemy on a large scale, and it was suspected that the area selected for this attack would be in the vicinity of St. Quentin. Every effort was therefore made to prepare all ranks for this assault, a series of staff rides were held—appropriately enough over the very ground where the Regiment was destined to fight in a short time. Orders arrived for the troops to stand to at one hour's notice, and on 20th March the 15th Hussars were suddenly turned out as a test, and marched to their position of readiness at Aix farm. It will thus be seen that when the German assault actually did take place, it came as no surprise to the British armies.

From experience of defensive warfare, both of our own and of other armies, it had been realised that the front-line system was easily overrun by the assaulting infantry, and to pack this position with troops and try to defend it to the last, as a rule only led to increased casualties. In consequence the first line was only held as an outpost line, and it was the duty of the troops which occupied it to hold out as long as possible, in order to give the reserve troops time to occupy the rear defences, which constituted the line of resistance, and where it was decided the actual struggle should take place. This position was as a rule some way back from the front line, so as to avoid if possible the destructive effects of the preliminary bombardment. It was never anticipated that the front line would be able to hold up the enemy's advance for a long time, but it was hoped that by the time the enemy had reached the line of real resistance, his attack would be so broken up that the reserve troops would have ample time to occupy their battle positions, and any further advance of the enemy would be impossible.

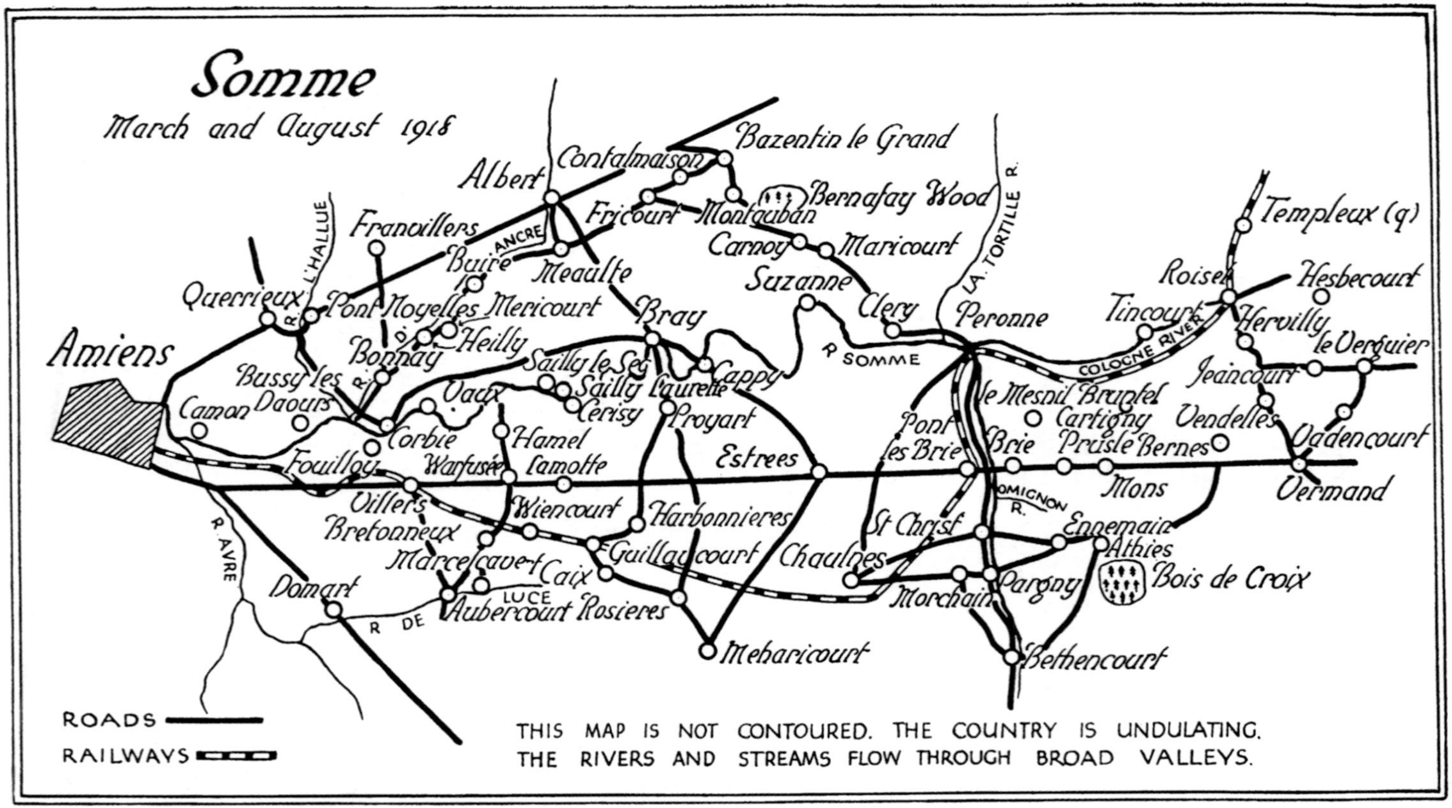
Somme
March and August 1918
Amiens
Querrieux
Pont Noyelles
Francvillers
Albert
Contalmaison
Bazentin le Grand
Fricourt
Montauban
Bernafay Wood
Carnoy
Maricourt
Buire
Meaulte
Mericourt
Heilly
Bonnay
Bussy les Daours
Camon
Corbie
Vaux
Bray
Sailly le Sec
Sailly Laurette
Cappy
Cerisy
Suzanne
Clery
Peronne
Fouilloy
Villers Bretonneux
Warfusée
Hamel
Lamotte
Proyart
Estrees
Wiencourt
Harbonnieres
Guillaucourt
Marcelcave
Caix
Aubercourt
Rosieres
Domart
Chaulnes
Mehariourt
Pont les Brie
St Christ
Morchain
Pargny
Bethencourt
Brie
le Mesnil Bruntel
Cartigny
Prusle
Bernes
Mons
Ennemain
Athies
Bois de Croix
Tincourt
Roisel
Templeux (q)
Hesbecourt
Hervilly
le Verguier
Jeancourt
Vendelles
Vadencourt
Vermand
R. AVRE
R. L'HALLUE
ANCRE
R. SOMME
LA TORTILLE R.
COLOGNE RIVER
OMIGNON R.
LUCE
R DE
ROADS
RAILWAYS
THIS MAP IS NOT CONTOURED. THE COUNTRY IS UNDULATING.
THE RIVERS AND STREAMS FLOW THROUGH BROAD VALLEYS.

As had been anticipated, the German attack was launched early on 21st March. Copying our methods the enemy did not indulge in a long preliminary bombardment, but relied on overwhelming our resistance by the concentrated fury of artillery fire, before the assault of his infantry.

The day dawned very foggy, which considerably hampered our defence, it was impossible for our artillery to find out exactly what was taking place, or how far the Germans had advanced.

At 4.50 a.m. the full fury of the enemy's bombardment fell upon our front trenches and back areas, a large number of gas shells were used, and the whole countryside became drenched with poison gas.

Covered by this bombardment, and favoured by the fog, the German infantry advanced to the attack in successive waves. In this initial assault, the enemy overran our front-line system in many places. In certain localities determined parties of men held out, all of these were eventually forced to surrender or were annihilated. The Germans advanced with far greater rapidity than had been expected. In this area our trench systems were not very elaborate, and the consequence was that the enemy quickly smashed through our defensive positions, and in a short time a situation arose, which was almost open warfare, a type of fighting with which our troops were unacquainted. It was thus inevitable that a certain amount of confusion ensued, and the enemy's advance became more rapid than anyone anticipated.

The 15th Hussars in their huts at Le Mesnil were awakened at dawn by the terrific bombardment. The orders to saddle up were received at 7.45 a.m. and came as no surprise. Everything was packed up as rapidly as possible in readiness for a move, and the men stood by their horses awaiting further orders. It was fortunate that time was given for the men to have their dinners, and for the horses to be watered and fed, for it was not until 12.55 p.m. that orders were received to march to the position of readiness at Aix Farm. Meanwhile the horses of those who were on the digging party had been sent to Vendelles, where the men mounted and rejoined the Regiment.

About midday as far as could be judged, we were holding a line which ran roughly from Vadencourt, through Le Verguier and Cote Wood to Templeux quarries. The XIX Corps reported that Fervaque Farm was in the hands of the enemy.

At 4.15 p.m. the 9th Cavalry Brigade moved forward to Hervilly, with orders to hold the Brown Line. This line, a defensive system of trenches clearly marked on all maps, was in reality only in the course of construction, and consisted simply of the outlines of a trench, although in most places plenty of wire had been put up.

Towards evening the 15th Hussars and a section of machine-guns marched to Roisel, which was reached about 6 p.m. At this place the Regiment came under the orders of the 197th Infantry Brigade. Regimental headquarters were established in the village, whilst the squadrons halted just west of it. The Regiment remained saddled up all night, ready either to reinforce the Brown Line or hold the village of Roisel.

When night fell the situation still remained obscure, but as near as could be ascertained the position of our troops in the vicinity of Roisel was as follows : About two hundred and sixty men of the 2nd Cavalry Division (who had formed part of their working parties) were in Carpeza Copse, and were holding a line to the south of it ; men of the 9th Manchester and of the Suffolks were north of them holding Trinket Redoubt ; the 2/5th East Lancashire were holding a line just south of Templeux, the village of Hesbecourt was still in the hands of the Suffolks ; as already related, the 15th Hussars were about Roisel, and the rest of the 9th Cavalry Brigade about Hervilly.

Early in the morning of 22nd March, it was decided to send the led horses back to Bernes, as the enemy's shell-fire had increased considerably during the night. It soon became apparent that the Regiment would have severe fighting during the coming day, and as it seemed doubtful whether the supplies could be delivered, the men were ordered to break into their iron rations. Breakfasts were eaten as soon as it became daylight, and hardly had the men finished, when the enemy renewed his attacks all along the front.

The report that Hervilly was captured arrived very shortly afterwards, and this brought about a situation of some seriousness, as the Brown Line was thus pierced. The 8th and 19th Hussars assisted by tanks made a dismounted counter-attack to recover this lost village, which they succeeded in doing, after a most gallant fight.

The enemy, however, continued his pressure at all points, and finally succeeded in capturing the Brown Line in several places. The German attack was particularly successful north of Roisel, where they advanced to some depth.

At 7.35 a.m. the 15th Hussars were ordered to retake the Brown Line east of Roisel. Owing to the very unfavourable situation in other parts of the line, it did not seem likely that the attack even if successful could effect any material change, as it appeared that the party making it would become quite isolated. Nevertheless, as the situation was desperate, the counter-attack was ordered to take place, in spite of the almost hopeless conditions under which it had to be carried out. The regimental headquarters and dressing station were in Roisel village, and A and C Squadrons were on the eastern edge of the village, with B Squadron in support. Roisel itself was under very heavy fire, and on both flanks the enemy could be seen advancing in considerable numbers. Major J. Godman,[1] who led the attack, took with him A Squadron and four machine-guns. B Squadron covered the advance on the left or northern flank, whilst C Squadron remained in reserve. By 9.30 a.m. the attack was in progress. It was Major J. Godman's intention to secure the high ground north of Hesbecourt, and having secured the high ground, he intended to turn east and attack the Brown Line.

In spite of the heavy hostile fire the attack succeeded and A Squadron occupied the Brown Line, but as was anticipated, they found themselves isolated. By this time it had become quite manifest that any attempt to hold the Brown Line was doomed to failure, as north of Roisel the enemy had overrun our positions, and was already well established west of the railway. Meanwhile both sides had concentrated their artillery fire into the village of Roisel, which had become absolutely untenable.

At 1.30 p.m. orders were received to abandon the village, and to take up a position behind the marshy ground which lay to the west of Roisel. Owing to the intensity of the fire, it was found impossible to communicate with Major Godman, and he and his men had perforce to be left to their fate. Although soon surrounded on all sides, the squadron continued to fight on alone and unaided, and manfully upheld the traditions of the Regiment. The enemy attempted time after time to rush and annihilate this small handful of men, whose determined resistance was causing them so much loss. Our own artillery, quite unaware that there was a party of men still holding out, so far behind the advance of the enemy, shelled the area thoroughly, and the plight of the squadron soon became desperate in the extreme. But the men refused to surrender, and accounted for very large numbers of the enemy. Towards evening the Germans brought up a number of trench mortars, and commenced a systematic bombardment of the miserable trench occupied by A Squadron. This fire was most destructive, as the Germans were able completely to surround the position with their mortars, and finally they succeeded in rushing the shattered trench, but not until all the ammunition of the squadron had been expended, and no further effective resistance could be offered. The Germans were highly indignant at the opposition displayed by this handful

[1] Now Lieutenant-Colonel J. Godman, late Commanding Officer 15th Hussars.

of men, and at first their attitude was distinctly menacing; finally however those who were left were marched off as prisoners to Germany.

B and C Squadrons did not suffer very severely, although Captain C. H. Liddell and Lieutenant R. Harvie had both been wounded in the earlier stages of the fight.[1]

Meanwhile the Regiment concentrated about Cartigny, where the horses were found, the men mounted and rode to Ennemain, and at this spot a short halt was made in order to water and feed the horses.

Owing to the rapid advance of the enemy, it was decided to fall back behind the river Somme, and to defend the crossings. With this intention the 1st Cavalry Division was concentrated about Athies. It was perhaps unfortunate that the whole of the Cavalry Corps could not have been collected together as a corps in order to oppose the enemy on the Somme, for the cavalry still had many officers, N.C.O.'s and men who understood and had been trained to open warfare, and there can be no doubt that a highly efficient mobile force, such as the cavalry then was, could have offered very considerable opposition to the enemy's advance across the river. But the cavalry were so urgently required everywhere, the 2nd Cavalry Division also was too deeply engaged in the fighting further south to be withdrawn, in consequence there was only a small force of cavalry to oppose the Germans on the Somme. Many cavalrymen as well had been employed on digging parties and had been caught in the enemy's onrush, and were therefore unable to rejoin their units.

As soon as all the units of the 1st Cavalry Division had been collected together, they were ordered to throw out an outpost line covering the Brie crossing, and at 10 p.m. the 9th Cavalry Brigade took over the section Ennemain to Prusle, with patrols pushed out towards the enemy. The 15th Hussars were kept as a mounted reserve at Ennemain.

The advance of the Germans had been almost continuous throughout the day, and in the course of time the old regimental camp at Le Mesnil Bruntel fell into their hands. A considerable amount of heavy baggage had been abandoned, and this now became the spoil of the enemy; amongst other loot, they captured the whole of the regimental band instruments. The wagons indeed of echelon B only just got away across the Somme in time to avoid capture.

[1] The Officers with Major J. Godman (prisoner of war) were Captain C. H. Liddell (wounded), Lieutenants R. Rhodes, W. Alcock, W. Lowe (prisoner of war), R. Harvie (wounded), D. Tennant, M. Gatonby, J. Thomson, Second Lieutenant W. Pickering (prisoner of war).

During the night of 22nd/23rd the enemy did not press the outpost line very strenuously, but as soon as day dawned his attacks recommenced. Meanwhile along the whole of the British front in the vicinity of the Somme, a general retirement on a large scale had taken place, and there were many gaps in our line ; even opposite the Somme crossings there were in places no formed body of troops ready to oppose the enemy.

At 5.15 a.m. on 23rd March the 1st Cavalry Division was ordered by the XIX Corps to concentrate west of the Somme, and to fill in a gap by Morchain, which had occurred between the XIX Corps and the XVIII Corps.

The 1st Cavalry Division had therefore to cross the Somme, and whilst this operation was in progress, the 9th Cavalry Brigade covered the division as rear guard. The 15th Hussars took over the section from the Omignon river to Prusle. B and C Squadrons took over the outpost line under Captain J. Arnott, with A Squadron in support at Ennemain. By 9 a.m. the division was safely west of the river, and the outpost line was withdrawn. The Regiment crossed at Pargny and concentrated at Morchain, where an opportunity was given to water and feed the horses.

The 1st Cavalry Division was now responsible for holding the crossings of the Somme at Bethencourt and Pargny, and the orders were for the 2nd Cavalry Brigade to hold Bethencourt and the 9th Cavalry Brigade Pargny.

The cavalry were informed that the 8th Division would shortly arrive in buses to take over the defences of these crossings, and it was hoped that they would arrive about nightfall. The actual task of holding the bridge at Pargny was allotted to the 19th Hussars, the remaining two regiments of the brigade being in support about Morchain. At this time units of the 20th Division were holding the Somme from about Bethencourt, and the 30th Division was holding the villages of Esmery Hallon and Verlaines, these troops and the cavalry being covered by about seven batteries of artillery. Further orders were issued that as soon as all our troops had crossed these bridges they were to be destroyed.

The 19th Hussars found that they were forced to occupy the high ground on the east side of the river which overlooked the bridge in order to deny it to the enemy. During the morning the pressure on this regiment slowly increased and the shelling became more intense. About 1.45 p.m. it reached the proportions of a heavy bombardment, covered by which the enemy launched an attack against Pargny from the Bois de Croix, advancing in successive waves of infantry. This attack was eventually brought to a standstill by the fire of the 19th Hussars. This regiment was very hard pressed and situated as it was on the east side of the river its position was most dangerous. It was further reported by the patrols that in many places our infantry were being driven from their positions and were retiring across the Somme. At 3 p.m. the 8th Hussars were sent mounted to the eastern side of the Somme and the Queen's Bays were sent from the divisional reserve to support the 9th cavalry Brigade ; at the same time the 15th Hussars were ordered to line the bank of the canal at Pargny, dismounted, and with them was a battalion of the Worcestershire Regiment, which had arrived at an opportune moment.

In anticipation of the destruction of the bridges over the Somme a certain amount of explosive material had been collected in their vicinity. But so heavy had been the fire of the enemy against the position at Pargny that this material had been exploded by the hostile shells, and the bridge having been practically destroyed by their gun-fire, it was rendered impassable for cavalry, although still passable for infantry.

The 8th and 19th Hussars on the far bank of the Somme had by this time become opposed by large masses of Germans who had brought up several batteries of artillery, and these, firing over open sights, caused heavy casualties to the two regiments, and as can well be imagined, their position was no enviable one, with ever-increasing enemies to their front, broken bridges and an unfordable river to their rear. Their retirement now became absolutely imperative if they were to avoid annihilation. The leading two squadrons of the 8th Hussars somehow managed to cross the bridge, but by the time the rear squadron had come up, the enemy's guns had done their worst and the bridge was quite impassable for cavalry. The men of this last squadron were therefore forced to abandon their horses, and each individual man had to make his way as best he could over the broken bridge. It was impossible for the 19th Hussars to cross at this spot, and in order to shake off the enemy, they mounted and drawing swords, moved forward towards the hostile infantry. In spite of the severe machine-gun-fire, this threat of a mounted charge had the desired effect, for on the appearance of the cavalry, the Germans hurriedly abandoned their positions, and thus allowed the 19th Hussars to gallop for the bridge at St. Christ, where they were able to cross the Somme.

The enemy now moved down in masses towards Pargny bridge, quite disregarding the heavy fire which was directed against them, and which caused them heavy losses. The bridge was still practicable for infantry, and its final destruction became now most urgent. From the packs with the led horses fresh explosives were brought up, and a last effort made to destroy the bridge. This in the end was accomplished, but not until the gallant young engineer officer entrusted with its demolition had lost his life in the performance of his duty.

At 5.30 p.m. the 9th Cavalry Brigade was relieved by the 24th Infantry Brigade of the 8th Division, and at 6 p.m. the 15th Hussars withdrew to Curchy, where they bivouacked. The knowledge that a general retirement was taking place was slightly depressing, but the day had been fine, and as the Regiment had been in reserve most of the time the casualties were not heavy.

While the 1st Cavalry Division had been fighting at the crossings of the Somme, serious events had taken place in other parts of the line. During the whole course of the retreat the higher military commanders were continually faced with the terrific problem of finding formed troops to fill the gaps in our line, for no sooner was one gap successfully filled than a fresh one was created by the enemy in some other part of our fluctuating line. It was occasions such as these that proved the value of a mobile cavalry.

The 1st Cavalry Division was concentrated and ready to move, and at 2.35 a.m. on 24th March the XIX Corps informed it that, owing to another gap in the line to the north, it was placed under the orders of the VII Corps, which ordered it to march forthwith to Carnoy.

The march of the 1st Cavalry Division commenced at 5 a.m., the 9th Cavalry Brigade being the last to move. At 4 a.m. the 15th Hussars were saddled up ready to march. The roads were terribly congested and many scenes which recalled those that had taken place in 1914 were being enacted once again. Down the roads, fleeing from the battlefield, came crowds of civilians, with all their household goods packed into every conceivable type of conveyance ; and mixed up with them were endless lines of motor lorries, wounded, labour battalions, empty ammunition limbers, and even motor ploughs—all making their way to the rear, while marching forward with difficulty against this stream were the fighting troops, attempting to reach the scene of the struggle. Unfortunately the tide of war had once again reached the battlefield of the Somme and owing to the labyrinth of old trenches, the acres of barbed wire, and the countless shell holes, movement except by the roads was quite impossible.

A considerable delay took place before the 15th Hussars could get on the move, and it was not until 7.15 a.m. that they were able to proceed. The Regiment marched by Chaulnes and Proyart to Cappy.

On arrival at the last-named place, it appeared that the enemy had been attacking with vigour north and south of the Somme, and that the 21st Division was being very hard pressed north of Clery, which village was in the hands of the Germans; whilst the 31st Division was barely holding on along the Somme from Feuilleres to Barleux. In consequence the 1st Cavalry Division was concentrated east of Cappy, with orders to support the troops either north or south of the Somme. Owing to the nature of the country any action with large mounted forces was impossible, a strong detachment was therefore detailed by the 1st Cavalry Division to act dismounted with the infantry; the 15th Hussars contributed seven officers and one hundred and fifty other ranks under the command of Lieutenant R. F. Rhodes; the divisional detachment was commanded by Brigadier-General D'Arcy Legard. At 1 p.m. on 24th March this detachment rode to Maricourt. In order to avoid confusion, the adventures of this party will now be chronicled, from the time it left the Regiment at Cappy until it rejoined a few days later.

At 4.30 p.m. on the 24th Brigadier General Legard was ordered to fill in a gap which had occurred between the left of the 9th Division and the right of the V Corps, about Trones Wood. The detachment moved mounted towards Montauban, with patrols well to the front, and from the information sent in, although the situation was somewhat obscure, the right of the V Corps appeared to be at the cross roads north of Bazentin le Grand, the line running through High Wood; the left of the 9th Division appeared to be one mile south-east of Montauban. The detachment therefore occupied a position from the Briqueterie on the Maricourt road to Montauban, including Bernafay Wood. This position was taken up by 9 p.m. Mounted patrols were pushed forward as far as Longueval and Bazentin le Petit. Touch was obtained on the right or southern flank, but the left or northern flank was in the air; in consequence the cavalry detachment was forced to form a defensive flank facing north. It was further discovered that the enemy was holding Delville Wood in some force.

The night of 24th/25th March passed fairly quietly, but at dawn on 25th the mounted patrols were quickly driven in by the advancing enemy. The shell-fire gradually increased in intensity, and at 7 a.m. the led horses, which began to suffer casualties, were sent back to their regiments. It soon became certain that the enemy intended to attack, and just before 8 a.m. he opened artillery and machine-gun-fire, and after a short preparation his infantry advanced to the attack. The fact that the left flank was completely in the air made our position both difficult and dangerous to hold. The hostile attacks developed into an attempt to envelope Bernafay Wood, in which the 19th Hussars held a position with the 15th Hussars on their left, facing north, in order to form the defensive flank. The critical attack was driven off, but as it soon became evident that the Germans intended to renew their assault, the few reserves were hurriedly brought up to strengthen the exposed left flank. At 8.45 a.m. the enemy again resumed the attack on Bernafay Wood, and began to work round the exposed flank. The Germans were able to make considerable progress, owing to the broken nature of the ground and the numerous old trenches of which they could make use, so that shortly after 9 a.m. the small party of cavalrymen in the wood were almost surrounded. There was nothing else to be done but to withdraw from this exposed position.

It was with considerable difficulty that the troops were enabled to break off the engagement and effect their retirement, but by severe fighting this was eventually done, and the cavalry fell back on to the road running south from Montauban, abandoning Bernafay Wood, which was at once occupied by the enemy. A readjustment of the line now took place and every effort was made to strengthen the left flank which still remained so exposed. Men of the 1st and 2nd Cavalry Brigades were sent up to try and strengthen this line.

No sooner had the Germans occupied Bernafay Wood than they began to attack the right flank, and for a time the situation was precarious, as they succeeded in breaking through, but a splendid counter-attack delivered by a battalion of the 9th Division from Talus Wood was successful, and relieved all pressure in this quarter. Our batteries meanwhile afforded all the assistance they possibly could, and continued to maintain a heavy fire against the enemy. The guns were fought magnificently, many of them fighting in the open. By midday the men of the 9th Cavalry Brigade were still holding the eastern exits of Montauban, supported by men from the 5th Dragoon Guards and the 11th Hussars, while further on the left were men from the 2nd Cavalry Brigade.

Meanwhile the 1st Cavalry Division had formed a small mobile reserve back with the horses, which was now sent up to support the sorely-tried dismounted detachment.

About 1.30 p.m. the enemy again attempted to debouch from Bernafay Wood, but was repulsed by our fire. He repeated the attempt at 2 p.m., after a heavy burst of artillery fire ; advancing in strength, he moved forward across the open and attacked with great determination. Severe fighting took place, which lasted about three hours, but everywhere the Germans were repulsed, and at 5 p.m. our line ran as follows : from the northern edge of Montauban across the Bazentin road, and thence south down the Maricourt road. The village of Maricourt itself was held by some men of a Highland brigade. There was at this time a certain amount of confusion, as both cavalry and infantry were mixed together, and it was decided to reorganise the line as soon as darkness had fallen. During the fighting Lieutenant H. N. Gatonby was severely wounded.

The Germans could be seen in large numbers massing in and about Bernafay Wood, their artillery fire was still very heavy, and they still continued to work round our left flank ; the situation was anything but reassuring, because it was quite evident that eventually this enveloping movement was bound to succeed. Nevertheless as night fell, the cavalry still continued to hold the greater part of the positions which had been maintained throughout the day.

At 8.45 p.m., before the organisation of the line could be carried out, orders were received from the VII Corps that, owing to events which had occurred further north it had been decided to withdraw to the line Albert–Bray. The rear guards covering this retirement had orders to remain in their positions until 2 a.m. on the 26th.

The withdrawal commenced at 10 p.m. Strong rear guards were left behind to cover the retirement, and patrols sent out to keep touch with the enemy ; the artillery also kept up a heavy fire until far on into the night. The retirement was carried out slowly and systematically, and so secretly that the enemy continued to fire on our positions long after they had been evacuated. By 1.15 a.m. on 26th the whole of the cavalry detachment was concentrated at Carnoy, whence it marched to Meaulte. Meanwhile orders had been received which directed the cavalry to concentrate, as it was the intention to collect the whole Cavalry Corps together, and in accordance with these orders the men were to rejoin their Regiments.

The general officer commanding the artillery of the 9th Division had very kindly placed a number of G.S. wagons at the disposal of the cavalry and in these the men were conveyed as far as Buire, where the led horses were found. After a short rest and a meal, the men rode to Bussy les Daours, which they reached about midday, and there rejoined their regiments.

To return now to the movements of the rest of the 15th Hussars on the 24th, after the detachment under Brigadier-General Legard had left. It must be realised that at this time the information was very vague, and no one knew how deep into our line the enemy had penetrated. It was therefore imperative to keep the Regiment as mobile as possible—ready to advance into action when and wherever ordered.

At 6.45 p.m. on 24th March the 1st Cavalry Division was ordered back to Cerisy. This place the 15th Hussars reached soon after dark, where they bivouacked, after having thrown out an outpost line for their own protection. The following morning at 6.30 a.m. the Regiment continued its march, and reached Bussy les Daours at 1 p.m.

The 15th Hussars remained in bivouacs during the 26th. The general situation had by this time become so threatening that another flying column was formed (known as General Beale Brown's column) and to this force the 15th Hussars contributed four officers and seventy other ranks, under the command of Captain J. Arnott. This column received orders to march at 11 a.m. on 26th.

It will now be necessary to follow the movements of Brigadier-General Beale Brown's column. The men were mounted, and fought as cavalry ; the task for which they were detailed was to cover the right flank of the 21st Division (VII Corps) and in the event of this division being forced to fall back, the mobile column was to conform to the movement, and cover the right of the division as far south as the Somme, in order to keep touch with the Fifth Army. The column got well away, and soon came in contact with the Germans, who were advancing in every direction. A line of trenches had been found, which ran from Sailly le Sec to Mericourt ; it was in fairly good condition, and well wired, and thus there was a position on to which the column could fall back if necessary. At 11 a.m. the party from the 15th Hussars pushed on straight to Heilly, from which place one troop under Lieutenant J. C. Thomson was sent on to Sailly-Laurette, in order to hold the bridge over the Somme ; they also pushed forward patrols towards Cerisy and Lamotte. Meanwhile the enemy had occupied Bray and Meaulte, and strong columns of the Germans were advancing in the direction of Morlancourt. The 15th were not seriously engaged during the afternoon, and at 6 p.m., in accordance with orders, the troop at Sailly-Laurette withdrew to Heilly, where it rejoined the rest of the party. It had been decided that the infantry would fall back on the river Ancre and in consequence the cavalry was ordered to retire on to the Sailly–Mericourt line. The 15th Hussars withdrew shortly after 7 p.m. and very soon became engaged with the advancing Germans. The hostile pursuit became very energetic, and the men of the 8th and 19th Hussars were sent up to the support of the 15th ; a sharp contest now ensued in the twilight, just east of the Bois de Gessaire, fought at fifty yards range. The Germans showed the greatest determination, and our rear guard was only enabled to fall back by dint of strenuous fighting ; when darkness came on the enemy pressure ceased, and the men were enabled to fall back on to the Mericourt–Sailly line. Late in the afternoon the attacks on General Beale Brown's column had become so vigorous that at 7.30 p.m. the 2nd Cavalry Brigade had been sent up to their support. The fighting had been particularly severe about Morlancourt, which place the enemy had vainly attempted to capture. By midnight on the 26th a mixed force of cavalry and infantry was holding the Sailly-Mericourt line, with cavalry patrols well to the front ; the 21st and 35th Divisions were holding the line of the Ancre, whilst Morlancourt was in the hands of the enemy. The line was held during the next day without the enemy making any very serious attempt to capture this portion of it. Reinforcements of Australian troops began to arrive, and at 7 p.m. on 27th the men composing Beale Brown's column were relieved, and rejoined their regiments which by this time had also become involved, and were fighting hard to hold this same line.

To revert once again to the doings of the Regiment back at Bussy, after Beale Brown's column had left them. Shortly after this column had marched away, the men who had been fighting under Brigadier-General Legard returned, as has already been related. Owing to casualties, A Squadron was reduced to thirty-six men, it was therefore broken up and the men and horses divided up between B and C Squadrons. The surplus horses and baggage were sent away, many of the spare horses had to be evacuated tied to the wagons, as there were no men to lead or ride them.

The 1st Cavalry Division now received orders that it was to be responsible for holding the ground between the Ancre and the Somme. The division therefore moved off to occupy its position. The 9th Cavalry Brigade remained where it was in reserve to the division.

The 15th Hussars marched from their bivouacs at Bussy at 5 a.m. on the 27th and moved by Daours and La Neuville to the low ground east of Bonnay, where the horses were watered and fed.

The 1st Cavalry Division now came under the orders of the Cavalry Corps again in the process of concentration ; units of the cavalry had been pulled out of the battle from all parts of the front, and mounted, and were marching from all directions to come under the orders of the Cavalry Corps.

How serious the situation was required no demonstration : it was quite evident to all ranks that unless the German advance could be checked it would be a very great disaster to our armies ; all had seen the abandoned guns and dumps, the long lines of retreating traffic congesting the roads, and all knew that the enemy was by this time perilously near the town of Amiens. The men therefore required no encouragement to fight to the utmost.

The Germans were pressing their attacks on either side of the Somme and Ancre with determination, and it was only with difficulty that our troops were holding their own. The Third Army was most anxious that the line Sailly–Mericourt should be held at all costs, and the Staff hoped a line in advance of this could be occupied. The 1st Cavalry Division was ordered to attack vigorously and occupy the Chipilly Spur ; the 1st Cavalry Brigade was entrusted with this operation, and the 9th Cavalry Brigade ordered to support it.

The 15th Hussars marched at 11.25 a.m., and proceeded to a position north-east of Vaux sur Somme. It soon became apparent that it would be impossible to carry out the attack as ordered, because the pressure of the enemy was increasing in strength and intensity, and large forces could be seen advancing from all directions ; his artillery fire also became very heavy all along the line. The news from other parts of the front was disturbing in the extreme, and so far from its being a question of our advancing, it even became doubtful whether our line could still hold on. At 4.30 p.m. the situation in this area was as follows : the 4th and 5th Dragoon Guards were hanging on to the cemetery west of Sailly Laurette, and the 11th Hussars were about to deliver a counter-attack to relieve the situation in this quarter ; the 2nd Dragoon Guards had been ordered to cross the canal at Sailly le Sec, and hold a line from that place to Hamel. The advance of the Germans made the situation very critical, and the 8th and 15th Hussars were ordered into Sailly le Sec to assist in the defence of that place.

In the midst of this fight information arrived that the Fifth Army line north of Harbonnieres had been broken, but that an effort was being made to establish a fresh line further back. Aeroplanes also reported large forces of the enemy all advancing to the attack. The 1st Cavalry Division was therefore ordered to break off its action north of the Somme, cross the river, and stop the enemy's advance by Harbonnieres.

This operation was eventually successfully carried out, but it was one of great difficulty, as the troops in Sailly Laurette were fighting almost hand to hand with the Germans, and they were only enabled to shake off the enemy and effect their retirement by launching a vigorous counter-attack.

The 15th Hussars crossed the Somme at Sailly le Sec, and by 7.30 p.m. had taken up a position from Hamel to the main Amiens road, which position they at once began to consolidate. The 8th Hussars prolonged the line to the north, and the 19th Hussars were in support.

A mixed force had been extemporised which consisted of instructors and pupils of army and corps schools, American railway engineers and stragglers collected from all parts. This force, known as "Carey's Force," was holding a line from the Somme to west of Warfusee Abancourt and the orders which the 9th Cavalry Brigade received were to support it.

The trenches occupied by "Carey's Force" had been dug some time previously, but consisted only of a shallow ditch ; the

NO MAN'S LAND

position was, however, well wired. The 15th Hussars spent the night of 27th/28th in a sunken road about six hundred yards behind this line, and during the night they worked hard at improving their position, and rendering it defensible. It had been decided that the 61st Division, together with the 1st Cavalry Division, should counter-attack the enemy at dawn on 28th, with the object of capturing Lamotte en Santerre and Warfusee Abancourt. It was hoped that this attack would relieve the 39th Division, which was maintaining a position in front of the general line held by the Third and Fifth Armies.

During the night strong patrols were sent out to reconnoitre the country and discover the exact position of the enemy. Detailed orders for the attack were issued at 3 a.m., and by 5 a.m. the Regiment stood to, all surplus equipment was dumped on the ground, and in the early dawn the men awaited the order to advance. But at the last moment these orders had to be cancelled, as there was no possibility of the 61st Division arriving in time, and the 1st Cavalry Division was not strong enough to carry out the attack unaided. Ther orders were therefore altered and the cavalry were asked to push out strong mounted patrols, closely supported by squadrons, with the hope that a certain amount of ground might thus be gained. The patrols from the 15th Hussars were ordered to operate just north of Warfusee, and they were supported by B Squadron from the Regiment. The 19th Hussars remained mounted in close support, in order to take advantage of any gap that might be found in the enemy's line.

This operation began about 9.45 a.m. Everywhere the Germans were found to be in great strength and alert, and very soon the patrols were driven back by their fire. The men of B Squadron (who were acting dismounted) were soon exposed to heavy machine-gun-fire, and in their turn were forced to fall back and occupy a trench just south of the Bois de Tailloux, which was also held by American engineers. It was thus found impossible to establish any line in advance of the one already held. Meanwhile the hostile artillery fire had increased to such an extent that at 12.30 p.m. it was decided to send away the led horses, whose presence now only constituted a danger ; they were therefore marched away to the west of Fouilloy and the rest of the fighting was done on foot.

During the morning the Bedfordshire Yeomanry appeared on the scene once again. It will be remembered that just before the Germans launched their attack in March, it had been decided to dismount the Yeomanry, and they had all been sent away to the base. But luckily this order had not yet been fully carried into effect, and they were thus available to support the cavalry. The arrival of the Bedfordshire Yeomanry at this crisis of the battle was most opportune.

Meanwhile the enemy, with long columns of artillery, could be seen moving south, and large forces began to concentrate behind Warfusee and Lamotte. All indications pointed to the fact that the enemy intended to attack on either side of the main Amiens road, from the direction of Warfusee towards Villers Bretonneux. At this period " Carey's Force " was holding the line, and the cavalry was distributed all along the trenches mixed with this force. The 15th Hussars, still only two squadrons, had one in the front trench and one in close support ; the whole of the 19th Hussars were in support to the brigade.

At 4.30 p.m. the enemy began a heavy bombardment of the trenches, which was kept up until 7.30 p.m., when his infantry advanced to the attack. To many of the troops holding this roughly constructed trench, the massed attack of the enemy was a new experience, the heavy preliminary bombardment had caused several losses, and most of the officers had become casualties. In the darkness and consequent confusion many of the men fell back, and B Squadron was thus isolated. C Squadron and the 19th Hussars were at once rushed to their support, and with them came a number of American engineers, and after a short struggle this attack was eventually repulsed.

Nevertheless for some considerable time the situation was perilous in the extreme, as there were large gaps all along the line, and it was very weakly held. It was lucky that those few men holding the line were determined, and were enabled to check the enemy, but it was an anxious night for all concerned as the left of the line was in the air. Somehow during the darkness, men were collected, and sent to the trenches in small batches to fill in the gaps, and later the 18th Hussars as well as the Bedfordshire Yeomanry came into the line ; fresh American troops also arrived. But even with these reinforcements there were not enough men to occupy the trenches in any strength, the line was absurdly weak.

Stragglers kept arriving with the news that the enemy had broken the line both north and south, and there were many reports and rumours of the most alarming nature. The Germans had indeed broken through our line between Warfusee and Marcelcave, but this gap had been bridged by units of the 2nd Cavalry Brigade, Canadian machine-gunners, and machine-guns from the 1st Cavalry Brigade.

As day broke on the 29th, the line from the Somme to the Luce was held as follows :

Left Sector : Queen's Bays, 600 details from the 10th Division, 11th Hussars, 100 American troops.

Centre Sector : 200 American troops, men from the Corps Schools, and the 9th Cavalry Brigade, Bedfordshire Yeomanry, Essex Yeomanry with the 184th Infantry Brigade in reserve.

Right Sector : Royal Engineers, Field Survey Company, details from the Corps Schools, Detachment of Royal Engineers, details from the 66th Division were in reserve.

The 2nd Cavalry Brigade was in reserve to the whole front. This force, composed of men from all units, was at this time all that stood between the enemy and the town of Amiens.

The 29th passed without any further hostile attacks, which

gave an opportunity of organising the line, and getting the men into their positions. It was quite evident that the Germans intended to renew their attacks, as they spent the whole day registering our positions, and evidently reforming their troops for the coming assault.

As soon as darkness came on, the cavalry effected a relief, and Captain J. Arnott brought up the men who had been with the led horses. This exchange was carried out without interference from the enemy. Meanwhile, as the force holding the line was very mixed and composed of men from all units, who were very short of leaders, picked N.C.O.'s and men from the cavalry were distributed along the front, and in the fighting which ensued the services of these N.C.O.'s were of the greatest value. At daylight on the 30th the enemy began a heavy bombardment which continued at intervals throughout the day. The Germans could be seen moving about in Warfusee, evidently trying to get machine-guns into position in the ruined houses, from which to enfilade our lines, but this was successfully prevented by our fire.

At 10.35 a.m. on the 30th the enemy advanced to the attack, opposite the position occupied by the 15th Hussars, but he was easily repulsed and the attack came to nothing. Again at midday the enemy renewed the bombardment with increased intensity, and shortly afterwards attempted to rush our lines, only to be driven off with heavy casualties. During this attack, whilst gallantly leading his men, Captain J. Arnott fell dead, shot through the head. Lieutenant T. F. Frost was wounded about the same time.

The number of men holding the trenches had been seriously depleted by the casualties which had occurred, and the 8th Hussars were sent into the front line to support the Regiment. They suffered heavy losses on their way up, as the hostile artillery fire continued to be very heavy.

The enemy apparently was determined to break through our line at this place if it were possible to do so and continued to shell the trenches unmercifully. At 4 p.m. the Germans again launched an attack, which was met by our steady fire, and came to no better fate than the former ones.

Nevertheless the enemy did not intend to abandon the struggle, and at 4.30 p.m. the hostile artillery once more began to fire upon the trenches, knocking them to pieces. After a short but intense bombardment the barrage lifted and for the last time the Germans advanced to the attack. But the men of all corps fought stubbornly, and our rifle and machine-gun-fire swept the oncoming ranks and in spite of all the efforts of the enemy this attack withered away in a very short time, and soon after 5 p.m. the infantry attacks ceased.

The hostile bombardments had quite destroyed the trenches and all ranks had now to work hard to repair the damage, and to throw up some form of defensive cover. Throughout the night the enemy continued to shell the trenches, and numerous casualties were the consequence. During the night Australian troops began to take over part of the line, as the Anzac Divisions had arrived for the defence of Amiens.

At 4 a.m. on 31st the 18th Hussars relieved the 15th from the front trench, and the Regiment moved back into support.

The very fine fight put up by "Carey's Force" is perhaps worthy of record. Although composed of men from many different sources, they showed the most determined spirit under particularly trying and arduous conditions. This was especially noticeable where N.C.O.'s who had had previous experience of a modern battle were in a position to take command. The behaviour of the American troops was magnificent, in their first experience of the horrors of modern warfare.

The rest of the day was passed by the Regiment in the support trench; except for a continual and harrassing artillery fire the enemy took no other action. At 5 p.m. the 15th Hussars were relieved by the 1st Field Squadron and the Essex Yeomanry. On completion of the relief the men marched to Fouilloy, where the Regiment was held in reserve. The led horses had been sent back to Bussy les Daours, and the men spent 1st April quietly in their billets at Fouilloy.

The advance of the Germans had been so rapid that they had outrun their ammunition and supplies, and behind them lay the destroyed areas, with all the difficulties of communication, so by this time the enemy attacks lost their vigour and the battle on this front quietly died down.

During the night of 1st/2nd April the 15th Hussars found a working party which was employed digging a second line behind the front one. On the following day the Regiment was addressed by the divisional commander, who thanked them for the work they had done; he stated that the infantry commanders under whom the Regiment had served had nothing but the highest praise for its behaviour.

During the evening of 3rd April the 14th Division finally relieved the 1st Cavalry Division, and at the same time "Carey's Force" was also withdrawn. The Regiment marched back to Bussy les Daours, which place was reached at 10 p.m. This area was under constant shell-fire, but luckily the Regiment suffered no casualties.

In the rush and continuous fighting which had taken place since the German attack on 21st March a very considerable amount of equipment had been abandoned or lost ; the Regiment was short of many indispensable articles, and the whole of 4th April was spent in drawing stores and refitting.

In the evening orders came for the 15th Hussars to march into Amiens, and bivouacs about the Citadel were reached about 8 p.m. At this time the town of Amiens was under shell-fire, and as the inhabitants were abandoning their homes, excellent billets were found in the empty houses and it was possible to get some of the horses under cover.

The decision which had been arrived at early in March to break up the Yeomanry regiments had been deeply deplored by all cavalrymen. The disbandment of this fine old historical force was distressing, more especially as it was composed of the finest material in the country. The losses of all cavalry units in the recent fighting had been heavy, and the reserve regiments and base depots were quite unable to make good these losses, for they were practically empty of recruits. As the war dragged on and the chance of cavalry being employed seemed apparently to become more and more remote, the recruits had been sent to other branches of the service, where they were more urgently needed. Luckily the men of the disbanded Yeomanry regiments had not yet been absorbed, and as the cavalry now urgently required reinforcement, these men were distributed among the various regiments. The 15th Hussars received seven officers and one hundred and one other ranks from the Bedfordshire Yeomanry, to whom the Regiment owes a deep debt of gratitude. No better reinforcement could be desired, and officers and men showed the greatest loyalty to the regiment of their adoption, with whom they served to the end of the war.

The 5th April was spent in reforming A Squadron, and re-organising the others. At 2 p.m. C Squadron was suddenly turned out. It was thought that the 1st Cavalry Division might be asked to protect the flank of the Fourth Army if a further retreat became necessary, and for this eventually the squadron was sent to reconnoitre the area Sains en Amiennois–Boves. The British line had by this time become firmly locked, and on 6th April the squadron rejoined the Regiment.

Lieutenant-Colonel H. D. Bramwell was now unfortunately obliged to give up the command of the Regiment. The wound which he had received so long ago as the Battle of Ypres 1915 had in reality never completely healed, the strain of the past days had seroiusly affected him, and by the orders of the medical authorities he was evacuated to England ; he never entirely recovered, and to the deepest regret of all ranks he died in 1921.

On 7th April Lieutenant-Colonel H. Combe[1] (3rd Hussars) took over the command of the 15th Hussars.

The Germans continued to bombard the town of Amiens, and the whole countryside was abandoned by the populace, who fled, leaving behind them large quantities of live stock; the men were therefore enabled to supplement their rations with many luxuries, it being considered that if our men did not eat the numerous chickens which were wandering about they would only fall to the Germans.

The fighting round Amiens died down for the time being. But the enemy turned his attention to other parts of our front, and launched an attack against the Second Army in the north, at the outset with some success. The reports which came from the Second Army were anything but reassuring, and the cavalry received orders once again to march to the sound of the guns.

A GAY HUSSAR

(In the trenches)

[1] The late Lieutenant-Colonel H. Combe, D.S.O.

Chapter VIII

THE SUMMER OF 1918
THE FINAL BATTLES

THE 15th Hussars saddled up on 10th April at 2 p.m. and moved to the new scene of activity. They marched by Villers Bocage and Occoches to Villers l'Hopital, which village was reached at 11.15 p.m., and here the men bivouacked in pouring rain. At 1 p.m. the next day the march was resumed to indifferent billets in Rebreuve. On 12th April the Regiment remained saddled up for some time before orders were received to move, and it was not until 1.20 p.m. that the march was continued to Fontaine lez Hermas, where the Regiment remained until 16th April.

By this time the German onrush against the Second Army had been stayed, and large numbers of French reserves had also arrived. It was not therefore intended to employ cavalry unless the enemy succeeded in penetrating all our defensive positions. This never happened and the cavalry was not employed in this area.

Upon the arrival of the 24th Division, a readjustment of the billets became necessary, and the 15th Hussars moved to the following two villages, headquarters, A and B Squadrons to Flechin, C Squadron to Pippemont (later changed to Boncourt).

The Regiment was now once again in comfortable billets behind the fighting line. The countryside looked lovely in the early spring, and these peaceful quarters seemed far removed from war. Nevertheless night and day the boom of the guns could be heard, and the cavalry expected to be turned out at any moment. The battle on the Second Army front, however, slowly died down. Fresh battles soon began again, but in places far removed from the peaceful billets of the 15th Hussars.

Meanwhile there was ample time to refit, organise, and train the new reinforcements.

The attempt of the enemy to break through to the Channel Ports had again definitely failed, and no fear was felt that anything untoward would happen in the north. The cavalry was therefore ordered to march south, nearer to those areas where exciting events were taking place, and on 21st May the Regiment marched to Monchy Cayeux, and on the following day to Genne Ivergny, where billets were found.

The time passed on the whole uneventfully in this village.

Towards the end of June the 15th Hussars were attacked by the influenza scourge, then known as P.U.O. Practically every officer and man was laid low by this malady, and it was with the greatest difficulty that the ordinary duties of the Regiment could be carried out. The 9th Cavalry Brigade was for some time quite immobile, and for the time being ceased to be a fighting unit. Every effort was made by the medical authorities to deal with this epidemic, and a camp was formed to which the patients were sent. Luckily the disease was not in its most serious form, and a week sufficed for most men to recover.

Meanwhile events were moving rapidly. Marshal Foch's great counter-attack had been launched, and once again the Allies had taken the offensive, which was to continue until the Armies stood on the Rhine. But these great battles for the present had very little effect on the 15th Hussars, buried away as they were in quiet villages.

On 13th July the 19th Hussars held a sports meeting, in the middle of which orders were received for the 9th Cavalry Brigade to march to a fresh area the following morning. The Third Army front had been much weakened by many of its divisions being sent to other and more important parts of the line ; it was therefore decided to move the 1st Cavalry Division up closer to the trenches in order to support the weakened line.

The 15th Hussars marched at 7.45 a.m. by Auxi le Chateau to Famechon, where they bivouacked. The next few days were spent in reconnoitring the trenches and back defensive areas, and all the arrangements were made, in the event of an enemy attack, for the 15th Hussars to occupy their defensive positions. On 20th July there was another move ; the Regiment marched to Boisbergues, where they still remained in support of the front line, and were prepared in the event of any hostile attack to march at once to the trenches.

The first few days of August passed quietly in bivouac ; no one in the Regiment was aware that important events were about to take place, the secret of the impending British attack was very well kept indeed, and when the orders arrived to march for what was evidently a battle, they came as a complete surprise to all.

The great success of the Franco-American counter stroke made all ranks realise that the German offensive had been brought to a standstill, and it was anticipated that next year, when the American armies would reach their full strength, the Allies' offensive on a large scale would begin, but nobody realised that the British Army was itself about to launch a vigorous and successful assault on the German positions.

At 3 p.m. on 4th August the Regiment received a warning order to be ready to march ; B Echelon Transport was taken away and divisionalised, which gave a hint to all that active operations were intended.

At 10 p.m. on 5th August the Regiment begun the usual unpleasant night march, moving by Fienvillers to St. Leger, which was reached at 3 a.m., and where bivouacs for the day were found.

The next night the march was continued by St. Vaast to Longpre, where the Regiment went into billets, and where every effort was made to hide the horses from the view of hostile aircraft.

So far no hint had been given as to the forthcoming operations, and it was not until 2 p.m. on 7th August that the brigadier-general assembled all his officers together in the little school at Longpre, and disclosed to them the plan of the battle which was to develop at dawn the next day.

The Fourth Army intended to attack the enemy positions between Morlancourt and the Amiens–Roye road, and the cavalry was to follow close behind the assaulting infantry. The First French Army was to co-operate in this attack. Directly the infantry had reached its objectives, the cavalry was to move forward and seize the old Amiens defence line. A very large number of tanks were taking part in this operation, and the 3rd Tank Brigade was allotted to the Cavalry Corps, the 6th Battalion (Lieutenant-Colonel C. Truman, 12th Lancers) being detailed to the 1st Cavalry Division.

The orders for the 1st Cavalry Division were to follow close behind the 2nd Canadian Division and to exploit their success. The 9th Cavalry Brigade was the leading brigade of the division, and the 15th Hussars formed the advance guard to this brigade. The route which they were to follow ran south of the Amiens–Chaulnes railway. The 3rd Cavalry Division was operating south of the 1st Cavalry Division, and the 1st Cavalry Brigade was moving north of the railway and on the left of the 15th Hussars.

At 10 p.m. on 7th August the Regiment with a section of machine-guns moved from Longpre, and marched in the darkness through the shattered town of Amiens. Progress was slow and exasperating as the streets were crowded with troops and there were endless blocks and delays. The march was carried out in dead silence, and in utter darkness, as no lights of any sort were permitted. If the Germans had only realised what was taking place on that night, and that the streets of Amiens, usually quite deserted, were packed with dense masses of silently marching troops, they could have caused the greatest loss and confusion. But they were all unaware of the blow which was about to fall upon them, and the night was particularly quiet. Occasionally a Verey pistol flare illuminated the horizon for a few seconds, and occasionally a lonely shell crashed into the town, but the marching hosts of the British Army silently moved onwards, and were not interrupted in their march by the Germans.

About 3.30 a.m. on 8th August the 15th Hussars reached the forward concentration area, just east of Longeau. Here in the darkness there slowly concentrated an imposing force of cavalry, whose presence could be felt rather than seen. The night was

GERMAN ARTILLERY, AUGUST 8TH, 1918

noticeably quiet except for the uneasy movement of the horses, the clank of a sword scabbard or bit, the whispered words of command, no sound was to be heard, and the distant firing of a solitary gun seemed only to lend emphasis to the silence of the night. For a brief space of time the Regiment rested, and the men tried to snatch what sleep they could in anticipation of the strenuous work before them. Just before dawn orders were given to tighten girths, and in the increasing daylight all gave a final look round their equipment, and with nerves well braced, awaited the raising of the curtain for the great drama which was about to be enacted.

At 4 a.m. with a resounding crash the British bombardment opened on the German trenches, and in a few seconds the sky line was lit by our bursting shells, whilst in the air rose and fell unceasingly the enemy's calls for help, which were not answered.

The Regiment at once mounted and marched for Achy, B Squadron (Captain H. Brace) formed the advance guard, followed by C Squadron (Captain the Hon. F. A. Nicolson), and then A Squadron (Major F. W. Barrett). With the advance guard was a section of machine-guns.

It was a foggy morning, and the Regiment had great difficulty in keeping the proper direction whilst moving over broken ground. The 8th Hussars had detailed a squadron to accompany the advance guard and fill in trenches, cut the wire and clear the way. The work soon became too much for one squadron to accomplish, the men had to pick their way as best they could through mazes of barbed wire, and to scramble in and out of trenches and amongst shell holes. Some of the pack horses found this too difficult and were left lying in the bottom of the trenches. It was quite obvious that the day was going well for us. The scream of our shells passing overhead was incessant, and few enemy shells were coming back in reply. The German dead were lying about in considerable numbers, and there appeared to be very few khaki casualties, the walking wounded were all most cheerful and full of optimistic information.

At 7.30 a.m. the 15th Hussars reached a position just south at Villers Brettoneux, and the patrols from B Squadron were in close touch with the victorious Canadians, who were about to assault Marcelcave. This place was soon captured, and keeping in close touch the Regiment moved forward behind the advancing infantry.

The leading squadron was now enabled to advance more rapidly, the advance guard troop proceeding between Marcelcave and the railway was fired at from north of the railway. Although the Canadians had cleared the village of Marcelcave, small detachments of the enemy still held out in odd corners of the ruins, for whom the advancing cavalry formed an excellent and exceptional target. In consequence a troop had to be sent south of the village to clear it, before the Regiment could continue the advance.

With B Squadron still leading the Regiment passed through Marcelcave towards Wiencourt, the men moving forward in the loosest of formations in order to cross the numerous trenches and make their way over the broken ground. Wiencourt was soon cleared by the Canadian infantry, and the 15th Hussars entered the village directly afterwards.

Now, after many weary years of waiting and months of fruitless endeavour, the aim of the cavalry had at length been achieved, for it was now quite apparent that the Regiment was behind the enemy trench system, and that in a few moments the 15th Hussars would again be fighting as cavalry in the open. Meanwhile the Canadians advanced into Guillaucourt, and proceeded to clear the village. The advance patrols reported that parties of the enemy with machine-guns still held out in the ruins at the eastern end of the village, and that the road between Wiencourt and Guillaucourt was under the direct fire of these machine-guns. Captain Brace led the advance guard at full gallop between these two villages, and the other squadrons going as hard as they could, swept into Guillaucourt behind B Squadron. Although the distance between the two villages was well over one thousand yards, most of the way under direct fire of the enemy, there were practically no casualties, and the men were able to reform behind the ruins of the village. Meanwhile the advance guard pressed on, sending back reports that the enemy was retiring and that the Canadians were about to reach their final objective (the Red Line). Lieutenant-Colonel Combe then gave the orders for the 15th Hussars to gallop to the Old Amiens Defences, which was the final objective of the cavalry.

B and C Squadrons formed line of half squadrons, B Squadron on the left, and C Squadron on the right, with A Squadron in reserve. This formation was rapidly taken up, and the 15th Hussars, breaking into a fast gallop, dashed forward. There is little doubt many felt that this moment was worth all the years of waiting. As the 15th swept past the position just captured by the Canadians, these latter leapt to their feet, and loudly cheered the Regiment as it passed by.

The distance to be covered was about two thousand yards, and almost at once the 15th came under machine-gun-fire, a few men and horses fell, but the momentum was gained, the forward rush continued, and in a remarkably short time all squadrons reached their objectives, dismounted and occupied the old trenches. C Squadron came under heavy fire from the right in the valley of Guillaucourt, and the men were forced to dismount and reach their objective on foot, after having exchanged a few shots with the enemy, and with the help of the covering fire of the machine-guns. B Squadron, whose objective was the railway bridge, found it to be held by the enemy ; by a gallant charge they succeeded in obtaining a foothold on the bridge. For a time they had some difficulty in holding on, but finally the enemy was driven off and the position secured.

Both squadrons reached the final cavalry objective by 11.30 a.m., and A Squadron was therefore ordered to push forward to Rosieres, but before these orders could be carried out it was found necessary to send A to support B Squadron, which was very weak. As this left flank of the Regiment was in the air, a flank facing the north had to be formed, more especially as here the enemy could be observed rallying their scattered units. The regimental reserves were therefore soon all used up, the machine-guns had also been sent to strengthen the line held by 15th Hussars.

On the north of the position held by the Regiment the Australians had advanced victoriously, and the 5th Dragoon Guards achieved a notable success about Harbonnieres. Meanwhile the 19th Hussars had advanced close behind the 15th, and on debouching from Guillaucourt galloped for their objectives south of the line held by the 15th Hussars.

AUGUST 8TH, 1918

They came under considerable machine-gun-fire, but upon the arrival of the whippet tanks, the German machine-guns were soon put out of action, and the 19th were also enabled to reach their final objectives. The 8th Hussars were kept in brigade reserve, but were forced to send strong detachments to protect the flanks of the brigade. The objectives having been reached, the men proceeded to dig themselves in and improve the trenches, which had fallen into a considerable state of disrepair.

As the orders to the cavalry were most definite, that the primary consideration was to reach the objectives at all costs, no time could be spent in collecting prisoners or capturing booty. As the Regiment swept forward it had passed by numbers of Germans, guns and material of all sorts, which were later collected by other troops. A complete motor-pigeon loft, crowded with carrier-pigeons, was captured by C Squadron. These pigeons were promptly killed and eaten by the troops who relieved the squadron in the evening.

The opposition offered by the enemy had not been of a very desperate nature, but the hostile machine-guns had held on until the last moment.

Patrols pushed forward in the direction of Rosieres met with considerable resistance, machine-guns and snipers from hidden positions in the village shot at them. A battery of artillery, which was in action in the open, kept up an intermittent fire on the Regiment throughout the day, but did not cause much damage. The battery fired at about two thousand yards range, and rifle-fire was not able to silence it. Meanwhile from the position occupied by the 15th Hussars, the men could watch the less brave of the enemy leaving the battlefield in large numbers and the efforts of their officers to rally them could be clearly seen, and caused some amusement to all ranks.

The 15th Hussars held a long line, and as the day wore on the numbers became very weak, for what with horse-holders and casualties, none of the squadrons could muster more than twenty-five rifles. All ranks realised that a great victory had been achieved, and that this day was indeed a black one for the German Army, as the British Army had broken the German line and penetrated to a depth of nearly nine miles between dawn and midday.

At 5 p.m. the Canadian Infantry arrived and relieved the 15th Hussars in their positions, and the Regiment concentrated in a valley south of Guillaucourt. It was some considerable time before a place could be found where the men might bivouac for the night, and darkness had long since fallen when the men lay down by their horses to snatch what sleep they could before the sun rose. In this action 2nd Lieutenant J. Marshall was killed, and 2nd Lieutenant H. W. Palmer very severely wounded. The day had been a particularly trying one for the horses, there had been no opportunity of watering them since the night before, prior to the Regiment leaving its billets. The day, moreover, had been exceptionally hot, and it was distressing that there was not a drop of water to give the thirsty horses.

By 4 a.m. on 9th August the 15th Hussars were saddled up awaiting further orders. It had originally been intended that the cavalry should advance on Chaulnes, and strong patrols had been sent out before dawn to cover this advance. These patrols discovered that the enemy's positions had been much strengthened during the night, that reinforcements had arrived, and that there was considerable opposition. The tide of battle had now once again reached the old battlefields of the Somme and the country off the roads was quite impassable for mounted troops, a fact which hindered the cavalry far more than any resistance which the enemy might offer. The orders were therefore changed; the infantry was to continue the advance towards the line Roye–Chaulnes, and the cavalry was to follow behind in close support, and exploit any success that might occur.

The 1st Cavalry Division was ordered to advance on a two-brigade front, roughly on the line Vrely–Fouquescourt–Hattencourt, the 2nd Cavalry Brigade on the right, and the 9th Cavalry Brigade on the left. The delay caused by this change in the orders enabled the Regiment to water the horses in the river Luce.

The advance of the British Army began soon after daylight, and the infantry had to fight hard in order to gain ground forward; as they slowly advanced the 9th Cavalry Brigade moved forward behind them from position to position as they were captured by our troops. The 8th Hussars were the advance guard regiment to the brigade, and their leading troops moved forward with the infantry.

Rosieres was captured by 1 p.m., and the 9th Cavalry Brigade moved to the south-east edge of this village. An attempt was now made to launch the cavalry, and the 8th Hussars succeeded in galloping the village of Meharicourt; they came under very considerable fire during this movement. After the capture of Vrely, the 2nd Cavalry Brigade also moved forward. The troops were now fighting in an area which had been so cut up in former battles that it was almost impossible for mounted men to leave the roads, and furthermore the resistance of the enemy was becoming more obstinate.

As the afternoon slowly wore on it was realised that a rapid cavalry dash, such as had taken place the day before, was not practicable. Towards evening the 15th Hussars received orders to halt where they were for the night, and to throw out an outpost line. By 10.20 p.m. the men and horses were settled for the night, no fires could be lit, neither could the horses be watered. Meanwhile in conjunction with the infantry, an outpost line was established and the Regiment occupied the road from Rosieres to Meharicourt, A Squadron on the right, B in the centre, and C Squadron on the left. The outpost line was well situated, for a captured German canteen was located in the centre of the line; it was filled with all the luxuries which the German Empire could produce at this time, dug-outs and shelters were also numerous. The battlefield was an extraordinary sight, and even for those well used to the horrors of war, the spectacle was remarkable. The German dead and wounded lay about in large numbers, for they had been given no time to evacuate them ; the ground was also covered with abandoned equipment and war material. Throughout the night the groans of the German wounded resounded on all sides, and at the time there was no opportunity of succouring them. Except for the continual bombing by enemy aeroplanes the night passed quietly.

Shortly after daylight on 10th August orders were received for the Regiment to withdraw, as it had been decided to move the cavalry to some locality where the horses could be watered. In consequence the 15th Hussars saddled up at 5 a.m. and marched to the valley of the Luce, in which river the horses were at last watered.

The day passed quietly in this valley, and the men were enabled to wash and shave, and to indulge in the luxury of a hot meal.

The Cavalry Corps had been ordered to keep a cavalry division ready to move at a moment's notice, and the 1st Cavalry Division was detailed for this duty. The Regiment therefore remained at one hour's notice.

At 4 p.m. orders came to saddle up and march, as it appeared the infantry attack was progressing very well.

The 9th Cavalry Brigade marched to Caix and halted in a grassy valley. Late in the afternoon orders arrived for the 9th Cavalry Brigade to retire, and by nightfall the 15th Hussars were in bivouacs along the river Luce.

The British Army had penetrated so deeply into the enemy's line that the question of supply became very serious. The roads, railways and bridges had all been destroyed, and the authorities experienced the greatest difficulty in moving forward the supply columns. The watering arrangements also were very bad, and it was decided to withdraw the cavalry closer to their railhead. Orders were therefore issued for the 1st Cavalry Division to march by night back to Amiens. The 15th Hussars marched at 9 p.m. on 11th August. It was no easy march, the route led by narrow tracks over the old battlefield, the men had to thread their way through large areas of twisted barbed-wire, scramble in and out of the battered trenches and over innumerable shell-holes. In the darkness progress was very slow. Throughout the night the German air squadrons hovered over the cavalry, lighting up every movement by flares which they dropped from their machines, thus making long columns of horsemen an excellent target for the airmen's bombs. It would be difficult to imagine anything more unpleasant ; the troops were confined to the narrow tracks and were regulated to a slow pace, whilst bombs of various calibres rained on them from the sky with little intermission, and they were powerless to retaliate in any way. The Regiment fortunately escaped lightly, and had only to deplore the loss of one man killed. Bivouacs were finally reached at Camon, where the men settled down for the night; the next day everybody managed to get under cover.

At 3 p.m. on 14th August the 15th Hussars formed up in their horse lines, and were inspected by the Commander-in-Chief, who thanked them for what they had done at the Battle of Amiens.

The British armies did not remain inactive after the battle of Amiens, and fresh assaults were organised in other parts of the front. The chief difficulty with which the cavalry had to contend was not so much the opposition which might be offered by the enemy as the broken nature of the ground over which the battles were about to be fought. Our troops had to batter their way through a broad belt of elaborate and highly organised trench systems and over an area already tremendously cut up by the former fierce battles. In consequence there was a very large extent of country over which the movement of mounted troops was confined to the roads and tracks, and where it was impossible for any force of cavalry to be effectively deployed for battle. Yet it was hoped that a situation might arise which would justify the employment of cavalry, so that for the next few weeks the Regiment was constantly on the move from one battlefield to another, and the whole time remained on the alert, ready to seize the opportunity if it should arise.

On 16th August the 15th Hussars left Camon at 8.15 p.m. and made a night march to Hem, where good billets were found. On 18th August the Regiment formed up in a hollow square in a field nearby, and a memorial service was held for those who had fallen in the recent operations. The 15th made another night march on 19th August to Thievres, and bivouacked in a damp field near the river.

The Third Army was about to launch into a fresh battle, and the 1st Cavalry Division came under the direct orders of this army. It was intended to push the enemy back in the direction of Bapaume as rapidly as possible in order to prevent him destroying the roads and railways.

In the first place the IV and VI Corps were to seize Bucquoy and the Ablainzeville–Moyenville spur, and if this operation was successful, tanks and infantry were to push forward and seize the line Irles–Bihoucourt–Gomicourt, and from thence northwards along the Achiet le Grand–Arras railway. The IV Corps was at the same time to seize the Serre–Miraumont Ridge.

The orders for the 1st Cavalry Division were to take advantage of any opportunity to exploit the success of the infantry and pass through the IV or VI Corps and seize the line Irles–Bihoucourt and Gomicourt, and if possible to push on towards Bapaume, any line gained was to be held until the infantry came up in relief.

In accordance with orders the 9th Cavalry Brigade detailed the 19th Hussars to keep in close touch with the 63rd Division and C Squadron 15th Hussars to keep in touch with the 5th Division. The remainder of the 9th Cavalry Brigade remained under the direct orders of the G.O.C. 1st Cavalry Division, ready to exploit any success gained by the 63rd Division.

During 20th August the 15th Hussars remained in bivouac, but officers and N.C.O.'s went up to the front line to reconnoitre the various cavalry tracks. At 5.30 p.m. a large working party from the Regiment left to prepare the cavalry track behind the assaulting infantry.

At 11.15 p.m. the 15th Hussars saddled up and marched to Souastre, where the brigade concentrated about 1 a.m. on the 21st. From here C Squadron proceeded through Fouquevillers to just west of Essarts. The march of the cavalry was much delayed by the heavy traffic on the roads, and in the darkness movement across country was impossible. When 21st August dawned a thick mist which did not lift until well on in the day covered the whole scene of the operations. This made it difficult for the cavalry patrols to watch the actual progress of the battle. On the other hand, the large forces of cavalry present on the battlefield were never accurately located by the enemy, and the remarkably few casualties suffered by the cavalry were undoubtedly due to the friendly cover offered by the mist.

The story of the Regiment on this day can be told in a few words, for on this occasion the cavalry achieved practically nothing, and its presence had but little effect on the battle. C Squadron awaited the hour of zero at Essarts, and directly the bombardment opened advanced behind the infantry, with its patrols in the closest touch with the assaulting troops of the 5th Division. Bucquoy was reached at 6.25 a.m., by which time the attack was proceeding with every prospect of success, but here a check arose. Owing to the extremely broken nature of the country any movement by mounted troops except by road was absolutely out of the question. It would indeed have been difficult for a man on foot to have made his way over the shattered and broken trenches, and through the dense belts of barbed wire. The village of Bucquoy was under heavy and continuous fire from the German artillery, and the roads through the village were completely blocked by several of the largest type of tanks, which had been knocked out by hostile shell fire. Progress through the village by any force of cavalry was therefore impossible, but a few patrols did manage to scramble through. Meanwhile the rest of the squadron remained just west of Bucquoy. Once again the value of cavalry patrols was incontestably proved, for these patrols kept in close touch with the firing line and sent back a constant stream of information which was both timely and accurate.

The 5th Division advanced with some celerity, and soon occupied Achiet le Petit and the railway embankment beyond. But towards the afternoon a strong counter-attack by the enemy drove our men from the embankment ; the 5th Division were forced to dig themselves in about Achiet le Petit, and a further advance was no longer probable.

During the day the enemy employed a quantity of gas shells, and the men of the leading troop and patrols were forced to don their gas masks. The cavalry carried no gas masks for the horses, but although the patrols passed through several gas barrages, the horses did not appear to suffer.

Meanwhile the Regiment less C Squadron moved off from Fonquevillers about 7 a.m. to a valley due east of Essarts, where they remained throughout the day, without anything worthy of record taking place. Towards evening it became apparent that the enemy was holding his own along the whole front. Orders were therefore issued for the cavalry to withdraw. The 15th Hussars in consequence marched back to Amplier, which they reached about 10.50 p.m. C Squadron also rejoined during the night.

Throughout the whole of the operations there had been no opportunity of watering the horses, and the day had been very hot ; as soon as the mist lifted in the morning the sun beat fiercely down on the Regiment, and there was no shade of any kind. Considerable distances were covered, especially by the patrols, the endurance of the horses was therefore severely taxed, but they suffered no ill effects.

The cavalry had achieved no success, as on 8th August, but in reality there was no chance, the countryside was quite unsuited for the movement of mounted troops, and unless the German Army had broken into complete rout, there had never been any possibility of the cavalry effecting anything of consequence.

The Regiment remained in bivouacs during 22nd and 23rd August under orders to move at a moment's notice. Once or twice the men were ordered to turn out and saddle up, but the Regiment did not actually march until 7 p.m. 24th August.

It was now apparent that although a state of open warfare had not yet been reached, the long period of trench warfare was rapidly approaching termination. The enemy's power of resistance was weakening, and everywhere our attacks were meeting with considerable success.

There still remained a large belt of fortified country, as well as the elaborate Hindenburg trench system, and the enemy had to be driven from these before a state of open warfare could be reached. By this time all corps felt the need of mounted troops, a need that had not been felt during the long period of trench warfare. Certain regiments were therefore detailed as Corps mounted troops, and the 15th Hussars were detailed to the VI Corps.

In consequence the Regiment marched to join this Corps, and marching by night reached bivouacs about Douchy les Aylette at 12.30 a.m. 25th August.

Throughout the march the enemy night bombing squadrons were most active, and during the hours of darkness their machines hovered over the marching Regiment, the crash of their bursting bombs resounded on all sides, but fortunately there were no casualties.

The 15th Hussars were now acting once again as divisional cavalry, and A Squadron was broken up into different detachments, with the Guards Division, the 2nd Division, the 3rd Division and 62nd Division, whilst B Squadron sent one troop to Humbercamp for escort duty with prisoners of war.

The attachment of the 15th Hussars to the VI Corps did not last for long, as the 1st Cavalry Division was withdrawn from the Third Army and came under the orders of the Cavalry Corps. The 15th Hussars were therefore ordered to rejoin the 9th Cavalry Brigade. The Regiment was relieved by the Oxford Hussars, and at 6.30 p.m. on 25th August made a night march in pouring rain to Humbercamp, where the various troops rejoined during the night, all soaked to the skin.

The 15th Hussars marched again by night to Dernier, which was reached early on 27th August. The men got into billets, but the horses were in the open.

The Regiment remained in this village for some time, once or twice the men were turned out and saddled up, but nothing serious occurred. Rain fell in torrents towards the end of August, and the horse standings soon became feet deep in mud, which necessitated constant changing of the lines.

On 16th September the 15th Hussars left their billets at Dernier, and marched to Conchy sur Canche. The move of the Regiment on this occasion was not to a battle, but to take part in a field day. A large mixed force had been collected together, chiefly armoured cars and cavalry, to practise a rapid advance after a retreating enemy. The Commander-in-Chief was present during these manœuvres. The Regiment had an early start on 17th, the day was a long one and tiring both for men and horses, and towards evening all were glad to reach bivouacs at Le Ponchel. Although the day had been a long one it had been very fine and the absence of shells and bullets made the day on the whole rather enjoyable.

On the 18th the Regiment marched to Barley, where the men billeted ; they were, however, unceremoniously turned out of their comfortable billets to make room for other troops on the 20th and marched to Hem, where everybody managed to get under cover.

At nightfall on the 24th the 9th Cavalry Brigade again marched to the battlefield. The 15th Hussars marched in the darkness to Coigneux. This village was located just at the edge of the war zone, and was considerably shattered. The following night the march was resumed to Becordel, where about midnight the men settled into bivouacs. Still marching by night on the 26th the Regiment moved to the Bois de Hennois, which place was reached about 2 a.m. on the 27th. The line of march was through the old battlefields and scenery of the most depressing nature. Throughout the night rain fell in torrents, not much shelter was available, and the men and horses spent the rest of the night under the trees, sheltering as best they could against the storm.

The great battles which had so far taken place had driven the enemy from position to position, and almost every day had recorded the successful advance of our troops. By this time only one line of fortifications was left to the Germans, the elaborate system of the Hindenburg Line, behind which lay the open country. But the Hindenburg trench system had been prepared by the labour of prisoners of war, it was as elaborate and formidable as foresight and care could make it, and its capture was an undertaking of considerable difficulty. The higher military authorities had, however, decided that the time had now arrived when this formidable fortification system should be assaulted, and a great battle was impending which was to drive the Germans from their last entrenchments and throw them back over their own frontiers.

The actual tasks allotted to the different armies from north to south were as follows :

The First Army was to force the crossings of the Canal du Nord and seize the high ground about Sailly–Haynecourt–Oisy le Verger. From there the eventual object was to secure the general line Morenchies–Blecourt and Aubenchal au Bac, and if this operation was successful the First Army was to push further forwards and secure its flank on the Sensee River, and from there operate so as to protect the flank of the Third Army.

The objectives of the Third Army (from north to south) were as follows :

The XVII Corps and VI Corps were to attack with the object of gaining the bridge-heads over the Canal de l'Escaut in the direction of Rumilly and north of that place. The IV Corps was to clear the Hindenburg Line as far east as the Couillet Valley, and was then to continue its advance to Welsh Ridge, its attack conforming with the advance of the VI Corps across the Canal de l'Escaut. The final advance of the Third Army was to be in the direction of Le Cateau–Solesmes.

The Fourth Army was to attack the Hindenburg defences between St. Quentin and Vendhuile with Le Tronquay–Le Vergies–Wiancourt–Beaurevoir as their objectives.

The Cavalry Corps (less the 2nd Cavalry Division, whose units were detailed to act as corps cavalry) was to be in a position of readiness along the Tortelle and Somme rivers by 28th September, and was to be prepared to exploit any success gained by the attacks of the British Armies. It was not anticipated that the cavalry would be employed until the situation had become one of open warfare.

In accordance with the above orders the 15th Hussars marched by Bossu to near Roisel, where the men bivouacked. As the weather by this time was ideal all superfluous kit was stored and marching order cut down, all ranks moving as light as possible. The place where the Regiment bivouacked was in practically the same spot where A Squadron had been surrounded the previous March.

Meanwhile the attacks of the British Armies had progressed with the greatest success ; the 1st Cavalry Division was in readiness about Roisel and the 3rd Cavalry Division about Bihoucourt.

In the event of the battle proving successful the rôle of the cavalry was as follows : they were to pass through the Fourth Army and were to advance in the general direction of Le Cateau, securing the railway junction at this place and at Busigny; they were further to operate on the flanks and in the rear of the enemy opposing our Third and First Armies, and to cut the hostile communications about Valenciennes. It was decided that during the earlier stages of the battle the cavalry formations were to be under the orders of the Armies with which they were operating, but when once launched they would come under the direct orders of G.H.Q.

The detailed orders for the 1st Cavalry Division were to move by Hervilly and Hesbecourt to Bellicourt ; from this place to advance to Le Cateau, seize the railways at this junction and, if possible, send detachments northwards in the direction of Valenciennes and cut the railway communications of that place.

On 1st October the 15th Hussars were warned that they would be required the following day. By 5 a.m. 2nd October the men were all saddled up awaiting the orders to advance. It must be realised that for some days a great battle had been raging, and that the cavalry was only intended to take part during the final stages ; its movements depended entirely on the success of the infantry assaults.

The men remained standing by their horses until 9.15 a.m., when the Regiment moved forward to Riqueval, only to be ordered back to bivouacs later in the day. A very large number of troops had been collected for this battle, with the result that all the roads and tracks were jammed with traffic, and to complicate matters numerous delay-action mines had been buried by the enemy in his retreat. These exploded at the most inopportune moments, which added considerably to the difficulties and dangers of the march. A very large number of transport animals were also concentrated in this area, which complicated the watering arrangements. A very long and weary time was spent before the Regiment got its turn at the watering troughs.

The 15th Hussars were turned out again on 3rd October at 10.50 a.m. and marched to their position of readiness at Riqueval. The orders were for the 9th Cavalry Brigade to lead the division, and the 19th Hussars were the leading regiment of the Brigade. The enemy offered the most strenuous opposition about Montbrehain and Beaurevoir, and no great advance could be made, so the cavalry was not employed. Throughout the day the 15th Hussars had remained off-saddled by the side of the road, and had not been employed in any way. The return march in the darkness was accomplished with some difficulty, and it was not until well after midnight that all units were bivouacked once again at Roisel.

The Regiment remained in bivouac for the next few days, anxiously awaiting news as to the progress of the great battle. Orders eventually arrived at 2.15 p.m. on 7th October, when the 15th Hussars marched across country to a valley east of Villeret, where the men bivouacked after darkness had fallen. Enemy aeroplanes vigorously bombarded the whole area during the night, but there were very few casualties—none in the 15th

Hussars. In this bivouac there was not a drop of water for the horses, and it was difficult to foresee when there would be a chance to water them, especially if the cavalry became engaged. The orders had not been changed and the objective for the cavalry was still Le Cateau. The Third Army was attacking towards Caudry, and the Fourth Army towards Bohain, whilst the French First Army was moving in the direction of Essigny le Petit and Fontaine Uterte. The 1st Cavalry Division was to lead the Cavalry Corps and was advancing in the form of an arrow-head, with the 9th Cavalry Brigade in advance, and the 1st and 2nd Brigades echeloned on right and left.

The 19th Hussars were the leading regiment of the 9th Cavalry Brigade, and they were to keep in close touch with the assaulting troops of an American Corps and the XIII Corps, and it was anticipated that as soon as the villages of Serain and Premont were in our hands, the whole of the 9th Cavalry Brigade would be able to advance, and eventually move towards Le Cateau.

Shortly after 3 a.m. on 8th October the men saddled up, and the Regiment moved to a valley between Nauroy and Joncourt. The attack was launched, and following behind the advancing infantry the 15th Hussars moved to near Wiancourt, and thence to Geneve and by 9.37 a.m. they halted at Ponchaux. Meanwhile reports had arrived that the enemy was retiring from Serain and Premont, and that our infantry was approaching the two villages. It appeared that a successful advance of the cavalry would take place, and the 19th Hussars were ordered to pass through the lines of advancing infantry to their first objective and the remainder of the 9th Cavalry Brigade prepared to follow them.

To the British troops as they advanced the countryside presented an attractive appearance, the broad belt of destroyed and devastated areas had now been left behind, and stretched out to view lay the rolling, highly cultivated countryside of agricultural France, untouched by war since 1914. Numerous villages dotted the horizon, the steeples and unbroken roofs showing above the surrounding trees. From the distance the view was quite peaceful, and except for the presence of the observation balloons, and the occasional bursting shells, there seemed at first glance to be no sign of war. Nevertheless this peaceful prospect was deceitful, for the German retreat was not by any means disorganised, and the rear guards were most skilfully placed. Machine-guns were cleverly hidden in the houses and behind fences and trees, and all approaches were swept by a deadly fire. Behind these machine-guns, batteries of field artillery were in action, which, firing over open sights, caused very heavy casualties to the advancing cavalry.

Directly the 19th Hussars moved forward, they were held up by heavy fire, and all three squadrons soon became heavily engaged. Every effort to advance either mounted or on foot failed, and it became evident that a direct advance through either Serain or Premont was not feasible. It was therefore decided that the whole of the 19th Hussars should attempt to turn the flank of the enemy occupying these two villages. The squadron of the 19th, fighting on the outskirts of Serain, rejoined the rest of the Regiment. A Squadron of the 15th Hussars under Major Barrett replaced it, and at 11.25 a.m., advancing to the edge of Serain, soon became engaged with the enemy. The orders were to push through the village if possible, and seize the high ground (Hill 160) beyond it, but if the squadron could not do this, it was closely to engage the enemy, keep down his fire, and prevent him interfering with the 19th Hussars whilst carrying out their turning movement. Detachments of infantry which had reached the outskirts of the village were found to be very weak in numbers and short of ammunition, the regimental ammunition packs were therefore sent up to replenish them. Lieutenant Anderson with his troop attempted to rush the main street of the village dismounted, but he himself fell wounded at once, as did six of his men, and the attempt failed. Major Barrett therefore decided to work forward slowly from house to house, and keep as many of the enemy engaged as possible.

Meanwhile a similar state of affairs had occurred in other parts of the battlefield. The 1st Cavalry Brigade south-east of Premont, and the 2nd Cavalry Brigade north-west of Serain, were also trying to find a weak spot in the German rear guards, through which they might break through, but everywhere they were held up by machine-guns and shell-fire. Whilst they were manœuvring, strong hostile air squadrons hovered over them, and attacked them with bombs and machine-gun-fire. As the cavalry was unable to make any effective reply to this form of attack, and the led horses were particularly vulnerable, and there was no cover, the casualties were fairly heavy.

As soon as the 19th Hussars were assembled, they proceeded to carry out the turning movement round Premont. This movement pivoted on Fraicourt Farm, and attempted to outflank Premont from the south-east and east. About midday the 19th Hussars tried to advance in the direction of the railway west of Bohain, towards Busigny, but everywhere found themselves confronted by enemy machine-guns. A desperate attempt was made by one of the squadrons to charge the machine-guns.

This charge was met by heavy fire, which almost annihilated the attackers, all the officers being either killed or wounded. Shortly afterwards Lieutenant-Colonel Franks personally led another desperate charge in a vain effort to break through the enemy's resistance. This gallant effort also failed, the colonel himself falling at the head of his men. A handful of troopers did indeed succeed in reaching a hostile battery which surrendered to the swordsmen, but the German gunners soon realised the small number of their assailants and attacked them with hand grenades : the 19th were driven from the captured battery, most of the officers and men being killed or wounded. It was soon clear that the courageous attempt of the 19th Hussars to break through was doomed to failure, and about 2 p.m. the remnants of this gallant regiment were withdrawn to the railway north-east of Brancourt.

Whilst this fight was in progress the 15th Hussars, less A Squadron which as already narrated had moved to Serrain, marched to a position just west of Premont. During the whole time the Regiment was under the direct observation of German balloons, with the inevitable result that they were heavily shelled throughout the day. The men were kept constantly on the move in order to avoid if possible the heaviest shell-fire.

During the afternoon it was feared that the enemy might be contemplating an attack against Serrain, and the Regiment therefore proceeded to the help of A Squadron in that village.

The 9th Cavalry Brigade now received orders not to engage more than one regiment, as it was hoped that the turning movements which were being carried out by the 1st and 2nd Cavalry Brigades would be successful, in which case the 9th Cavalry Brigade would be required for the pursuit. The 15th Hussars were therefore ordered to withdraw and come into divisional reserve.

As the afternoon wore on, and all the efforts of the cavalry to break through the German rear guards failed, it became quite clear that the resistance was too great to be swept aside by the comparatively small force of cavalry present on the battlefield. The American Corps and the XIII Corps therefore proposed to renew their attacks, and smash through these German rear guards. But as the day was drawing to a close, and some time must necessarily elapse before these fresh attacks could materialise, it was decided to postpone the battle until the next day.

The infantry threw out an outpost line on the battlefield and the cavalry withdrew. Between the left of the 25th Division and the right of the American Corps, there existed a gap which the 15th Hussars were ordered to fill and they were to form part of the outpost system during the night. The men therefore dismounted and the led horses were sent to a sunken road south of Serain, and the Regiment occupied a line between Serain and Premont. The rest of the 9th Cavalry Brigade retired to Beaurevoir.

Throughout the night the German air squadrons vigorously bombarded the back areas and the led horses of the Regiment were also subjected to intermittent shell-fire. The 15th Hussars suffered a few casualties both in men and horses.

On the whole the day had been a disappointing one for the cavalry. Although nothing much had been accomplished, the Regiment had suffered serious losses. After the infantry had achieved that great feat of arms—the storming of the Hindenburg Line—and had driven the enemy into the open, it was anticipated that the cavalry would be able to sweep forward victoriously and carry out an energetic pursuit. The battle had not ended as all had hoped and the desperate efforts of the 19th Hussars to break down the enemy's resistance had only ended in failure, and it was but natural that all ranks felt disappointed that so little had been accomplished.

At 3.30 a.m. on 9th October the 15th Hussars were relieved by the 20th Battalion Manchester Regiment, and rode back to Beaurevoir. Here the horses were watered for the first time since early on 7th October. During the night the German rear guards retired to fresh positions, and thus our advance met with but slight opposition at first. On 10th October the advance of the cavalry was led by the 3rd Cavalry Division, who succeeded in gaining ground towards Le Cateau. After severe fighting the Canadian Cavalry Brigade was enabled to break through and reach the river Selle and the outskirts of the town of Le Cateau.

The 9th Cavalry Brigade was not actively engaged and remained in reserve. The 15th Hussars did not march on this day until 10.30 a.m., when they moved slowly forward from valley to valley, some way in rear of the assaulting troops. There was plenty of time to water the horses, and even to graze them, as there was abundant grass. At 6 p.m. the men got into bivouacs in a damp field just south of Maretz. This village was standing practically untouched by war, and the inhabitants were still living in their houses. In 1914 the villagers, as they stood by the doors of their cottages, had watched the British troops retiring after the battle of Le Cateau, now once again they watched British soldiers passing through their village, but this time it was columns of victorious troops pressing on in pursuit of a beaten enemy. A man of the 11th Hussars was found in Maretz, where he had remained hidden since 1914; he was now enabled to rejoin his old Regiment, which had been in action near his hiding place. The 15th Hussars remained in bivouacs at Maretz, without being employed, until the 13th, when the whole of the cavalry were withdrawn to rail-head.

The enemy had occupied a hastily prepared position about the Selle river, and some time must necessarily elapse before the armies were ready to assault this position. During the past few days the troops had outrun their supplies. The railways had been smashed and torn up, all the bridges had been destroyed, and the roads were in a dreadful state. The supply arrangements were therefore most complicated, and it was imperative to call a halt in order to bring up the necessary munitions and supplies. The cavalry was therefore ordered to withdraw to rail-head until wanted again.

In consequence of these orders the 15th Hussars paraded at 5.30 a.m. on 13th October, and marched across country to Trefcon. Before the German onslaught on 21st March, Trefcon had been the winter camp of a cavalry regiment, and at one time the huts and stables had been fairly comfortable, but twice since that date a battle had raged over the camp and little was left of it save the remnants of its hutments. Nevertheless the men managed to settle in and construct some form of shelter both for themselves and their horses.

The Regiment remained in this camp for some time, during which period strenuous training was carried out. The 9th Cavalry Brigade paraded on 21st October and the corps commander presented ribbons[1] to the officers and men of the Brigade, three officers and fifteen other ranks of the Regiment were so decorated. Men and horses were all very fit and ready to respond to any call which might be made on them.

By this time it was quite clear that victory for the Allies was certain. The daily telegrams recorded success after success in the various theatres of war, and the inevitable collapse of the Central Powers now became only a question of time.

All ranks felt rather anxious lest they should fail to be in at the death, for it looked as though the end might come and find the 15th Hussars in their rather dreary bivouacs at Trefcon. But orders eventually arrived for the Regiment to march and, as everyone realised, to take part in the final act of the long-drawn-out drama of the war.

On 6th November the whole of the 1st Cavalry Division moved north. The 15th marched by Ephey to Vaucelles, where the men bivouacked. The weather was abominable, and heavy rain fell throughout the march. Very little cover

[1] His Majesty the King personally presented the decorations to the majority after the War.

was found in the bivouac as the village had been utterly destroyed. The next morning the march was continued by Cambrai to Brunemont. The march on this day led through a country quite new to all ranks, a country which was terribly devastated. Brunemont, a shattered village, offered a certain amount of shelter, and cover of sorts was provided for all. On the 8th the march continued, through Douai, to Ennevelin. This march was most interesting, as the areas destroyed by war were left behind and the Regiment passed through a countryside which appeared quite peaceful and unaffected by the devastation of battles. Towns and villages were entered, which until now had lain far behind the German lines. Ennevelin, where the 15th spent the night, had been used by the enemy as a veterinary hospital, and was still well supplied with all the requisites of a large horse depot. Everybody found comfortable billets.

On this day the whole of the 9th Cavalry Brigade was placed under the orders of the Fifth Army. The 15th Hussars were placed at the disposal of the III Corps, and were ordered to march into Belgium the following day.

Leaving billets at 8.15 a.m. on the 9th the 15th Hussars marched to Rumes where they halted for some time. At 2.30 p.m. the march was continued through Tournai to Gourain Ramecroix, where just before dark the Regiment got into billets. When the Regiment entered Tournai the town was decorated, the flags of the Allies being displayed from nearly every house. The Germans had not long left the town, and in their retreat had blown up all the bridges. They had further made every effort to destroy the roads and had exploded huge craters at every cross-road and corner. These craters made it very difficult for the supply columns to proceed. The men had therefore to wait some time before the rations turned up, which was not until far on into the night.

By this time the Germans were in retreat along the whole of the front, and the cavalry were in small detachments covering the British Armies. The 9th Cavalry Brigade was broken up, and the 15th Hussars, with a section of Y Battery, Royal Horse Artillery, and a field troop of Royal Engineers, were ordered to operate the following morning with the 55th Division.

This division had already formed a mobile force, known as "Stockwell's Force," which had been in action with the enemy for some days, and kept in close touch with the Germans during the night. This force was composed of King Edward's Horse, Cyclists, Machine-Gun Companies, and the 2/5th Lancashire Fusiliers, as well as a complement of artillery and other units. On the arrival of the 9th Cavalry Brigade the command of this force passed to the G.O.C. 9th Cavalry Brigade, and became known in future as "Legard's Mobile Column." During the night the 15th Hussars received orders to act as advance guard to this column, and to push on and seize the crossings of the river Dendre about Ath.

The Regiment marched at 6 a.m. on 10th November, B Squadron (Captain Brace) as advance guard. The 15th Hussars passed through the outpost line of "Stockwell's Force" just as daylight was breaking, and almost at once got into touch with the enemy. The general line of advance was the main Leuze–Ath road, the advance guard squadron sent a troop to either flank, whilst the main body marched down the road. A detachment of Royal Engineers marched with the advance guard to destroy German mines which it was known had been placed under all cross-roads and bridges.

Directly the advance guard moved the enemy abandoned the small town of Leuze, and as he left, the leading files of the 15th Hussars entered the main street. Immediately every house displayed the flags of the Allies, the inhabitants poured out from the houses, and in a few moments the men were surrounded by a dense mass of the populace almost delirious with joy. The troopers could hardly make their way through the crowd, the people clung to their stirrups and were wildly excited. The pursuit of the enemy was still taking place, and these exhibitions of delight were most embarrassing to men yet engaged in the stern task of war. Once clear of Leuze the advance continued. Aeroplanes reported that there were still small parties of the enemy about Ligne, and as the advanced scouts approached the village they were fired on by hostile machine-guns.

The country on the whole was not very suitable for cavalry, as it was dotted with innumerable small farms, and cut up by fences and wire hedges. The enclosed nature of the country also gave the most excellent cover for the hostile machine-guns, a rapid pursuit of the enemy was therefore not very easy.

The advance guard was held up outside Ligne, and in order to support them C Squadron was sent forward. The Regiment then advanced on a two-squadron frontage. A certain amount of firing took place, but the enemy soon fled towards Ath. Here again, even before the Germans abandoned the village, and whilst bullets were still whistling down the streets, women and children rushed from their houses and flung themselves on the men, and an active pursuit became most difficult.

Once clear of Ligne, the chase continued towards Ath. The enemy retired rapidly, and it was not until the outskirts of Ath were reached that the hostile opposition stiffened. The advance was here finally checked, the town was walled and almost completely surrounded by the river Dendre, and the only entrances were over the bridges and through the gates. All these entrances were carefully defended with machine-guns covering all approaches. The German artillery was in position east of the town, with observation posts which overlooked all the roads, and they were thus enabled to bring a heavy fire to bear on anyone advancing towards the town.

The 15th Hussars cautiously approached Ath. The bridges were found barricaded, and everywhere the troops were met by a heavy fire. It did not take long to realise that any attempt to force an entrance into the town would lead to heavy casualties, and would probably be unsuccessful.

The guns of Y Battery were brought into action, but the enemy were far superior in artillery, and very soon smothered our guns under an accurate and heavy fire ; the officer in command and the greater part of the detachments soon became casualties, and the guns were put out of action.

Owing to the effective way in which the enemy had destroyed the roads, ammunition and supplies were only brought forward with great difficulty. The Germans on the other hand were falling back on to their supplies, and had no transport difficulties to contend with. Throughout the day their artillery fire was fairly heavy, but was not carefully directed, and the whole countryside was impartially bombarded. The 15th Hussars did not suffer very heavily, but a shell sometimes landed amongst the led horses and caused casualties.

By midday the Regiment was roughly disposed as follows : C Squadron on the right had one troop on the railway, which attempted to enter Ath by this route, but was held up by machine-gun-fire, and was unable to advance ; two troops were astride the main road, and one troop was in reserve. B Squadron which was on the left, had one troop in a farm about the second kilometre stone of the Mainvult–Ath road, and the remainder of the squadron was about one mile south-west of this farm. A Squadron was halted about the fifty-fifth kilometre stone on the Leuze–Ath road, with a troop on either flank.

Throughout the operations the Regiment was supported by a company of cyclists, who, moving down the main road, were engaged with the enemy the whole time, and rendered the most valuable assistance. One troop of B Squadron (Lieutenant Haggas) tried to gallop a farm, but was met by heavy machine-gun-fire, and forced to take cover ; it remained in an isolated position until dark. The horse ridden by Lieutenant Haggas was killed, and he himself, rendered unconscious by the fall, lay pinned underneath. Owing to the enemy fire it was found impossible to extricate him and he was thus forced to remain in his uncomfortable position until rescued after nightfall some hours later.

During the afternoon the Germans brought up trench mortars and increased their fire, which drove the patrols back on to their squadrons. It was now quite evident that the capture of Ath was far too big an undertaking for one cavalry regiment, without proper artillery support. By this time a battalion of infantry had reached the scene of action, and General d'Arcy Legard decided to launch them in an effort to carry the bridges. A large number of machine-guns were placed in position, and under cover of their barrage fire, the infantry advanced to the attack. It was soon found that the enemy was too strongly posted and to attack without proper artillery preparation was hopeless. As little artillery was available at the time, the attack did not develop, and the infantry confined itself to gaining ground forward by fighting from house to house.

As darkness descended the enemy opened a final and heavy bombardment and for some time shells of every calibre rained down on the countryside. The men huddled behind the banks and ditches, and endeavoured to find what cover they could against the storm of shells.

It was quite evident that this exhibition of hate was unaimed, and that the Germans were firing off their ammunition dumps. The crash of bursting shells slowly ceased, the machine-gunners fired their last belts, and except for the occasional shots from the snipers in the houses outside Ath, all sounds of battle and strife died away. As far as the 15th Hussars were concerned the last shots of the war had been fired.

About 5 p.m. the infantry put out an outpost line watching the bridges at Ath, and the Regiment withdrew to Villers St. Amand ; one troop remained out all night on the main road just west of Ath. Although at times the shelling had been very heavy, the fighting on the whole had not been severe, and until the outskirts of Ath were reached the enemy made no very determined effort to hold up the advance. The country on the whole was not suitable for rapid cavalry movement, and as the enemy never stood long enough for the turning movement to materialise, the captures were not very numerous, only a few prisoners and some machine-guns being taken. The casualties suffered by the Regiment were not very heavy, the led horses being the chief sufferers.

At St. Amand the 15th Hussars were billeted in a convent, and the nuns placed a large dormitory at the disposal of the officers where the night was comfortably spent.

On 11th November at 5.30 a.m. the 15th Hussars saddled up and awaited further orders, but the Regiment did not move until 8 a.m., when orders came to march to Ath, which the enemy had abandoned during the night. As the Regiment entered the town it was found that a dense mass of people crowded the square and the streets leading to it, whilst the Mayor and Town Council stood in the centre to greet the British troops. The men had some difficulty in forcing their way through the population, made almost too enthusiastic by their delight. Some German prisoners were only rescued from the mob who wished to tear them in pieces by the ready wit of the Staff Captain 9th Cavalry Brigade.

The Regiment advanced slowly, all bridges and culverts had been destroyed, and at every cross-road mines with delay-action fuses had been buried, and the dull sounds of their explosions could be heard on all sides.

About 10.30 a.m. the 15th Hussars reached Maffle, and turned into a field, where the horses were off-saddled, the other units of the 9th Cavalry Brigade also concentrated about this village.

At 11 a.m. orders were received that hostilities had ceased, the trumpeters of the Regiment sounded the Regimental call, and then the Cease Fire ; the men gave a loud cheer. The call to stables was sounded, and all then proceeded prosaically to groom and look after the horses.

The 15th Hussars remained in the field until the afternoon, when the men went into billets about Maffle. Although the Cease Fire had sounded, the outpost lines continued to fire at each other for some considerable time, as every individual wished to be the one who had fired the last shot in the war.

The field near Maffle, where the trumpeters of the Regiment sounded the Cease Fire, was not far distant from the neighbourhood of Mons, where, in 1914, the 15th Hussars had first exchanged shots with the grey-clad Uhlans, the advance guard of the invading German armies.

Many weary months had passed since those far-off days, and many gallant officers and men who had so bravely marched from Longmoor were no longer with the Regiment to celebrate the victory which they had helped to win.

Chapter IX

THE MARCH INTO GERMANY
THE WATCH ON THE RHINE

THE 12th November dawned cold and frosty, when the Regiment marched back through Ath to billets about Rouillon.

Most of the villages were decorated, the inhabitants showed their enthusiasm to the best of their ability, and all ranks looked forward to comfortable billets. Alas, they were disappointed, for Rouillon, the village allotted to the 15th Hussars, lay just across the border in France, where there had been severe fighting. The village was quite shattered and deserted by the inhabitants, German dead were still lying in the streets where they had fallen, and it was as uncomfortable a place as could well be imagined. Nevertheless everybody managed to get some sort of cover in the ruined houses.

Orders were received that the 15th Hussars would only remained halted for a few days and then the advance into Germany would begin. Everyone realised how important it was that the Regiment should make as imposing an appearance as possible for the march.

The next few days were spent in hard work, bits and log chains were burnished, saddlery polished and new clothing issued when possible ; the State trumpets were also fetched from England.

It was decided that the Second and Fourth Armies would march to the Rhine, and that the Cavalry Corps would cover this march. All the precautions of war were to be observed, with proper advanced guards on the move, and outposts at night.

At 7.15 a.m. on 17th November the 15th Hussars began their march to the Rhine. The weather was cold and frosty, the roads in consequence were very slippery. Throughout the march through Belgium, the Regiment met with the greatest enthusiasm. The church bells of every village rang out their welcome as the advance guard was seen to approach. In the larger towns and villages the Mayor and Councillors in full dress met the head of the column, and welcomed the 15th Hussars in the name of the inhabitants ; suitable sentiments were exchanged in the speeches, and cheers given for the Allies. In many places the local band headed the march through the town and the various societies and guilds turned out with their banners and full regalia.

After a two-days' march the Regiment reached the pleasant little town of Ecaussines Lalaing, where there was a formal reception at the Hotel de Ville, and in the evening the local authorities gave a dance. During the early hours of 19th November orders were suddenly received instructing a squadron to march forthwith to Nivelles, to take over and guard a quantity of war material which the Germans were about to surrender. C Squadron was detailed for this duty, and marched at 7 a.m. passing through the outpost line. On arrival at Nivelles the usual dense crowd assembled, making progress very difficult, but at length the German rear guard was reached just east of the town. No greater contrast could be imagined between the well-mounted, perfectly equipped, smart-looking men of the 15th Hussars who drew up across the road with drawn swords, and the untidy, miserable, war-worn German soldiers whom they relieved. Staff officers from the Cavalry Corps and the Canadian Corps came to take over the surrender, and some German Staff officers were present to hand over. The enemy surrendered a very large quantity of war material, comprising an aerodrome, with numerous aeroplanes, many of them quite new; three railway stations and sidings packed with trains loaded with all kinds of war material, a large number of machine-guns, artillery of every description, and a considerable amount of transport wagons, cookers and other impedimenta. The task of guarding all this equipment, which covered a considerable area, fell to the lot of C Squadron. In addition the squadron had to protect the lives of the five German officers who remained behind from the fury of the mob.

The crowd soon got completely out of hand and commenced to loot and destroy the premises of those whom they had supposed had shown any friendliness to the enemy. The local authorities lost all control, and strong patrols had to be found to police the town; in consequence there was little rest for the men of the squadron that night.

The following day the rest of the Regiment reached Nivelles before midday, and the war material could then be protected and the streets properly policed.

On 21st November the Regiment handed over to the Canadian troops, and then marched to Quatre Bras. On this historic site the Regiment passed in review before the G.O.C. 1st Cavalry Division (Major-General R. Mullens, C.B.). Afterwards the 15th marched to Cortil Noirmont. A troop of B Squadron had to be detached to Grand Manil, to guard war material which the enemy had abandoned at this place. Later on in the day another detachment had to be sent to Gembloux, at which place the enemy had abandoned three hundred and six truckloads of artillery, and a very considerable amount of material; there was no formal handing over by the Germans—the whole of this material had just been abandoned by them. A number of prisoners of war were also found in the hospital at Gembloux; the poor fellows were in a very bad state, although the inhabitants had treated them with every kindness and done all that was possible for them.

On the 22nd the march was resumed to Cortil Wodon. While passing through Gembloux, the Regiment was received in state, and given a great ovation.

The stricken battlefields had now been left far behind, the countryside looked peaceful and pleasant, indeed prosperous, and the inhabitants did not appear to have suffered too great hardships. The people reported that the German Army was retreating in great disorder, the red flag much in evidence; the officers appeared extremely depressed, and were forced by their men to don the red cockade.

Meanwhile a great difficulty arose, which had not been unforeseen. It was found almost impossible to supply the advancing troops. Owing to the complete destruction of the railways, all supplies had to be carried very great distances by mechanical transport, which had to proceed over roads wholly or partially destroyed, with the inevitable result that the supply columns were on the verge of breaking down under the strain. In many cases it was found impossible to deliver supplies, and resort had to be made to requisitioning, but the country was not in a position to supply very much, and it sometimes happened that men and horses had to go very short indeed.

Even if the Germans had not signed the Armistice, it is a question whether the British Armies would have been in a position to carry out an energetic pursuit. When marching slowly under approximately peace conditions and with no question of ammunition supply, it was found exceedingly difficult to keep the leading troops properly supplied with rations. It seems therefore very doubtful whether the question of supply would have been solved under war conditions.

Owing to these difficulties, the 3rd Cavalry Division was ordered to halt on the line they had reached, and the 1st Cavalry Division alone covered the advance of the Second Army to the Rhine, in consequence this division had to take over a wider front.

By 8 a.m. on the 24th the Regiment was once again on the march, and on arrival at Briaves, formed part of the outpost line, along the Huy–Hannaut road.

The 15th remained halted until 27th, when after a long and tiring march they reached the outskirts of Liege about Embourg. The three regiments of the 9th Cavalry Brigade here found the outpost line along the Sprimont–Liege road, of which the 15th Hussars formed the left sector ; but were not able to gain touch with the French Army, with which our left was supposed to join. Pouring rain fell throughout the day, and the men were all soaked to the skin.

The 28th was spent in billets. The mob got entirely out of hand, and the local authorities lost all control, strong patrols had therefore to be found during the night to support the Belgian police. On this day the Belgian Army entered Liege in state.

On the 29th the Regiment after another long march reached Membach on the German frontier. Everywhere the 15th met with a most enthusiastic reception, especially in Verviers, where there was a halt, and where the men were soon surrounded by crowds of delighted townsfolk. A very large number of prisoners of war were found in this town. During the whole of this day's march, as the Regiment advanced towards the Rhine, it passed a continual stream of men who had been released from Germany and were making their way back to France and Belgium. These men were of all nationalities, French soldiers still dressed in the old kepi and scarlet trousers of 1914, Italians, Serbians, Roumanians, and many Russians—these latter looking the most woebegone of all.

Neither the civilian population nor the returning prisoners at first recognised the Regiment as British, for the uniform had undergone some change since 1914. The 15th Hussars as they marched along had all the appearance of mediæval horsemen, a fact commented on by all the local newspapers. With polished leather jerkins, black field boots and steel helmets, the men looked most workmanlike, the horses were in excellent condition, the saddlery as smart as trouble and care could make it, and the whole appearance of the Regiment was most effective. On arrival at the frontier an outpost line was thrown out along the Malmedy–Eupen road.

The 30th was spent in billets, where full instructions were issued regarding the march through Germany, the control of the civil population, and the demeanour to be observed by the troops.

The 15th Hussars paraded at 8 a.m. on 1st December, and at 9 a.m. crossed the frontier into Germany. The Membach Town Band accompanied the Regiment across the German frontier, and did not leave them until the outskirts of Eupen, the first town the Regiment entered in Germany. After leaving Eupen, the Regiment formed the advance guard to the brigade.

The march lay through hilly and wooded country, where the scenery was most attractive. At first the inhabitants were slightly anxious and curious as to the attitude the British troops would adopt, but directly they realised that their attitude was perfectly correct, the people became perhaps almost too friendly, whilst the local authorities did all in their power to carry out the demands made upon them. The troops carried with them proclamations which laid down regulations for the control of the civil population. These orders the inhabitants made every effort to obey.

During the march evidence of a certain amount of demoralisation in the German Army became apparent, for guns, transport wagons, and material of every description had been abandoned on the side of the road. On entering Germany these signs became even more marked, for numbers of men, discarding their equipment, left their units and returned to their homes. Dead horses in considerable numbers were met with in the tracks of the German Army.

From Eupen the march lay through Rutgen, and the 9th Cavalry Brigade threw out an outpost line from Kestmich to Stolberg. Of this the Regiment formed the left sector, with headquarters at Kornelmunster and the squadrons in the villages round about.

During 2nd and 3rd December the Regiment halted on the line occupied, and the district was searched for arms. A certain number were found and collected. The country was wooded and hilly, and the outpost line was located along the ridges in a thick forest.

On 4th December the march was continued to Merkem and the usual outpost line was found. The hills and forests were left behind, and the next few marches were through a dull flat country, but highly cultivated.

On 5th December the 15th marched to about Bedburg, with an outpost line along the Eerft Canal.

The Regiment remained halted during the 6th.

On the 7th the 15th Hussars marched to the Rhine, and placed an outpost line along the banks of the river from Zous to Sturzelburg, with headquarters at Nivenheim.

According to the proclamations issued by the British authorities, all traffic up and down the Rhine was to be regulated. But where the 15th Hussars were the Rhine was a great river, with ocean-going steamers awaiting permission to make their way to the sea. The Ships' Captains were most anxious to obey the orders issued, but it is difficult to see how the cavalry pickets on the banks of the Rhine could have enforced them.

On the 9th the 15th Hussars marched to Cologne and occupied the Artillery Barracks at Riehl in the suburbs. These barracks were clean and tidy, as a certain number of German soldiers had been left behind to keep them in good condition, and they were busily engaged in painting and cleaning up.

The 15th Hussars remained here until the 12th during which period every effort was made to smarten up as much as possible for the ceremonial crossing of the Hohenzollern Bridge.

On the 12th the men paraded at 9.45 a.m., marched through Cologne and passed in review before the G.O.C. Second Army,[1] who stood at the western edge of the bridge. The band of the Royal Horse Guards played at the saluting point. As the Regiment came up the trumpeters sounded the salute on the State trumpets. The whole of the 1st Cavalry Division (less the 1st Cavalry Brigade) passed in review, and it must be owned that their appearance was very fine. Men and horses were all perfectly turned out and in excellent condition ; the German populace could not believe that they were looking at Regiments who had been through the whole of the campaign.

The division had hardly crossed the bridge when the rain, which had been threatening for some time, came down in torrents. The Regiment marched to the outpost line about Opladen. The inhabitants were on the whole much relieved at the appearance of the British troops, whose arrival saved them from anarchy. The Spartacus[2] group had been very active in this industrial area, and red flags were flying in all the towns. On the arrival of the Regiment all disturbances ceased, the red flags vanished, and everybody appeared only too anxious to obey any orders issued by the British authorities.

On 13th December the march was continued to Hohscheld ; this was the final perimeter of the bridge-head, as laid down by the Armistice Commission, and the Regiment became responsible for the sector from the railway east of Sollingen to the railway west of Haan. The next day two companies of the 6th King's Own Scottish Borderers and two companies of the Black Watch reinforced the outpost line.

On the 15th the Regiment handed over to the infantry and returned to the artillery barracks at Cologne, crossing the Rhine at Mulheim.

On the 16th the march was continued to Bedburg. Good billets were found in this small town, the local authorities were obliging, and the men were all most comfortable. Here the Regiment remained for the winter.

[1] Now Viscount Plumer of Messines, G.C.B., G.C.M.G., G.B.E., G.C.V.O.

[2] The extreme Revolutionary Party in Germany.

The band arrived from England, and was most welcome. Sahagun and Christmas Day were kept in a way worthy of the "Great Victory." The end of the year found the men awaiting demobilisation, but content and happy. Efforts were made to keep everyone amused by games and entertainments in the evening. The only difficulty was the shortage of food, it was almost impossible to buy any in the country, for the inhabitants were in great want, all ranks were therefore entirely dependent on their rations and on their parcels from home. Unfortunately, owing to the destruction of the railways in France and Belgium, the railway service was not yet in thorough working order, and the supply trains took some considerable time on the journey. With so many hungry people about, the temptation was too great to be resisted, and it was seldom that food parcels arrived which had not been tampered with and the rations often arrived very short indeed. This state of things improved as time went on.

There was a certain amount of anxiety about demobilisation amongst the older men who had families and jobs awaiting them at home. In theory the Government scheme of demobilisation was most excellent, but in practice many men who had only served for a short period were released before those who had volunteered at the very commencement of the campaign. This caused a certain amount of grumbling, and in some cases led to serious breaches of discipline. The troubles caused on the lines of communication and at home did not affect the Regiment, and the men patiently waited at Bedburg for any orders they might receive.

The Regiment received the orders to demobilise on 7th March and parties of men left for civilian life. When the actual moment of departure came, all ranks were genuinely sorry to leave the old Regiment. Those left behind had a difficult job, for the numbers available for duty became very few, horses were sent away for disposal, but fresh horses continued to arrive from the Regiments returning to England, and at one time the 15th Hussars were reduced to one man to ten horses, luckily on 3rd April one hundred men from the Argyll and Sutherland Highlanders arrived to help the Regiment carry on.

Meanwhile demobilisation had gone on apace. Those regiments due for foreign service left for England and their stations abroad, the Cavalry Corps was broken up, and the 1st Cavalry Division became the cavalry of the Rhine. The units of the 9th Cavalry Brigade were dispersed to all parts of the world, and a new brigade was formed, known as the Hussar Brigade, composed of the 3rd Hussars, 10th Hussars and the 15th Hussars.

Major-General Sir William Peyton,[1] Colonel of the 15th Hussars, assumed the command of the cavalry in Germany, and on 14th April Brigadier-General T. T. Pitman[2] took over the command of the Hussar Brigade. The same day Brigadier-General d'A. Legard, on relinquishing command of the 9th Cavalry Brigade, visited the Regiment, and wished all ranks farewell.

The 15th Hussars left Bedburg on 7th April, the march was carried out with some difficulty, owing to the few men of the Regiment able to ride. Moving by Sindorf, the 15th Hussars reached their final destination, Kerpen, early in the afternoon. This village is situated on the main Duren–Cologne road, and all ranks were soon very comfortable. The headquarters were situated at Schloss Lorsfeld, just outside the village.

The summer passed very pleasantly. Every effort was made to keep the troops amused, theatrical companies constantly visited the Regiment, a cinematograph theatre was installed in the village, polo was started, and Cologne soon became the centre for many polo tournaments, horse shows, and every sort of amusement.

A mobile force was formed to which the 15th Hussars supplied a strong troop of three officers and seventy other ranks, besides a Hotchkiss Gun Detachment.

When it seemed likely that the German delegates at Versailles might refuse to sign the treaty, the cavalry mobile column concentrated at Cologne, and the 15th Hussars troop left on 16th June. The cavalry moved on to the Perimeter, with orders to march into Germany if the Germans did not sign.

Peace however was signed on 28th June, all precautions were relaxed, and on 1st July the mobile column rejoined.

On 5th July five men of the Regiment left for Paris, to take part in the "Victory March." The men selected were all old soldiers, who had served some time with the 15th Hussars.

Meanwhile demobilisation continued, the horses were all classified, some to be sold on the continent, and a few to be taken to England.

In August a composite squadron was formed for a ceremonial parade before the Secretary of State for War. After a little practice the squadron was able to put up a very good show, and the parade passed off as successfully as any show at Aldershot before the war.

Definite orders arrived on 15th August for the Regiment to

[1] The late General Sir William Peyton, K.C.B., K.C.V.O., D.S.O. (Colonel of the Regiment).

[2] Now Major-General T. T. Pitman, C.B., C.M.G.

proceed to Ireland. All ranks were sorry to leave Germany, the summer had been pleasant, and the time had passed quickly. Horse shows, race meetings, and Polo tournaments at Cologne had given amusement and occupation to all.

On 29th August the equipment and baggage of the Regiment left by train for Ireland. On 2nd September the personnel entrained at Buir for Kilkenny, and on 5th September the horses entrained at Horrem for Ormskirk.

On 6th September the Regiment arrived in Ireland. After five years on active service the 15th Hussars returned to the British Isles. But for them there was no welcome, such as is usually conceded to those returning home as victors after a long war. Instead the Regiment marched to the barracks with loaded rifles, and once inside the barracks the gates were shut, and the armed sentries took their posts on the walls.

The Regiment was in a hostile country, once again engaged in a kind of warfare, although different, nevertheless equally unpleasant.

The long and dreary years of the war were over, and a peace had come, which at times seemed almost impossible. To many the war meant ideals utterly destroyed and illusions shattered. But throughout all, in times of stress and in periods of disappointment, and finally in the hour of victory, the Regiment had tried to uphold the traditions handed down from former times, and it is certain that in the future all ranks will uphold its motto, as they have done in the past—" Merebimur."

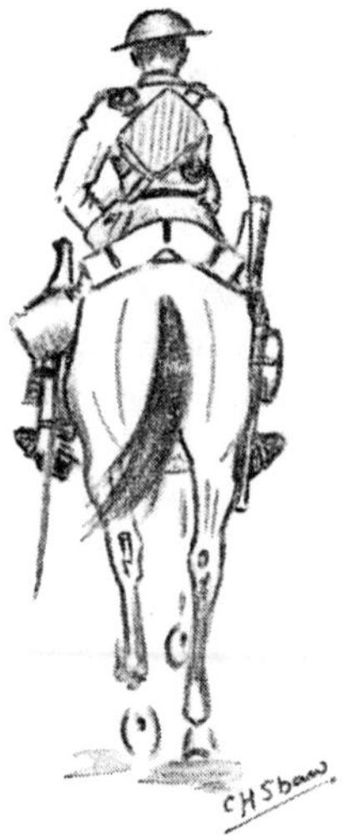

ON TREK

POSTSCRIPT

ON arrival in Ireland the 15th Hussars found two troops for duty at Fethard and two troops for duty at Waterford, which made training very difficult. On demobilisation, the majority of the regular N.C.O.'s and men, whose time had expired, took their discharge, and their places were filled by large drafts of recruits, mostly quite young boys and conscripts. In consequence there were no old soldiers to show them the way they should go, and practically no qualified instructors. A large number of horses were sent to the Regiment, mostly untrained, and there was nobody to train them.

The situation would have been difficult enough if the Regiment had been stationed in comfortable and peaceful barracks in England, but it was infinitely more difficult in Ireland in 1919. The Irish Republican Army was very active at the time. Daily there were accounts of police barracks assaulted and burned, of ambushes and of murders. This naturally gave cause for apprehension, for there was always the danger of the military barracks being attacked. The Regiment had to find armed guards and pickets, escorts and patrols, and there was hardly a man in the Regiment at this time who knew how to ride, or use his arms. Luckily, the I.R.A. ignored the 15th Hussars, and nothing happened.

Lieutenant-Colonel F. C. Pilkington joined the Regiment on 10th October and assumed the command of the 15th Hussars, with whom he had served so long and with so much distinction.

Lieutenant-Colonel H. Combe, who had commanded the 15th Hussars during the last battles of the war, and led them to the final victory, handed over the Regiment on the 11th October, and left to take command of the 5th Dragoon Guards.

During the winter training continued under great difficulties. As soon as men became even slightly trained they had to be dispatched to the 19th Hussars in India, where men were wanted as badly as in Ireland.

Eventually orders came for the 15th Hussars to move to Dublin ; Headquarters and B Squadron moved on 10th February, 1920, A Squadron on 17th February, and C Squadron on 9th March.

The Regiment was stationed in Marlborough barracks. The plate and pictures were unpacked, and every effort was made to get the Regiment back to the pre-war standard.

The situation also was easier in Dublin. Training facilities were ample ; quartered in the barracks were a battery of artillery and an armoured car company, so that the men were relieved of many guards, pickets and fatigues. Time therefore could be devoted to training. But to those persons who knew Marlborough barracks before the war their appearance at this time would have appeared very odd. Barbed wire, sandbag emplacements, trenches, and machine-guns in position, turned the barracks into a fortress.

The whole of the British Army in Ireland was composed of recruits, and every unit demanded time for training. The British Government therefore raised the Auxiliary Police, known as the " Black and Tans." The Royal Irish Constabulary were almost paralysed, not so much by the attacks against themselves, but by the cruel attacks made against their women and children. The Army in Ireland was untrained, and in 1920 the only force able to meet the gunmen was the " Black and Tans."

This force for some reason had a bad press in England, but it was a well-disciplined and a brave force, and undoubtedly " got murder by the throat." In any case, it gave the Army time to train. So the 15th Hussars in Marlborough barracks and Phoenix Park trained day and night, and steadily the raw recruits were turned into finished Hussars.

On the 18th May A Squadron marched to Kilbrew House and on the same day C Squadron marched to Enniskerry, County Wicklow. The troops were used to patrol the disturbed areas, and to assist the local Royal Irish Constabulary. The camps were protected by barbed wire and fire trenches, and by this time the men would have put up a good fight if attacked. Nothing happened however.

On 20th June A and C Squadrons returned to Marlborough barracks. B Squadron relieved A, whilst C Squadron was relieved by a company of infantry.

B Squadron remained at Kilbrew until the 20th July, when it rejoined, but left again for Dundalk on 13th September and remained there until 22nd March, 1921.

During the summer each squadron had an opportunity of spending a week or two in camp in the Wicklow Hills at Kilbride, where the whole day could be spent at musketry, and at the end of the time every man in the Regiment, if not a marksman, knew how to handle his rifle with precision.

By the year 1921 the British Army in Ireland was sufficiently trained to undertake operations on a larger scale against the Irish Republican Army. In April and June, 1921, the 15th Hussars took part in two drives, of which the following is a short and condensed account.

The towns were fairly free from organised rebel outrages owing to the ceaseless activities of the Auxiliary Police and Military forces, but it was reported that rebels were concentrating in certain country districts. The local police patrols were ineffectual and it was decided to form a Cavalry Column (3rd Cavalry Brigade) to encircle and drive certain areas—the prisoners to be identified by the local Constabulary.

The Regiment, commanded by Lieutenant-Colonel F. C. Pilkington, with transport and cyclists, marched from barracks through Rathcoole, and billeted for the night at Johnstown.

Continuing the next morning through Naas and Newbridge, the Regiment joined the 3rd Cavalry Brigade at Curragh Camp and now came under the orders of the G.O.C. 5th Division.

After a night's rest at the Curragh the march was continued through Kildare and Monasterevin to Portarlington.

Marching the next day, through Kileen Duff and Ballyshear, the Regiment billeted at Phillipstown for one night.

The next day's march was to Kilbeggan (route : Ballycommon and Skeahanagh), where operations commenced. R.I.C. patrols co-operated with the squadrons to drive from the line Ballycumber–Clara–Kilbeggan. Houses were searched in Clara, one of which was found to contain a large quantity of field dressings. Aeroplanes patrolled the area boundaries. After the drive the Regiment returned to billets at Kilbeggan. Several drives were carried out in this area with very satisfactory results. Regimental cyclists patrolled the roads at night.

An important drive was carried out towards Mullingar. The ground was very difficult to cover, being boggy, and it was found necessary to work most of the way dismounted. On conclusion of the drive the Regiment billeted in an area three miles south-west of Mullingar. After two days' rest the Regiment returned to billets at Kilbeggan, where operations were continued in a north-easterly direction about Rochfortbridge and Tyrrellspass.

From Kilbeggan further operations were carried out in a south-easterly direction to the Grand Canal at Phillipstown. Billets were found at Geashill for one night.

The next day the Regiment formed up dismounted on the Phillipstown–Ballyshear Road and drove the bog to the east, making several important captures. One man of A Squadron was wounded. The same night the Regiment billeted at Rathangan and operations were concluded.

Continuing the march eastwards the next day's billets were found at Johnstown. On the following day the Regiment marched into barracks at Dublin.

Owing to the success of the first series of operations it was again decided to utilise the Cavalry Column (3rd Cavalry Brigade).

The Regiment, commanded by Lieutenant-Colonel F. C. Pilkington, with transports and cyclists, marched from barracks in a north-easterly direction through Dunboyne to an area about Kilmore, where it billeted for the night.

Continuing the march the next day through Ballivor and Killucan, billets were found at Knockdrin, about five miles north of Mullingar.

After two days in this area the march was continued westwards through Bunbrosna, Ballinaleck to an area at Ballinalee, five miles north of Longford, where billets were found.

Marching the next day through Drumod, the Regiment bivouacked for two days near Drumsna, with Regimental Headquarters at Charlestown House.

On approaching the disturbed areas it was decided to march at night so that surprise operations could be commenced at daybreak.

Apart from an occasional horse and rider blundering into a bog during the darkness, nothing eventful occurred and there were no casualties. In places the roads were blocked by trees, and trenches were dug to impede the column. Fortunately, the heavy transport was not ambushed, but there were occasional delays. As, however, most of the supplies were requisitioned locally no one was inconvenienced.

Continuing through Carrick-on-Shannon and Boyle, some important drives were carried out in the Ballymote area. Here in many places, the Regiment was obliged to work dismounted owing to the steep hills and rocky ground. In spite of these difficulties some important captures were made.

During the drives in this area Regimental Headquarters were established at Rockingham House (near Boyle). From Boyle, marching in a north-easterly direction through Knockvicar Bridge, the Regiment bivouacked for one night (between the road and Lough Allen) in an area six miles north of Drumshanbo.

Continuing northwards the next day through Tober, billets were found about two miles east of Black Lion.

After two days' rest the march eastwards was resumed, through Belcoo to Lisnaskea, thence to billets at Donagh after the completion of another drive. The next day's march brought the Regiment to Ballyleck House, one mile west of Monaghan, having passed through Newtown Butler and Clones.

Continuing in a southerly direction through Ballybay, an important drive was carried out after which the Regiment rested for a day at Tully House, six miles south-east of Ballybay. The next morning, after another drive, billets were found at Carnagh, four miles north of Castleblaney.

From this place the night marches were continued southwards through Castleblaney to Donaghmoyne House, thence through Carrickmacross, Lobinstown and Harlinstown to Slane, at which place the Regiment bivouacked for one night.

The operations had now finished and the next day the Regiment marched to Dublin and resumed former quarters at Marlborough barracks.

Eventually the British Cabinet decided to withdraw the troops from Ireland. This is not the place to discuss the reasons or the wisdom of this surrender to rebellion. The fact remains, the surrender took place.

Marlborough barracks were handed over, lock, stock and barrel, to the new Free State Government, and report says everything was promptly looted directly the troops had left.

The advance party left for Tidworth on 6th March, 1922, and the remainder of the Regiment followed on the 9th and 10th March. The withdrawal of the troops from Ireland was almost universally regretted throughout the country, except by the most fanatical ; it was, of course, a tremendous financial loss to Ireland, for the British troops brought a considerable amount of money into the country, every penny of which was spent in the country.

The Regiment was now quartered in Assaye barracks, Tidworth, on Salisbury Plain. The barracks were excellent, and at last, conditions were those of real peace. The Regiment resumed the ordinary regular routine of peace time soldiering ; thus there is only one more important event to record before closing this postscript.

For various reasons, it was determined by the Powers that be to reduce the cavalry, and after due consideration, it was decided to amalgamate certain regiments.

Thus on 11th April, 1922, was published Army Order No. 133 to this effect :

" His Majesty the King is graciously pleased to approve of the reconstruction of four Cavalry Regiments recently disbanded and for Regiments to be amalgamated as under :

15th Hussars, 2 Squadrons
19th Hussars, 1 Squadron } to form the 15/19th Hussars

Composite Regiment to be treated as a complete regiment, but each squadron to retain name of its original regiment in order to preserve its identity."

This brings to an end the second volume of the history of the

15th Hussars dealing with their story during the eventful years from 1914 to 1922.

There are few now serving in the ranks of the combined Regiment, who were with either the 15th Hussars or the 19th Hussars during the years of the "Great War."

The battles of Mons, Ypres and the Somme are but traditions to the present serving soldiers. It will be for another historian at some future date to continue the story of the combined regiment, and it is certain that it will continue to uphold the traditions of those two splendid old regiments, the 15th Hussars and the 19th Hussars.

CEASE FIRE

BATTLE HONOURS

OF THE

15TH THE KING'S HUSSARS

" EMSDORFF," " VILLERS-EN-CAUCHIES," " WILLEMS," " EGMONT-OP-ZEE," " SAHAGUN," " VITTORIA," " PENINSULA," " WATERLOO," " AFGHANISTAN, 1878-80."

The Great War—" Mons," " RETREAT FROM MONS," " MARNE 1914," " AISNE, 1914," " YPRES, 1914, '15," " Langemark, 1914," " Gheluvelt," " Nonne Bosschen," " Frezenberg," " BELLEWAARDE," " SOMME, 1916, '18," " Flers-Courcelette," " CAMBRAI, 1917, '18," " St. Quentin," " ROSIÈRES," " Amiens," " Albert, 1918," " Bapaume, 1918," " Hindenburg Line," " St. Quentin Canal," " Beaurevoir," " PURSUIT to MONS," " FRANCE and FLANDERS, 1914-1918."

MEREBIMUR

Appendix A

DIARY OF MARCHES, BILLETS, BIVOUACS

OF THE

15TH THE KING'S HUSSARS

FROM

26TH JULY, 1914, TO 6TH SEPTEMBER, 1919

Event.	*Place.*	*Date.*
		1914
Regiment together under canvas at ...	Nursery Camp, Aldershot	July 26–28
Preliminary orders to mobilise ...	Aldershot	July 29–31
Regiment marched from Aldershot to	Longmoor	Aug. 1
Mobilisation at	Longmoor	Aug. 2–15

Regiment broken up on 15th August, and the Squadrons became independent Units.

"A" SQUADRON.

Left Longmoor by train and embarked on the *Manchester Engineer* at ...	Southampton	Aug. 16
Sailed at dawn	At sea	Aug. 17
Disembarked and marched to camp at	Rouen	Aug. 18
Entrained at dusk	In the train	Aug. 19
Detrained at 3 p.m. at	Aulnoy	Aug. 20
Joined the 3rd Division and marched to	Gosnes	Aug. 21
Crossed the Belgian frontier and bivouacked at	(Bonnet) Hyon	Aug. 22
Battle of Mons, Squadron bivouacked at	Nouvelles	Aug. 23
Retreat. "A" Squadron suffered heavy casualties at Offignies. Survivors bivouacked at	Bavai	Aug. 24
Retreat. After long march Squadron bivouacked near	Le Cateau	Aug. 25
Retreat. 3rd Division fought at Le Cateau. Squadron bivouacked near	Jeancourt	Aug. 26
Retreat and rear guard fighting. Billeted in	Ham	Aug. 27
Retreat and rear guard fighting. Bivouacked near	Pontoise	Aug. 28
British Army halted, but "A" Squadron marched to	Cuts	Aug. 29
Retreat continued. Squadron crossed the Aisne and billeted at ...	Montoise	Aug. 30
Retreat and rear guard fighting. Bivouacked at	Vauciennes	Aug. 31
Retreat. I Corps fought at Villers Cotterets. Squadron bivouacked at	Villers St. Genest	Sept. 1
Pursuit slackened. Billeted at	Monthyon	Sept. 2
Squadron crossed the Marne at Meaux and bivouacked at	La Haute Maison	Sept. 3
Squadron on outpost duty all day ...	La Haute Maison	Sept. 4

Event.	*Place.*	*Date.*
"A" SQUADRON (continued).		1914
Marched all night through the Forêt de Crecy and at dawn reached ...	Chartres	Sept. 5
On outpost duty all day, engaged with hostile patrols. Billeted at night at	Chartres	Night of Sept. 5
Army advanced. Squadron engaged with enemy rear guards. Billeted at	Faremoutieres	Sept. 6
Squadron advanced and billeted at ...	Coulommiers	Sept. 7
Squadron advanced. Some fighting. Bivouacked at	Bussieres	Sept. 8
3rd Division forced the Marne at Nanteuil. Squadron bivouacked near	Champressy Farm ...	Sept. 9
Fighting with enemy rear guards. Squadron bivouacked at	Dammard	Sept. 10
Advance continued. Billeted at ...	Grand Rozoy	Sept. 11
Fighting for the passage of the Vesle at Braine. Squadron bivouacked near	Braine	Sept. 12
3rd Division, severe fighting to cross the Aisne. Squadron bivouacked near	La Tuillerie Chateau (near Vailly)	Sept. 13
Battle of the Aisne. Squadron bivouacked near	The bank of the river Aisne	Sept. 14
Battle of the Aisne. Squadron bivouacked near	The bank of the river Aisne	Sept. 15
Battle of the Aisne. Squadron bivouacked on the battlefield	The bank of the river Aisne	Sept. 16–17
Squadron moved into billets at ...	Braine	Sept. 18
Trench warfare. Squadron remained in billets at	Braine	Sept. 19–30
With detachment dug in at	La Tuillerie Chateau ...	Sept. 19–30
Left the Aisne at 6 p.m. and marched to	Arcy St. Restitute ...	Oct. 1
Marched in small parties to	Troesnes	Oct. 2
Marched to	Crepy	Oct. 3
Marched by night to	Roberval	Oct. 4
Marched. Entrained at	Compiegne	Oct. 5
Detrained about mid-day at Etaples and marched to billets at	Abbeville	Oct. 6
Remained at	Abbeville	Oct. 7
Marched by night to	Reigneauville	Oct. 8
Marched by night to	Pressy	Oct. 9
Marched by night towards	Busnes	Oct. 10
Halted at	Busnes	Oct. 11
Enemy encountered. Bivouacked on the battlefield near	Paradis	Oct. 12
Heavy fighting outside Bout Deville. Squadron bivouacked near ...	Rue du Ponch	Oct. 13
Fighting all day. A short advance. Squadron bivouacked	On the battlefield	Oct. 14
Slow advance, continued fighting. Squadron bivouacked on the battlefield near	La Bassée–Estaires road ...	Oct. 15
Enemy's opposition not very severe. Squadron bivouacked near ...	Rue de Bacquerot ...	Oct. 16
Heavy fighting all day. A short advance. Squadron bivouacked at ...	Aubers	Oct. 17
The advance held up. Squadron on outpost duty during the night near	Herlies	Oct. 18
Troops entrench. Squadron near ...	Herlies	Oct. 19

APPENDIX A

Event.	*Place.*	*Date.*
"A" SQUADRON (continued).		1914
Squadron engaged at Le Pilly. Retired during the night to reserve near ...	Herlies	Oct. 20
Heavy German attacks. Squadron in the trenches	Le Pluich Farm	Oct. 21
II Corps withdrew. "A" Squadron retired to	Rue de Bacquerot	Oct. 22
(Machine-Gun Detachment was not withdrawn until Oct. 23)		
No hostile attack but continued shelling. Squadron remained near ...	Rue de Bacquerot ...	Oct. 23
Trench warfare. Continued enemy attacks. Squadron remained near	Rue de Bacquerot ...	Oct. 24–30
3rd Division relieved by Indian Division. Squadron marched to	Meteren	Oct. 31
Squadron marched into Belgium and billeted near	Locre	Nov. 1–6
Squadron marched through Ypres and bivouacked near	The Halte on the Menin Road	Nov. 7
Squadron in the trenches about ...	The Menin Road (near Veldhoek)	Nov. 8
In the trenches all day. At nightfall returned to bivouacs near ...	The Halte	Nov. 9
Remained in bivouacs	The Halte	Nov. 10
(One Troop and machine-gun sent to trenches)		
Attack of the Prussian Guard. Squadron in action by	Herentage Chateau ...	Nov. 11
Squadron in the trenches near	Herentage Chateau ...	Nov. 12
Squadron in the trenches near	Herentage Chateau ...	Nov. 13
Squadron relieved, and after some alarms billeted at	The Farm near The Halte...	Nov. 14–18
Squadron in trenches	South of Menin Road ...	Nov. 19
Squadron relieved by French at 10 p.m. Returned to bivouacs	Near The Halte	Nov. 20
Squadron marched to	Westoutre	Nov. 21
Remained in billets at	Westoutre	Nov. 22–23
Squadron marched to	Berthen	Nov. 24
Squadron went into billets	Farm near Mont Noir ...	Nov. 25
Remained in billets	Mont Noir	Nov. 26 to Dec. 31
		1915
Remained in billets	Mont Noir	Jan. 1 to Feb. 4
Squadron in the trenches	South of Wytschaete ...	Feb. 5–7
Relieved and returned to billets ...	Mont Noir	Feb. 8
Remained in billets at	Mont Noir	Feb. 9 to April 12
Squadron marched to rejoin the Regiment and billeted near	Hondeghem	Apr. 13

"A" Squadron from this date took its place with the Regiment and ceased to be an independent unit.

"B" SQUADRON.

		1914
Left Longmoor by train at 4 a.m. and embarked on the *Orion* at ...	Southampton	Aug. 16
Sailed at dawn	At sea	Aug. 17
Disembarked and marched to Camp at	Rouen	Aug. 18

APPENDIX A

Event.	*Place.*	*Date.*
"B" Squadron (continued).		1914
Entrained at night	In the train	Aug. 19
In the train	In the train	Aug. 20
Detrained at 4 a.m. at	Vaux-Andigny	Aug. 21
Marched. Billeted at	Bavai	Aug. 22
Battle of Mons. Marched at 3 a.m. Forced march. Bivouacked at ...	9th kilometre stone, Mauberge–Mons road	Aug. 23
Retreated all day. Bivouacked at ...	Audignies	Aug. 24
Retreated and rear guard engagements. During the night fought at the bridges round	Maroilles	Aug. 25
Retreated and rear guard engagements. Billeted at	Etreux	Aug. 26
Retreated. Squadron on outpost duty during the night near	Mont Origny	Aug. 27
Retreated. A long march. Billeted at	Servais	Aug. 28
Halted. Squadron found patrols for outpost line	Servias	Aug. 29
Retreated. Rear-guard actions. Bivouacked near	Coucy le Chateau ...	Aug. 30
Retreated. Squadron crossed the Aisne and bivouacked at	Cutry	Aug. 31
Retreated. Fight at Villers Cotterets.	Antilly	Sept. 1
Retreated. Rear guard not engaged. Bivouacked near	Chaucomin	Sept. 2
Retreated. No incident. Squadron billeted at	Les Lacquais. (South-east of Pierre–Levee)... ...	Sept. 3
Retreated. In observation of the crossings of the Marne nearly all day. Billeted at	Villeneuve Farm	Sept. 4
Last day of the Retreat. Squadron billeted at	Marles	Sept. 5
The Army advanced. Squadron engaged with enemy rear guards. Bivouacked at	Rigny	Sept. 6
Advance continued, Squadron bivouacked at	La Vanne	Sept. 7
Advance continued. Squadron engaged with enemy rear guards. Billeted at	Boitron	Sept. 8
Advance continued. Marne crossed without much opposition. Squadron billeted at	Couprou	Sept. 9
Advance continued. Severe fighting with enemy rear guards. Billeted at	Monines	Sept. 10
Advance continued. An easy day. Billeted at	Beugneux	Sept. 11
2nd Division crossed the Vesle with some difficulty. "B" Squadron billeted at	Vieil Arcy	Sept. 12
2nd Division forced the Aisne. Heavy fighting all day. Squadron billeted at	Bourg	Sept. 13
Battle of the Aisne. Heavy fighting. Squadron remained on battlefield near	Verneuil	Sept. 14–17
Battle of the Aisne. Trench warfare began. Squadron moved into billets at	Bourg	Sept. 18

APPENDIX A

Event.	*Place.*	*Date.*
"B" Squadron (continued).		1914
Squadron remained in billets at ...	Bourg	Sept. 19 to Oct. 13
Marched at dark to	Fere en Tardenois ...	Oct. 13
Entrained at	Fere en Tardenois ...	Oct. 14
Detrained at	Hazebrouck	Oct. 15
Remained in billets at	Hazebrouck	Oct. 15–16
Marched to	Boeschepe	Oct. 17
Remained in billets at	Boeschepe	Oct. 17–19
Marched as advance guard through Ypres to Zonnebeke. Billeted at ...	Bryke	Oct. 20
Severe fighting in an attempt to advance. At nightfall Squadron retired to	Bryke	Oct. 21
Fairly quiet day. Squadron billeted at	Bryke	Oct. 22
French relieved 2nd Division. Squadron marched to	Verbranden Molen ...	Oct. 23
2nd Division relieved units of the 7th Division. "B" Squadron on outpost duty near	Gheluvelt	Oct. 24
2nd Division attempted to advance. Squadron stood to all night near ...	Hooge	Oct. 25
Fighting continued. Squadron bivouacked near	Hooge	Oct. 26
Battle of Ypres, and hard fighting. Squadron bivouacked near ...	Hooge	Oct. 27–30
Very heavy fighting. Squadron in line near	Externest	Oct. 31
Battle of Ypres continued. "B" Squadron bivouacked near ...	Potijze	Nov 1–10
Attack of the Prussian Guard. Squaddron engaged about Nonneboschen Wood. Bivouacked at night near	Hooge	Nov. 11
Squadron remained about	Hooge	Nov. 12–15
2nd Division relieved. Squadron marched to	Poperinghe	Nov. 16
Squadron marched to billets at ...	Hazebrouck	Nov. 17
Squadron remained in billets at ...	Hazebrouck	Nov. 18 to Dec. 21
Squadron marched to	Bethune	Dec. 22
Squadron remained in billets at ...	Bethune	Dec. 23–26
Squadron billeted in a farm near ...	Locon	Dec. 27
Remained in billets near	Locon	Dec. 28–31
		1915
Remained in billets near	Locon	Jan. 1 to Feb. 1
Moved and billeted in a watch factory at	Bethune	Feb. 2 to Apr. 12
Marched to rejoin the Regiment near	Hondeghem	Apr. 13

The Squadron from this date ceased to be an independent unit, but took its place with the Regiment.

"C" SQUADRON.		1914
Squadron left Longmoor at midnight	Longmoor	Aug. 15
In the train, reached Southampton and embarked on the	*Siptah*	Aug. 16

APPENDIX A

Event.	*Place.*	*Date.*
"C" SQUADRON (continued).		
		1914
Embarked and anchored outside Southampton. Sailed at dawn	At sea	Aug. 17
Disembarked; marched to camp outside	Rouen	Aug. 18
Entrained at dusk	In the train	Aug. 19
Squadron detrained about 3 p.m. at ...	Le Nouvion	Aug. 20
Squadron joined the 1st Division and marched to	St. Hilaire	Aug. 21
Marched at 4 a.m. Crossed the frontier into Belgium and billeted at ...	Rouveroy	Aug. 22
Battle of Mons. Squadron billeted for night at	Rouveroy	Aug. 23
Retreat. Squadron billeted at ...	Feignes	Aug. 24
Retreat continued. Engagement with enemy rear guards. Bivouacked at	Taisnieres	Aug. 25
Retreat continued. II Corps fought at Le Cateau. Squadron billeted at...	Oisy	Aug. 26
Retreat continued. Squadron heavily engaged about Bergues. Bivouacked near	Origny Ste. Benoit ...	Aug. 27
Retreat continued. A long march. Squadron billeted at	St. Gobain	Aug. 28
The Army halted. Patrols with outpost line	St. Gobain	Aug. 29
Retreat continued. A long march. Squadron billeted at	Pinon Chateau	Aug. 30
Retreat continued. 1st Division crossed the Aisne at Soissons, and Squadron bivouacked at	Croix de Fer	Aug. 31
Fight at Villers Cotterets. Squadron engaged all day in the forest. Bivouacked late at	Mareuil	Sept. 1
Retreat continued. No fighting of importance. Squadron billeted at ...	Meaux	Sept. 2
An easy march. Squadron crossed the Marne at La Ferte sous Jouarre and bivouacked at	Le Grand Glairet ...	Sept. 3
Retreat continued. Rear guard fighting. Squadron billeted at	Coulommiers	Sept. 4
Last day of the Retreat. A short march. Squadron billeted at	Rozoy	Sept. 5
Advance of 1st Division. Squadron engaged with enemy rear guards, and bivouacked at	Vendoy	Sept. 6
Advance continued. Skirmished with enemy rear guards. Squadron bivouacked at	Choisy	Sept. 7
Advance continued. Some fighting to cross the Petit Morin. Squadron billeted at	Flagny	Sept. 8
1st Division crossed the Marne. Squadron crossed at Saulcherry, and bivouacked at	Beaurepaire Farm	Sept. 9
Advance continued. 1st Division fought with enemy rear guards at Priez. Squadron billeted at	Priez	Sept. 10
A short and easy march. Squadron billeted at	Coincy	Sept. 11

APPENDIX A

Event.	*Place.*	*Date.*
"C" Squadron (continued).		1914
1st Division crossed the Vesle without difficulty. Squadron billeted at ...	Bazoches	Sept. 12
1st Division crossed the Aisne at Bourg. Squadron billeted at	Bourg	Sept. 13
1st Division severely engaged on the Aisne. Squadron bivouacked on the battlefield near	Vendresse	Sept. 14
Battle of the Aisne. Squadron bivouacked on the battlefield near ...	Vendresse	Sept. 15–18
Trench warfare began. Squadron billeted near Bourg at	Ferme de la Fabriquee ...	Sept. 19 to Oct. 14
Marched by night to billets at	Arcy St. Restitute ...	Oct. 15
Marched by night, and entrained at ...	Neuilly St. Front	Oct. 16
In the train	In the train	Oct. 17
Detrained at St. Omer and marched to	Cassel	Oct. 18
Remained in billets at	Cassel	Oct. 19
Marched as advance guard to ...	Poperinghe	Oct. 20
Formed advance guard to Langemarck. Fighting about Bixschoete. Bivouacked at	Boesinghe	Oct. 21
Heavy attacks against the 1st Division. Squadron occupied a line along the railway north of	Pilkem	Oct. 22
1st Division counter-attacks successful. Squadron bivouacked at ...	Boesinghe	Oct. 23
1st Division relieved by the French. Squadron marched through Ypres to billets south of	Zillebeke	Oct. 24
Squadron remained in a Farm near...	Zillebeke	Oct. 25
1st Division ordered to attack. Squadron advance guard, severe fighting. Squadron bivouacked in woods by	Hooge	Oct. 26
Battle of Ypres. Squadron bivouacked in woods near	Hooge	Oct. 27–30
Heavy attacks. Squadron bivouacked near	Hooge	Oct. 31
Heavy shelling. Squadron lost men and horses. Bivouacked at	Hooge	Nov. 1
Battle continued. Squadron moved to railway east of	Ypres	Nov. 2
Battle continued. Squadron remained near	Railway east of Ypres ...	Nov. 3–10
Attack of the Prussian Guard. Squadron about Veldhoek all day. At night retired to near	Hooge	Nov. 11
Battle continued. Squadron remained near	The Halte (Menin Road)...	Nov. 12–15
1st Division relieved. Squadron marched at 5 a.m. and billeted at... ...	Westoutre	Nov. 16
Squadron marched to billets at ...	Merris	Nov. 17
Squadron remained in billets at ...	Merris	Nov. 18 to Dec. 20
Half-squadron marched to	Bethune	Dec. 21
Half-squadron remained in billets at ...	Merris	Dec. 22
The whole Squadron collected together at	Bethune	Dec. 23
Remained in billets at	Bethune	Dec. 24–30

APPENDIX A

Event.	*Place.*	*Date.*
"C" Squadron (continued).		1914
Squadron moved up in close support of front line at	Cambrin	Dec. 31
		1915
Returned to	Bethune	Jan. 1
Squadron remained at	Bethune	Jan. 2–28
Owing to German attacks, Squadron remained in close support at	Beuvry	Jan. 29
Returned to billets at	Bethune	Jan. 30 to Feb. 1
1st Division relieved. Squadron marched to billets at	Auchel	Feb. 2
Remained in billets at	Auchel	Feb. 3–27
Marched to billets near	Hinges	Feb. 28 to Apr. 12
Marched to rejoin the Regiment near	Hondeghem	Apr. 13

The Squadron from this date ceased to be an independent unit, but took its place with the Regiment.

15th HUSSARS		1915
Regiment reassembled in billets. Squadrons in farms round about...	H.Q. Hondeghem	Apr. 14–22
1st German gas attack	4th Kilometre	
Regiment alarmed and marched via Poperinghe to bivouacs	Stone, Poperinghe–Elverdinghe road	Apr. 23
1st Cavalry Division placed under orders of the French. Regiment in reserve in	Woods S.W. of Woesten	Apr. 24
Regiment moved to support Belgians, retired at night to bivouacs at	Eyhoek	Apr. 25
At dark Regiment moved to reserve trenches (led horses remained at Eyhoek)	North of Woesten	Night of Apr. 26
Regiment relieved during the day, returned to bivouacs at	Eyhoek	Apr. 27
Cavalry withdrawn, Regiment marched in the evening to bivouacs at	Herzeele	Apr. 28
Regiment remained at 1–2 hours' notice in billets at	Herzeele Herzeele	Apr. 29 to May 1
Regiment marched to billets at	Esquelbecq	May 2
Regiment marched to billets at	Hondeghem	May 3
Regiment remained in billets at	Hondegham	May 4 5
Regiment (conveyed by motor lorries) worked during night (horses remained at Hondeghem)	Canal north of Ypres	May 6
Regiment again dug all night (horses remained at Hondeghem)	Canal north of Ypres	May 7
Regiment returned to horses at	Hondeghem	May 8
Regiment turned out at 2 a.m., marched to huts by Vlamertinghe, moved up dismounted and dug trenches all night near (horses returned to Hondeghem)	Wieltje	May 9
Regiment occupied trenches about	Wieltje	May 10
Regiment dug a fresh line and occupied it, east of former line about	Wieltje	May 11
At 1 a.m. Regiment moved to trenches near Warwick Farm, relieved at night and retired to reserve trenches near	Potije	May 12

APPENDIX A

Event.	*Place.*	*Date.*
		1915
Powerful German attack, Regiment ment engaged all day	South of Wieltje ...	May 13
Regiment retook abandoned trenches, dug a fresh line and occupied it ...	West of Verlorenhoek ...	May 14
Regiment relieved and retired to ...	Huts at Vlamertinghe ...	May 15
Regiment remained in huts	Vlamertinghe	May 16–17
Regiment took over front-line trenches	About Hooge	May 18
In the trenches	About Hooge	May 19–22
Regiment relieved during the night ...	C Squadron to G.H.Q. line. H.Q. and A and B Squadrons to Ecole de Bienfaisance	May 23rd (relief was not finished until daylight May 24)
Heavy fighting. German gas attack. Regiment severely engaged all day about	Hooge	May 24
Regiment relieved and withdrawn to ...	Huts at Vlamertinghe ...	May 25
Regiment in reserve	Huts at Vlamertinghe ...	May 26–27
Regiment moved by motor bus to billets at*	Wormhoudt	May 28
Regiment in billets at	Wormhoudt	May 29 to July 31

(A large working party from the Regiment was employed from June 30th to July 30th. They dug a rear system of defence about Elverdinghe.)

Regiment marched to the sea for training purposes and billeted at ...	Mardick	Aug. 1
Regiment returned to billets at ...	Wormhoudt	Aug. 2
Remained in billets at	Wormhoudt	Aug. 3 to Sept. 22

(A large working party of the Regiment was employed from Aug. 5th to Sept. 6th digging the Reserve system of defence about Elverdinghe.)

Regiment marched by night (for Battle of Loos) via Arneke–Renescure–Hevringham to billets at ...	Blendecques	Sept. 23
Regiment marched by night via Creques to billets at	Estree Blanche	Sept. 24
Battle of Loos. Regiment marched by Auchel and Bruay to bivouacs in	Vaudricourt Chateau Grounds	Sept 25
Regiment remained in bivouac in ...	Vaudricourt Chateau Grounds	Sept. 26–27
Regiment marched to a fresh bivouac...	Wood just south of Hesdigneul	Sept. 28
Regiment marched to billets in ...	Marles les Mines	Sept. 29
Regiment remained in billets at ...	Marles les Mines	Sept. 30 to Oct. 2

(A large working party was employed clearing the battlefield and was away from the Regiment from Oct. 2 to Oct. 5.)

Regiment (less working party) marched to billets at	Febvin-Palfart	Oct. 3
Regiment remain in billets at	Febvin-Palfart	Oct. 4–18

* NOTE.—The led horses had been moved from Hondeghem to Wormhoudt whilst the Regiment was fighting at Ypres. This movement was carried out with great difficulty owing to the shortage of men.

APPENDIX A

Event.	*Place.*	*Date.*
		1915
Regiment marched to fresh billets at ...	H.Q., Glomenghen ... A Squadron, Rebecq, B Squadron, Rincq C Squadron and Machine-Guns, Warne	Oct. 19
Regiment remained in billets ...	H.Q., Glomenghen, ... A Squadron, Rebecq, B Squadron, Rincq, C Squadron and Machine-Guns, Warne	Oct. 20 to Nov. 16
Regiment marched to fresh billets ...	H.Q., Doudeauville, ... A Squadron, Bezingham, B Squadron, Zotteau, Machine-Guns, Crandal, C Squadron, Doudeauville	Nov. 17

(On Dec. 9 a large dismounted party prepared for the trenches. The persons left in billets were those necessary to look after the horses, farriers, etc. A few men were also left behind as a reserve.)

Regiment (less horses) entrained at Devres and proceeded by rail to ...	Fouquereuil	Dec. 30
Regiment remained at	Fouquereuil	Dec. 31 to Jan. 1, 1916
		1916
Regiment moved up to huts at ...	Sailly La Bourse	Jan. 2
Regiment remained in reserve at ...	Sailly La Bourse	Jan. 3–4
Regiment went into front line trenches about	Vermelles (Hohenzollern Redoubt)...	Jan. 5
Regiment remained in front-line trenches about	Vermelles (Hohenzollern Redoubt)...	Jan. 6–8
Regiment relieved from front line and retired into reserve at	Sailly La Bourse	Jan. 9
Regiment remained in reserve at ...	Sailly La Bourse	Jan. 10–16
Regiment returned to front line trenches about	Vermelles (Hohenzollern Redoubt)	Jan. 17
Regiment remained in front line ...	Vermelles (Hohenzollern Redoubt)...	Jan. 18–20
Regiment relieved from front line and retired into reserve at	Sailly La Bourse	Jan. 21
Regiment remained in reserve at ...	Sailly La Bourse	Jan. 22–25
Regiment suddenly alarmed, and moved into support trenches	On the railway east of Vermelles	Jan. 26
Regiment moved into the cellars in ...	Vermelles	Jan. 27
Regiment remained in the cellars in ...	Vermelles	Jan. 28
Regiment moved into front-line trenches	Vermelles (Hohenzollern Redoubt)...	Jan. 29
Regiment remained in the front line ...	Vermelles (Hohenzollern Redoubt)...	Jan. 30–Feb. 1
Regiment relieved and moved into General Reserve at	Bethune	Feb. 2
Regiment remained at	Bethune	Feb. 3–7
Regiment marched into reserve trenches	West of Vermelles ...	Feb. 8
Regiment remained in reserves trenches	West of Vermelles	Feb. 9
Regiment moved up into the front line	Vermelles (Hohenzollern Redoubt)...	Feb. 10
Regiment in trenches. Heavy enemy bombardment	Vermelles (Hohenzollern Redoubt)...	Feb. 11

APPENDIX A

Event.	*Place.*	*Date.*
		1916
Regiment relieved by infantry. Retired to	La Bourse	Feb. 12
Regiment entrained at La Bourse and returned to their former billets	H.Q., Doudeauville ... A Squadron, Bezingham B Squadron, Zotteau Machine-Guns, Crandal C Squadron, Doudeauville	Feb. 13
Regiment remained in billets	About Doudeauville ...	Feb. 14–May 20

(Working parties were found by the Regiment during this period, at Sains en Gohelle, digging rear lines of defence. The Machine-Guns were withdrawn from the Regiment to 9th Cavalry Machine-Gun Squadron on March 20.)

Regiment marched to sea for training, camped at	Escault	May 21
Regiment in camp training at ...	Escault	May 22–28
Regiment returned to their billets ...	About Doudeauville ...	May 29
Regiment remained in billets ...	About Doudeauville ...	May 30–June 24
Regiment marched at night (for the Battle of the Somme) and billeted at	Voisin	June 25
Regiment marched by night to billets at	Beauvoir-Riviere	June 26
Regiment marched by night to billets at	Pernois	June 27
Regiment marched by night to bivouacs at	Querrieu	June 28

(On this day A Squadron joined 49th Division as Divisional Cavalry Squadron.)

Regiment remained in readiness in bivouacs at	Querrieu	June 29–30
Battle of the Somme opened. Regiment marched to La Houssoye. Returned at night to bivouacs at ... ... (A Squadron rejoined.)	Querrieu	July 1
Regiment remained in bivouacs at ...	Querrieu	July 2–4
Regiment retired via Amiens, Picquigny and Longpre to billets at	Bettencourt Riviere ...	July 5

(A working party was left behind at Hericourt under the XIII Corps.)

Regiment remained in billets at ...	Bettencourt Riviere ...	July 6–11
Regiment marched at night through Amiens to bivouacs at	Querrieu	July 12
Regiment marched at night to concentration point of 1st Cavalry Division bivouacked at	Buire sur l'Ancre	July 13
Regiment remained standing to in bivouacs at	Buire sur l'Ancre	July 14–23
Regiment retired to bivouacs at ...	Querrieu	July 24

(A working party moved on July 24 to Fricourt, where they were employed by the XIII Corps working round Montaubon until the middle of August.)

Regiment remained in bivouacs at ...	Querrieu	July 25–Aug. 8
Regiment marched to back area via Villers Bocage to bivouacs at	Long	Aug. 8
Regiment continued the march by Pont Remy and Vismes au Val to billets at	Gamaches	Aug. 10

APPENDIX A

Event.	*Place.*	*Date.*
		1916
Regiment remained in billets at ...	Gamaches	Aug. 11–Sept. 5

(Working parties were employed by Cavalry Corps during Aug. and Sept. at work on the Cavalry tracks, which were prepared over the captured German trenches.)

Regiment marched to the battlefield via Oisemont to billets at	Bettencourt Riviere ...	Sept. 6
Regiment marched through Amiens to bivouac about	Daours	Sept. 7
Regiment remained in bivouac at ...	Daours	Sept. 8–13
Regiment marched at dawn via Morlancourt to bivouacs in	Carnoy Valley	Sept. 14
Regiment remained all day ready to advance, but at night bivouacked in	Carnoy Valley	Sept. 15–16
Regiment withdrew to bivouacs about	Daours	Sept. 17
Regiment remained in bivouacs about	Daours	Sept. 18–22
Regiment marched via Amiens and Picquigny to bivouacs at ...	Conde-Folie	Sept. 23
Regiment marched via Domquer and Bealcourt to bivouacs at ...	Beauvoir-Riviere	Sept. 24
Regiment marched via Buire au Bois and Galametz to bivouacs at ...	Wail...	Sept. 25
Regiment remained in bivouacs (and later billeted) at	Wail...	Sept. 26–Oct. 18

(A strong working party left on Oct. 8 to construct a Cavalry Track on the Somme battlefield and rejoined Nov. 11.)

Regiment marched again for the Somme via Galametz-Frevent to ...	Barley	Oct. 19
Regiment marched via Occoches and Dollens to bivouac at	Naours	Oct. 20
Regiment remained in bivouacs at ...	Naours	Oct. 21–Nov. 7
Regiment marched back to back areas via Havernas, to billets at ...	Caours	Nov. 8
Regiment marched via Drucat to ...	Dompierre	Nov. 9
Regiment marched via Aix en Issart, Recques and Samer to about ...	Isques	Nov. 10
Regiment billeted as follows	H.Q., Isques ... ... A Squadron, Hesdin l'Abbe B Squadron, Hesdigneul C Squadron, Montaigu Farm (Ecames) Transport, Hesdigneul	Nov. 11–Dec. 31
		1917
Regiment remained billeted about ...	Isques ... ... (2 Troops B Squadron moved to Condette on Feb. 19)	Jan. 1 Apr. 4

(A working party left for Arras on Mar. 25 to prepare a Cavalry Track. They rejoined Apr. 19.)

Regiment marched for Battle of Arras via Parenty and Enquin to ...	Hucqueliers...	Apr. 5

APPENDIX A

Event.	*Place.*	*Date.*
		1917
Remained in bivouacs about	Hucqueliers...	Apr. 6
Regiment marched via Haningham, and Blangy to	Humereoille	Apr. 7

(A working party was sent to work under the Canadian Corps on the Vimy Ridge; the party left the Regiment on Apr. 3 and returned Apr. 19.)

Regiment marched via Le Bout Haut St. Pol and Tinque to billets at ...	Le Moulin Rouge (south-east of Aubigny) ...	Apr. 8
Battle of Arras. Regiment under Canadian Corps. Stood to during daylight and bivouacked at night near	Aubigny	Apr. 9–13
Regiment placed under XIII Corps but remained at	Aubigny	Ap. 14–15
Regiment withdrew, and marched via Tilloy and Frevent to billets at ...	Bourbers	Apr. 16
Regiment remained in billets as follows	H.Q., Bourbers ... ... A Squadron, Vacquerie le Boucq B Squadron, Vacquerie le Boucq C Squadron, Bourbers Transport, Bourbers	April 17–May 12
Regiment marched via Ecoivres to billets at	Conchy-Cayeux	May 13
(1st Cavalry Division transferred to First Army.)		
Regiment marched via Calonne, Marles-les-Mines to bivouacs	La Beuvriere	May 14
Remained in bivouacs at	La Beuvriere	May 15–June 3

(A strong working party left on May 12 to work near Ecoivre, and another party left on May 17 to work near Roclincourt, both these parties rejoined on June 3.)

Regiment marched via Hinges and Lestrem to bivouacs at ... ... (1st Cavalry Division transferred to Second Army)	Estaires	June 4
Regiment remained in bivouac about	Estaires	June 5–10
Regiment returned to First Army area and returned to bivouacs at ...	La Beuvriere	June 11

(Two strong working parties left on June 12 and June 13 to work under the XIII Corps at Ecurie; they rejoined on July 9.)

Regiment remained in bivouacs at ...	La Beuvriere	June 12 to July 15
Regiment marched via Locon and Lesterem to	Estaires	July 16
(1st Cavalry Division moved to support the Portuguese.)		
Regiment remained in billets at ...	Estaires	July 17 to Aug. 26

(On Aug. 6 a working party left for Elverdinghe, where they came under the orders of XIII Corps; they rejoined at end of September.)

Regiment marched to the back areas via St. Venant and Molinghem to billets at	Estree Blanche	Aug. 27

APPENDIX A

Event.	*Place.*	*Date.*
		1917
Regiment marched via Martinghem and Gourneay to bivouacs about ...	Ergny	Aug. 28
Regiment marched via Hucqueliers and Enquin to billets at	Frencq (one Squadron at Widehem)	Aug. 29
Regiment remained in billets about ...	Frencq	Aug. 30 to Oct. 5
1st Cavalry Division moved up towards Ypres. Regiment marched via Samer to billets about	Questrecques	Oct. 6
Regiment marched via Henneveux and Le Poirer to	Serques	Oct. 7
Regiment remained at	Serques	Oct. 8–10
Regiment marched to back areas and billeted at	Questrecques	Oct. 11
Regiment returned to their old billets at	Frencq (C Squadron moved to Rosamel on Oct. 15)...	Oct. 12
Regiment remained in billets about ...	Frencq	Oct. 13–Nov. 9

(A working party left on Oct. 19 to join the Fifth Army; they worked under the XIV Corps, and rejoined early in November.)

Regiment marched (for the Battle of Cambrai) to	Beaurain Chateau	Nov. 10
Regiment marched via Hesdin and Tollent to	Boisbergues	Nov. 11
Regiment marched via Havernas to ...	Frenchecourt	Nov. 12
Regiment remained in bivouacs until dark	Frenchecourt	Nov. 13
Regiment marched by night via Daours and Cerisy to	Morecourt	Nov. 14
Regiment marched via Villers Carbonel and Brie to	Les Mesnil Bruntel ...	Nov. 15
Regiment remained in bivouac at ...	Le Mesnil Bruntel ...	Nov. 16–19
Battle of Cambrai. Regiment concentrated at Fins. Moved to Metz and bivouaced in	Havrincourt Wood ...	Nov. 20
Regiment marched to Frescault. Moved to support the 9th Lancers in action about Noyelles. At dark Regiment dismounted in action near ...	Marcoing	Nov. 21
Regiment relieved and withdrew for the night to	Metz	Nov. 22
Regiment marched to Flesquieres, where led horses were left. Regiment moved dismounted via Graincourt and bivouacked at	Anneux	Nov. 23

(The led horses retired to Metz on November 24th. They remained there until dismounted party was relieved from Bourlon Wood.)

Regiment heavily engaged throughout the day and night in	Bourlon Wood	Nov. 24
Regiment heavily engaged all day, but relieved at nightfall, and retired to	Flesquieres	Nov. 25
Led horses brought up, and Regiment rode back to	Metz	Nov. 26
Regiment retired to bivouacs at ...	La Neuville	Nov. 27
Regiment remained in bivouacs at ...	La Neuville	Nov. 28–29

APPENDIX A

Event.	*Place.*	*Date.*
		1917
Regiment suddenly alarmed and marched via Peronne and Buire to	Roisel	Nov. 30
Regiment remained in bivouacs at ...	Roisel	Dec. 1
Regiment went into the trenches about	Gauche Wood	Dec. 2
Regiment in the trenches about ...	Gauche Wood	Dec. 3

(Horses of the Regiment remained at Roisel until Dec. 3, when they were withdrawn to La Neuville.)

Regiment relieved from the front line and retired to	Roisel	Dec. 4
Regiment remained in reserve to 21st and 16th Divisions, digging a defensive line about	Roisel	Dec. 5–15
Regiment returned by rail to	La Neuville	Dec. 16
Regiment remained in billets at ...	La Neuville	Dec. 17–20
Regiment marched to a hut camp at ...	Le Mesnil Bruntel	Dec. 21
Regiment remained in camp at ...	Le Mesnil Bruntel... ...	Dec. 22–31
		1918
Regiment remained in camp at ...	Le Mesnil Bruntel ...	Jan. 1–15
Regiment moved up in support of front line to	Vadencourt	Jan. 16
Regiment remained in support at ...	Vadencourt	Jan. 17–20

(During the whole period the Regiment were in the trenches, the horses remained in camp at Le Mesnil Bruntel.)

Regiment went into front-line trenches east of	Vadencourt	Jan. 21
Regiment remained in front-line trenches east of	Vadencourt	Jan. 22–25
Regiment relieved and returned by bus to	Le Mesnil Bruntel ...	Jan. 26
Regiment remained in camp at ...	Le Mesnil Bruntel ...	Jan. 27 to Feb. 14

(Strong working parties were found daily working at Le Verguier and Jeancourt.)

Regiment found a strong party for trenches east of	Vermand	Feb. 15
Regiment remained in trenches front line and support, east of ...	Vermand	Feb. 16 to Mar. 3
Regiment moved into reserve at ...	Vendelles	Mar. 4
Regiment remained in reserve at ...	Vendelles	Mar. 5–11
Regiment relieved and returned in motor lorries to	Le Mesnil Bruntel ...	Mar. 12
Regiment remained, ready to turn out at	Le Mesnil Bruntel ...	Mar. 13–20

(A strong working party was employed about Vendelles from Mar. 17 to Mar. 20.)

Germans launched their attack, Regiment marched to Hervilly, and later came under orders of 197th Infantry Brigade. Regiment in position at nightfall about ...	Roisel	Mar. 21

APPENDIX A

Event.	*Place.*	*Date.*
		1918
Regiment counter-attacked, and captured Brown Line, but were forced to retire. (Majority of A Squadron killed or captured.) Regiment concentrated at Cartigny. During the night Regiment in support of outpost line at	Ennemain	Mar. 22
1st Cavalry Division placed under orders of VII Corps. Regiment marched via Chaulnes and Proyart to concentration at	Cappy	Mar. 23
Regiment sent a strong detachment to Maricourt. Detachment ordered to hold gap between V Corps and 9th Division. By nightfall detachment in position about	Bernafay Wood	Mar 24
Remainder of the Regiment retired to	Cerisy	Mar. 24
Detachment heavily attacked. Driven from Bernafay Wood, detachment severely engaged about Montauban, which they held until 10 p.m. Detachment withdrawn to ...	Carnoy	Mar. 25
Remainder of Regiment retired to ...	Bussy les Daours	Mar. 25
Detachment rejoined the Regiment at Bussy. Another detachment left Regiment and became seriously engaged near Morlancourt at dark, occupied a line	Sailly-Mericourt	Mar. 26
Rest of Regiment at	Bussy les Daours	Mar. 26
15th Hussars engaged in severe fighting north and south of the Somme. Detachment rejoined in the evening. By dark the Regiment consolidated about	Hamel	Mar. 27
Regiment heavily engaged all day in position near	Warfusee	Mar. 28
(Led horses sent back to a position west of Fouilloy.)		
Regiment remained and consolidated their position about ...	Warfusee	Mar. 29
(Led horses sent back to Bussy les Daours.)		
Regiment heavily engaged all day, but maintained their positions about ...	Warfusee	Mar. 30
Regiment remained in support trenches but at night retired to	Fouilloy	Mar. 31
Regiment remained in reserve at ...	Fouilloy	Apr. 1
(A working party employed all night in digging a second line.)		
Regiment remained in reserve at ...	Fouilloy	Apr. 2
Regiment relieved at night and retired to	Bussy les Daours	Apr. 3
Regiment withdrew to	Amiens	Apr. 4
Regiment remained in billets at ...	Amiens	Apr. 5

(C Squadron marched to Fourth Army area, about Sains en Amienois and rejoined the Regiment on Apr 6.)

APPENDIX A

Event.	*Place.*	*Date.*
		1918
Regiment remained in billets at ...	Amiens	Apr. 6–9
Regiment turned out and marched via Villers-Bocage, Thalmas-Occoches to	Villers l'Hospital ...	Apr. 10
Regiment marched via Bonnieres and Frevent to	Rebreuve	Apr. 11
Regiment marched by Frevent, St. Pol, Pernes to billets at	Fontaine lez Hermans ...	Apr. 12
Regiment remained in billets at ...	Fontaine lez Hermans ...	Apr. 13–15
Regiment marched to fresh billets ...	H.Q., Flechin	Apr. 16
	A Squadron, Flechin	
	B Squadron, Flechin	
	C Squadron, Pippemont (Later on this squadron moved to Boncourt)	
Regiment remained in billets about ...	Flechin	Apr. 17 to May 20
Regiment marched via Heuchin, Anvin to bivouacs at	Monchy Cayeux ...	May 21
Regiment marched via Beauvois, Linzeux to billets at	Genne Ivergny	May 22

(Regimental headquarters moved out to a farm at Selandre about the end of May.)

Regiment remained in billets about ...	Genne Ivergny	May 23 to July 13
Regiment marched to Third Army area via Wavans, Auxi-le-Chateau, and Dollens to bivouacs at	Famechon	July 14
Regiment remained at	Famechon	July 15–19
Regiment marched to bivouacs at ...	Boisbergues	July 20
Regiment remained in bivouacs at ...	Boisbergues	July 21 to Aug. 5
Regiment marched during the night via Authieux and Fienvillers to ...	St. Leger	Aug. 6
Regiment again marched by night via Vignacourt and St. Vast to ...	Longpre	Aug. 7
Regiment marched at dark (Aug. 7) through Amiens to Longeau. Attack launched at dawn. Regiment advanced via Villers Bretonneux and passed through enemy lines near Marcelcave, Wiencourt and Gillaucourt, and occupied final objective near Rosieres. Regiment relieved at night and bivouacked near	Gillaucourt	Aug. 8
Regiment marched to Rosieres. Some fighting at dark. Regiment formed an outpost line between	Rosieres and Meh""aricourt...	Aug. 9

(Led horses remained at Rosieres.)

Regiment withdrew to Luce River, to water the horses. In the afternoon Regiment marched to near Caix, at nightfall retired to bivouacs ...	By river Luce	Aug. 10

APPENDIX A

Event.	*Place.*	*Date.*
		1918
Regiment marched at night to bivouacs	Camon (outside Athens) ...	Aug. 11
Regiment remained in bivouacs and billets at	Camon	Aug 12–15
Regiment marched via Poulan, Talmas, Beauval to billets at	Hem	Aug. 16
Regiment remained in billets at ...	Hem	Aug. 17–18
Regiment marched by night via Doullens, Amplier to bivouacs at ...	Thievres	Aug. 19
Regiment remained in bivouacs at ...	Thievres	Aug. 20
Regiment marched (actually 11.15 p.m. Aug. 20) via Famechon, Pas, Fonquevillers to near Essarts. Regiment retired at night to bivouacs at	Amplier	Aug. 21

(C Squadron marched via Essarts to Bucquoy, and withdrew at night to Amplier.)

Regiment remained in bivouacs at ...	Amplier	Aug. 22–23
Regiment ordered to join VI Corps, marched via Pas to bivouacs near	Douchy les Aylette ...	Aug. 24

(A Squadron sent 1 troop to Boiry St. Rictrude, 1 troop to Douchy les Aylette, 1 troop to Monchy au Bois, and 1 to Quesnoy Farm. B Squadron sent 1 troop to Humbercamp.)

Regiment withdrawn from VI Corps to Cavalry Corps and retired to bivouacs at	Humbercamp	Aug. 25
Regiment marched by night via Saulty, and Grand Rollencourt to billets at	Dernier	Aug. 26
Regiment remained in billets at ...	Dernier	Aug. 27 to Sept. 15
Regiment marched via Frevent to billets at	Conchy sur Canche ...	Sept. 16
Regiment took part in a long field day, and bivouacked at night at ...	Le Ponchel	Sept. 17
Regiment marched to billets at ...	Barley	Sept. 18
Regiment remained at	Barley	Sept. 19
Regiment moved to billets at ...	Hem	Sept. 20
Regiment remained at	Hem	Sept. 21–23
Regiment marched at night via Doullens, Sarton to bivouacs at ...	Coigneux	Sept. 24
Regiment marched by night via Forceville, Albert to bivouacs at ...	Becordel	Sept. 25
Regiment marched by Maricourt, Clery Moislains to bivouacs in ...	Bois de Hennois	Sept. 26
Regiment remained in bivouacs ...	Bois de Hennois	Sept. 27
Regiment marched via Bossu, Buire and Cartigny to bivouacs near ...	Roisel	Sept. 28
Regiment remained in bivouacs near ...	Roisel	Sept. 29 to Oct. 6

(The Regiment was turned out twice, and moved forward to Riqueval, but returned at dark to Roisel on Oct. 2 and Oct. 3.)

Regiment marched to bivouacs in a valley	East of Villeret	Oct. 7

APPENDIX A

Event.	*Place.*	*Date*
		1918
Regiment marched via Nauroy and Wiancourt and Ponchaux. Regiment engaged about Serain. At night Regiment formed an outpost line between	Serain and Premont ...	Oct. 8
(Led horses were at Beaurevoir).		
Regiment relieved and retired to Beaurevoir; later moved forward to bivouacs near	Maretz	Oct. 9
Regiment moved forward to Reumont, retired at dark to	Maretz	Oct. 10
Regiment remained at	Maretz	Oct. 11-12
Regiment marched back via Vermand to	Trefcon	Oct. 13
Regiment remained at	Trefcon	Oct. 14 to Nov. 5
Regiment marched by Ephey, Villers-Guislain to bivouacs at	Vaucelles	Nov. 6
Regiment marched by Masnieres, Rumilly and Cambrai to ...	Brunemont	Nov. 7
Regiment marched by Cantin, Douai, Faumont and Pont a Marcq to ...	Ennevelin	Nov. 8
Regiment marched via Templeuve to Rumes, and thence by Tournay to bivouacs	Gourain Ramecroix ...	Nov. 9
Regiment pursued enemy rear guards. Some fighting, moved via Leuze and Ligne. Regiment finally held up outside Ath. At dark Regiment billeted in a convent ...	Villers St. Amand ...	Nov. 10
Regiment marched to Ath, and thence to Maffle, where cease fire sounded. Regiment billeted in	Maffle	Nov. 11
Regiment withdrew via Ath, Stanne and Peruwel to billets at	Rouillon	Nov. 12
Regiment remained in billets at ...	Rouillon	Nov. 13–16
Regiment marched via Brasmenil, La Boiterie, Ruevancamps to about ...	Louvignies	Nov. 17
Regiment marched via Neuvilles and Lovesse to billets in	Ecaussines Lalaing ...	Nov. 18
Regiment remained in billets at ...	Ecaussines Lalaing ...	Nov. 19
(C Squadron were sent on Nov. 19 to Nivelles to guard surrendered war material.)		
Regiment marched via Feloy to guard stores at	Nivelles	Nov. 20
Regiment marched via Quatre Bras and Gentinnes to billets at	Cortil Noirmont	Nov. 21
(Detachments dispatched to Grand Manil and Gambloux to guard war material.)		
Regiment marched via Gambloux, Dhuy, **Leuze** to billets about ...	Cortil Wodon	Nov. 22
Regiment remained in billets about ...	Cortil Wodon	Nov. 23
Regiment marched by Forville and Ciplet to billets about	Briaves	Nov. 24
(The Regiment threw out an outpost line along the Huy-Hannaut road.)		

APPENDIX A

Event.	*Place.*	*Date.*
		1918
Regiment remained (with outpost line along the Huy–Hannaut road) in billets at	Briaves	Nov. 25–Nov. 26
Regiment marched via Chapon, Lexhy to billets at	Seraing (outskirts of Liege)	Nov. 27
(Regiment formed part of an outpost line along the Sprimont–Liege road.)		
Regiment remained in billets at ...	Seraing	Nov. 28
(Outpost line remained in position.)		
Regiment marched via Trooz, Pepinster, Verviers, Limbourg to billets on the German frontier at	Membach	Nov. 29
(An outpost line was thrown out along the Malmedy–Eupen road.)		
Regiment remained in billets at ...	Membach	Nov. 30
(Outpost line remained in position.)		
Regiment crossed the German frontier, and marched via Eupen, Rutgen to billets	H.Q., Kornelmunster A Squadron, Venwagen B Squadron, Busbach C Squadron, Zweifal	Dec. 1
(The outpost line was from Kesternic to Stolberg.)		
Regiment remained halted (with outpost line in position about)	Kornelmunster	Dec. 2–Dec. 3
Regiment marched via Gressnich and Langerwehg and billeted... ...	H.Q., Merkem A Squadron, Stammeln B Squadron, Pier C Squadron, Selgersdorf	Dec. 4
(An outpost line was in position from Auchem to Selgersdorf.)		
Regiment marched via Steinstrasse and Oberempt to billets at	H.Q., Bedburg A Squadron, Morken B Squadron, Kaster C Squadron, Haff	Dec. 5
(Outpost line along Eerft canal, from bridge at Morkem to bridge at Bedburg.)		
Regiment remained halted (with outpost line in position) about ...	Bedburg	Dec. 6
Regiment marched to the Rhine and billeted at	H.Q., Nievenheim A Squadron, Ukerath B Squadron, Delrath C Squadron Sturzelburg	Dec. 7
(Outpost line along the Rhine from Zons to Sturzelburg.)		
Regiment remained halted (with outpost line in position) about	Nievenheim...	Dec. 8
Regiment marched to Cologne and occupied	Artillery barracks at Riehl, on the outskirts of Cologne	Dec. 9
Regiment remained at	Riehl	Dec. 10–Dec. 11
Regiment crossed the Hohenzollern bridge and marched to billets at	H.Q., Opladen A Squadron, Quettingen B Squadron, Neu Kirchen C Squadron, Opladen	Dec. 12
(Outpost line from Bursheid to Opladen.)		

APPENDIX A

Event.	*Place.*	*Date*
		1918
Regiment marched to the Perimiter and billeted	H.Q., Sollingen A. Squadron, Sollingen B Squadron, Haan C Squadron, Wald	Dec. 13

(Outpost line from railway east of Sollingen to railway west of Haan.)

Regiment remained on the Perimiter billeted about	Sollingen	Dec. 14
Regiment marched to Cologne, billeted at	Artillery barracks at Riehl	Dec. 15
Regiment marched to billets at ...	Bedburg	Dec. 16
Regiment remained in billets at ...	Bedburg	Dec. 17–31
		1919
Regiment remained in billets at ...	Bedburg	Jan. 1 to Apr. 6
Regiment marched to fresh billets at ...	Kerpen ... ... H.Q. and Transport at Schloss and Lorsfield	Apr. 7
Regiment remained at	Kerpen	Apr. 8 to June 15
Regiment remained at	Kerpen	June 16

(Regiment supplied a detachment to the Mobile Column on the Perimiter. This column was away June 16 to July 1st.)

Regiment remained at	Kerpen	June 17 to Aug. 15

(A composite squadron marched to Cologne to take part in a ceremonial parade, and was away Aug. 15–18.)

Regiment remained at	Kerpen	Aug. 19–29

(Equipment and baggage of Regiment left by train for Ireland, Aug. 29.)

Regiment remained at	Kerpen	Aug. 30 to Sept. 1
Regiment entrained at Buir	In the train	Sept. 2
Regiment travelled	In the train	Sept. 3
Regiment embarked at Calais ...	At sea	Sept. 4–5
Regiment debarked at Waterford and entrained to barracks at	Kilkenny, Ireland ...	Sept. 6

The horses of the Regiment entrained at Horrem and debarked at Ormskirk (near Liverpool), where they were disposed of.

Appendix B

CASUALTIES

Officers

KILLED IN ACTION

Rank.	*Name.*	*Date.*	*Place.*
Lieut.	J. M. Tylee	... 23/8/1914	... Villers St. Gueslain
Capt.	O. B. Walker	... 23/8/1914	... ?
Lieut.	C. H. S. Whittle	... 24/8/1914	... Offignies
Lieut.	C. M. Hoare	... 24/8/1914	... Offignies
Lieut.	B. Osborne	... 11/11/1914	... Veldhoek
2/Lieut.	A. M. Gaselee	... 24/5/1915	... Nr. Ypres
Lieut.	Hon. A. G. Cubitt	... 24/11/1917	... Bourlon Wood
Lieut.	L. N. Kindersley	... 25/11/1917	... Bourlon Wood
Capt.	J. Arnott	... 30/3/1918	... Warfusee-Abancourt
2/Lieut.	S. J. Marshall	... 8/8/1918	... Rosieres
Capt.	J. N. C. Livingstone-Learmonth	... 24/8/1915	... Dardanelles
Capt.	A. E. Bradshaw (14th Lancers, Indian Army, attd. 15th Hussars...	... 13/10/1914	... Bout Deville
2/Lieut. (T/Major)	L. Parker (15th Hussars, attd R.F.C.)	7/1/1917	... ?

DIED OF WOUNDS

Capt.	W. A. Nugent	... 29/5/1915	... France
Lieut.	Hon. E. C. Hardinge, D.S.O. ...	?	... London

DIED

Capt.	M. A. Muir	?	... East Africa
Capt. & Adjt.	H. H. Jackson, M.C. ...	... ?/12/1918	... In England

WOUNDED

Capt.	R. P. Wells, D.S.O. (Twice)	... 23/8/1914	... Nr Villers St. Gueslain
Lieut.	Hon. E. C. Hardinge, D.S.O.	... 27/8/1914	... Bergues
Capt.	E. H. C. Bald, M.C. ...	... 9/11/1914	... Nr. Hooge
Brig.-Gen.	P. O. Hambro, C.B., C.M.G.	... 10/11/1914	... Nr. Ypres
Major	H. D. Bramwell	... 10/5/1915	... Nr. Wieltje
Lieut.	Sir J. F. Grey, Bt.	... 10/5/1915	... Nr. Wieltje
Capt.	Hon. W. A. Nugent ...	... 13/5/1915	... Nr. Ypres
Capt.	A. Courage, D.S.O., M.C.	... 13/5/1915	... Nr. Ypres
Lieut.	R. B. de B. Hodge	... 19/5/1915	... Nr. Ypres
Capt.	C. Nelson, D.S.O. (Twice) ...	... 21/5/1915	... Nr. Ypres
2/Lieut.	A. B. Smith	... 24/5/1915	... Nr. Ypres (gassed)
Lieut.	H. F. Brace, D.S.O., M.C.	... 24/5/1915	... Nr. Ypres
Capt.	H. F. Brace, D.S.O., M.C.	... 24/11/1917	... Bourlon Wood
2/Lieut.	S. P. L. A. Lithgow ...	... 10/12/1917	... Laneuville
Lieut.	C. H. Liddle	... 22/3/1918	... Roisel
Lieut.	R. B. Harvie	... 22/3/1918	... Roisel
Lieut.	H. N. Gatonby	... 25/3/1918	... Montauban
Lieut.	T. F. C. Frost	... 30/3/1918	... Warfusee-Abancourt
2/Lieut.	H. W. Palmer	... 8/8/1918	... Nr. Rosieres
Capt	R. V. Pollok (with Irish Guards)		

OFFICERS—WOUNDED (continued).

Rank.	*Name.*	*Date.*	*Place.*
Lieut.	R. F. E. Rhodes, M.C. ...	... 8/8/1918	... Nr. Rosieres
Lieut.	J. C. Rogerson	... 23/8/1914	... Nr. Villers St. Gueslain
Lieut.	P. Anderson ... ... (Beds. Yeomanry attd. 15th Hussars)	... 8/10/1918	... Serain

OTHER RANKS

KILLED IN ACTION

No.	*Rank.*	*Name.*	*Date.*	*Place.*
14033	Pte.	Andrews, J.... ...	... 25/11/1917	... Bourlon Wood
11537	L/Corpl.	Aplin, D.	... 25/11/1917	... Bourlon Wood
26500	Pte.	Archer, W. J. ...	... 22/3/1918	... Roisel
46378	Sergt.	Ashton, W. J. ...	... 25/11/1917	... Bourlon Wood
4457	Pte.	Baker, R.	... 13/10/1914	... Bourdeville
3961	S.Q.M.S.	Barker, G.	... 13/8/1914	... Aisne
2510	Pte.	Barrs, E. R. ...	... 24/5/1915	... Nr. Ypres
4631	Pte.	Beckwith, A. W. ...	... 4/11/1914	... Nr. Gheluvelt
11402	L/Corpl.	Berry, W., M.M. ...	... 8/8/1918	... Rosieres
8301	Pte.	Biffin, W. T. ...	... 25/11/1917	... Bourlon Wood
10807	Pte.	Binstead, T.... ...	... 30/3/1918	... Warfusee-Abancourt
331488	Pte.	Bottomley, S. ...	... 25/11/1917	... Bourlon Wood
16844	Pte.	Bowyer, C. J. ...	... 30/3/1918	... Warfusee-Abancourt
15003	Pte.	Brown, F.	... 25/11/1917	... Bourlon Wood
234	Pte.	Brown, G.	... 1/11/1914	... Hooge
46268	Sergt.	Byrne, F.	... 27/10/1917	... ?
10938	Pte.	Carter, J., M.M. ...	... 25/11/1917	... Bourlon Wood
46386	Corpl.	Caygill, J. D. ...	... 22/3/1918	... Roisel
3986	Pte.	Chelson, T.	... 10/9/1914	... Missy
27371	Pte.	Cherrett, E. ...	... 25/11/1917	... Bourlon Wood
10337	Trptr.	Cheshire, A. G. ...	... 30/3/1918	... Warfusee-Abancourt
24083	Pte.	Coghlan, T.... ...	... 25/11/1917	... Bourlon Wood
4232	Pte.	Cox, J.	... 24/5/1915	... Nr. Ypres
2907	Corpl.	Crowhurst, H. ...	... 24/5/1915	... Nr. Ypres
15984	Pte.	Dalgleish, W. S. ...	... 25/11/1917	... Bourlon Wood
1089	Pte.	Dalton, J. J. ...	... 1/11/1914	... Hooge
7311	Sergt.	Darley, W., D.C.M.	... 25/3/1918	... Bernafay Wood
21436	Pte.	Delafield, H. ...	... 8/8/1918	... Rosieres
619	Pte.	Doughty, H. ...	... 13/10/1914	... Bourdeville
5709	Pte.	Duthie, J.	... 11/11/1914	... Nr. West Hoek
29790	Pte.	Eatwell, J.	... 30/3/1918	... Warfusee-Abancourt
230	Pte.	Edwards, F. ...	... 22/3/1918	... Roisel
1020	Sergt.	Everest, E. E. ...	... 25/11/1917	... Bourlon Wood
23222	Pte.	Farmer, L. E.	... 22/3/1918	... Roisel
841	Pte.	Francis, W. C. G.	... 1/11/1914	... Hooge
4721	Pte.	French, F.	... 13/5/1915	... Nr. Ypres
604	Pte.	Gardner, W. G. ...	... 13/10/1914	... Bourdeville
4747	Pte.	Gurdin, L.	... 1/11/1914	... Hooge
29852	Pte.	Harris, F.	... 22/3/1918	... Roisel
8957	Pte.	Harrold, W. J. ...	... 25/11/1917	... Bourlon Wood
5924	Pte.	Handscombe, F. W.	... 8/4/1917	... ?
5381	Pte.	Hayes, A.	... 21/5/1915	... Hooge
9745	Pte.	Haynes, S.	... 24/8/1914	... Offignies
9723	Pte.	Hibbert, C. ...	... 25/11/1917	... Bourlon Wood
11229	L/Corpl.	Hide, P.	... 25/11/1917	... Bourlon Wood
34019	Pte.	Hill, S. H.	... 10/11/1918	... Ath
4262	Pte	Holmes, H J. ...	... 24/8/14	... Offignies.

APPENDIX B

OTHER RANKS—KILLED IN ACTION (continued).

No.	*Rank.*	*Name.*	*Date.*	*Place.*
29798	Pte.	Horwood, G. ...	... 8/8/1918	... Rosieres
2945	Pte.	Hudson, G. W. ...	... 25/11/1917	... Bourlon Wood
8861	Pte.	Hunt, J.	... 22/3/1918	... Roisel
9460	Pte.	Hurley, A. H. ...	... 8/10/1918	... Nr. Premont
2916	Corpl.	James, W. J. ...	... 24/5/1915	... Nr. Ypres
9488	Pte.	Kemp, W.	... 22/3/1918	... Roisel
1031	Pte.	Keymer, W. ...	... 11/9/1914	... Missy
108	Pte.	Lamb, G. W. ...	... 25/11/1917	... Bourlon Wood
4106	Pte.	Lapwood, S. T. ...	... 13/5/1915	... Nr. Ypres
29631	L/Corpl.	Light, D.	... 25/11/1917	... Bourlon Wood
9439	Pte.	Lowndes, E.... ...	... 8/10/1918	... Nr. Premont
15352	Pte.	Ludditt, F. C. ...	... 30/3/1917	... Vimy
6112	Pte.	MacDonald. J. T. ...	... 24/8/1914	... Offignies
46352	Pte.	Mackey, H. T. ...	... 25/11/1917	... Bourlon Wood
16738	Pte.	Mason, W.	... 12/4/1917	... Vimy
1269	Pte.	McFareland, G. ...	... 22/3/1918	... Roisel
5761	Pte.	McKerron, T. F. ...	... 11/11/1914	... Nr. West Hoek
3813	Pte.	Millar, J.	... 24/5/1915	... Nr. Ypres
4430	Pte.	Moore, W.	... 24/5/1915	... Nr. Ypres
46363	Corpl.	Mundy, C. M. ...	... 25/11/1917	... Bourlon Wood
6095	Pte.	Newman, A. ...	... 30/3/1917	... Vimy
21996	Pte.	Norris, R.	... 25/11/1917	... Bourlon Wood
1022	L/Corpl.	Oliver, A. E. ...	... 24/8/1914	... Offignies
1473	L/Sergt.	Padgham, R. B. ...	... 30/3/1918	... Warfusee-Abancourt
8704	Pte.	Parsons, A. E. ...	... 13/10/1914	... Bourdeville
1048	Pte.	Pegram, R. ...	... 1/11/1914	... Hooge
15059	Pte.	Penhorwood, W. ...	... 25/11/1917	... Bourlon Wood
15375	Corpl.	Phoenix, W. J. ...	... 22/3/1918	... Roisel
4300	Pte.	Prentice, C. J. ...	... 8/8/1918	... Rosieres
23819	Pte.	Regan, M.	... 8/8/1918	... Rosieres
5766	Corpl.	Robinson, J. M. ...	... 1/11/1914	... Hooge
46343	Corpl.	Robinson, L. ...	... 25/11/1917	... Bourlon Wood
7325	Sergt.	Rough, E. C. ...	... 22/3/1918	... Roisel
7344	Pte.	Saunders, A. F. ...	... 24/8/1914	... Offignies
8971	Pte.	Scholey, C.	... 11/8/1918	... Nr. Camon
782	Pte.	Shanks, R.	... 23/3/1918	... Nr. Pargny
5961	Pte.	Sharp, W.	... 25/11/1917	... Bourlon Wood
15097	L/Corpl.	Simmons, F. F. ...	... 30/3/1918	... Warfusee-Abancourt
3304	Sergt.	Sloan, R.	... 25/11/1917	... Bourlon Wood
7390	Pte.	Smith, G.	... 25/11/1917	... Bourlon Wood
10749	Pte.	Smith, T.	... 12/4/1917	... Vimy
4738	Pte.	Bennett, F.	... 30/6/1917	... Thelus (Arras)
11754	Pte.	Southcott, H. ...	... 9/10/1918	... Nr. Premont
8333	Pte.	Spicer, C.	... 30/3/1918	... Warfusee-Abancourt
6943	L/Corpl.	Stent, J. W.... ...	... 27/8/1914	... Bergues
8334	Pte.	Stringfellow, R. ...	... 13/9/1914	... Aisne
9720	Pte.	Sullivan, D. B. ...	... 23/8/1914	... Villers St. Gueslain
26685	Pte.	Sydall, J.	... 30/3/1918	... Warfusee-Abancourt
46275	Pte.	Tallowin, S. T. ...	... 22/3/1918	... Roisel
14024	L/Corpl.	Tolley, B.	... 25/11/1917	... Bourlon Wood
7297	Corpl.	Tuffley, A. ...	... 13/10/1914	... Bourdeville
46322	Pte.	Wallace, E.	... 22/3/1918	... Roisel
8620	Corpl.	Wallis, J.	... 25/11/1917	... Bourlon Wood
1016	L/Corpl.	Walters, T.	... 24/8/1914	... Offignies
46381	Pte.	Welch, H.	... 25/11/1917	... Bourlon Wood
526	Pte.	Wilkes, W.	... 27/8/1914	... Bergues
1007	Pte.	Wilkinson, W. ...	... 8/10/1918	... Nr. Premont

OTHER RANKS—KILLED IN ACTION (continued).

No.	Rank.	Name.	Date.	Place.
7335	Pte.	Wilkinson, G.	24/5/1915	Nr. Ypres
5929	Pte.	Wiseman, J. M.	31/1/1916	?
10339	Pte.	Wraight, R.	23/8/1914	?

DIED OF WOUNDS

No.	Rank.	Name.	Date.	Place.
219	Pte.	Abbott, A. H.	9/10/1918	
11371	Pte.	Amor, G. S.	21/4/1916	
15342	Pte.	Arnold, C.	1/8/1916	
1064	Pte.	Atkinson, G. J.	8/8/1918	
15556	L/Corpl.	Baker, H.	30/3/1918	
9922	Pte.	Barfield, S. P.	14/5/1915	
10916	Pte.	Beasley, J.	28/11/1917	
1067	Pte.	Bowman, J.	11/11/1914	
4113	Sergt.	Brear, E.	17/11/1914	In England
8345	L/Corpl.	Burgess, C. A.	26/5/1915	
15534	Pte.	Butcher, J. A.	27/3/1918	In German hands
23099	Pte.	Cummins, A. E.	1/4/1918	
11227	L/Corpl.	Darkins, B. F.	28/11/1917	
8633	Pte.	Davey, R. H.	11/4/1917	
255503	Pte.	Fowkes, W. H.	11/4/1918	
9681	Pte.	Fowles, A. T.	1/2/1916	
4003	Pte.	Freeman, F.	22/7/1917	
9141	Pte.	Greensmith, F.	4/6/1915	
9650	Pte.	Halsley, H. J.	13/9/1914	Blangies, Belgium
15705	Pte.	Henderson, H. F.	2/1/1918	
8608	L/Corpl.	Herriott, H. A.	28/8/1914	Mons
4525	Pte.	Kirkby, A. H.	6/6/1915	
23121	Pte.	Lyons, J.	25/11/1917	
11238	Pte.	Marsden, A. J. W.	16/10/1918	
9162	Pte.	Napper, C.	25/5/1915	
14039	Pte.	Pearcey, A.	1/6/1915	
10201	Corpl.	Pope, J.	13/5/1915	
8290	Corpl.	Rawlins, A.	3/6/1915	
44	Pte.	Riddle, J. E.	22/11/1914	
4446	Pte.	Sears, H.	14/5/1915	
46365	Pte.	Spurden, A.	23/3/1918	
8347	Pte.	Swire, E. G.	9/8/1918	
5567	S.S.	Lipton, J. V	24/8/1914	Blangies, Belgium

DIED

No.	Rank.	Name.	Date.	Place.
4339	S.S.M. (O.R.S.)	Allen, T. H.	2/2/1917	In England
26992	Pte.	Bailey, W.	14/10/1915	
5989	Pte.	Bland, C.	13/4/1915	Whilst prisoner of war
11550	Pte.	Edgley, C.	27/12/1917	
10895	Corpl.	Green, T.	14/12/1915	
11711	Pte.	Jeremiah, J. V.	31/10/1918	
8340	Pte.	Martin, S. A.	10/11/1914	
3894	Pte.	May, E.	3/6/1915	In England
46316	Pte.	McEvoy, B.	23/10/1918	In England
3875	Trptr.	Mead, G. F.	26/7/1915	In England
29352	Pte.	Payne, A. J.	14/6/1915	In England
26545	Pte.	Rumbold, H.	9/7/1916	Drowned at Etten-court Riviere
15585	L/Corpl.	Slade, G.	13/9/1918	Whilst prisoner of war
4730	Pte.	Smith, F.	7/10/1917	Liverpool
5561	Pte.	Stafford, T. J.	7/3/1915	
8717	Pte.	Vaus, N.	27/12/1914	

537303 L/Corpl. Turner, W. Killed whilst on patrol duty in Dublin.

OTHER RANKS (continued).

WOUNDED

WOUNDED THREE TIMES.

H/9148 Cpl. Dable, W., D.C.M.
H/2543 Pte. Sharp, C.

WOUNDED TWICE.

H/46312 Sgt. Arthur, F.
H/26258 L./Cpl. Appleby, H.
H/482 Pte. Baldwin, W., M.M.
4282 Pte. Bairstow, J.
H/14944 Pte. Buckingham, W.
H/15563 L/Cpl. Coles, G.
H/46261 FS./Sgt. Dennis, F. S.
H/9916 Pte. Evans, A.
H/7494 Sgt. Francis, J., D.C.M., M.M.
H/10891 Pte. Gent, F.
H/1614 Pte. Green, R.
H/46388 Pte. Gosden, H.
H/11522 Pte. Gower, H.
H/46329 Pte. Hardbattle, J.
H/11393 Pte. Hickey, E.
H/1862 Pte. Hensley, F.
H/10925 Pte. Hadingham, E.
H/495 Cpl. Johnson, J.
H/15628 Pte. Jacobs, H.
H/1289 Sgt. Kell, C.
H/1000 Sgt. Lewis, J.
H/2425 Cpl. Munn, A.
H/2262 Pte. McCarthy, W.
H/5751 S./Sgt. Nicholson, J.
H/1038 Pte. Neville, F., D.C.M., M.M.
H/1678 Sgt. Oliver, J., D.C.M.
H/2596 Sgt. Pangborn, J.
H/2935 Pte. Parsons, G.
4686 Pte. Parsons, S.
H/358 Sgt. Ryland, C.
H/7320 Pte. Sumner, H.
H/2937 Pte. Stenton, H.
H/6094 Pte. Scrivens, F.
H/3596 Pte. Thrussell, F.
H/26670 Pte. Titchener, W.
H/9649 Pte. Vickers, V.

WOUNDED.

H/5948 Cpl. Allix, H.
H/7358 Sgt. Appleton, I.
H/46264 Pte. Andrews, E.
H/46394 Pte. Abrahams, H.
L/31167 Pte. Abbott, H.*
H/10892 Pte. Ager, F.
H/2556 L./Cpl. Burridge, W.
4538 Pte. Batchelor, S.
H/6686 Cpl. Bunn, H.
H/1035 Pte. Barber, W.
H/224 Pte. Bell, E.
H/2294 Pte. Buck, S.
H/8075 Pte. Bailey, J.
H/46377 Pte. Burnett, D.
H/10767 SS./Cpl. Billings, G.
H/29328 Pte. Bullen, C.
H/989 Pte. Brookes, A.
H/23411 Pte. Boomer, W., M.M.
H/10573 Pte. Burgoyne, W.
H/11225 Pte. Baker, A.
4340 Pte. Baldwin, E.
H/23045 Pte. Bentley, E.
4518 Pte. Brewer, J.
H/21557 Sdr./Cpl. Barber, E.
H/29069 Pte. Bishop, G.
H/9556 Pte. Barfe, L.
H/7346 Pte. Cuthbert, A.
H/3718 Pte. Capps, W.
H/8090 Sgt./Cook Corbel, W.
H/9498 Pte. Causer, J.
H/4516 S.Q.M.S. Clark, E., D.C.M.
H/11504 Pte. Cunningham, E.
H/220 Pte. Cade, J.
H/9751 S./Sgt. Charnick, G.
H/46375 L./Cpl. Cradduck, S.
H/8628 Pte. Croxford, T.
H/10198 Sgt. Clayton, G.
H/7798 Sgt. Clarke, C.
H/46346 Pte. Cratchley, W.
H/46274 Pte. Coates, A.
H/11055 L./Cpl. Chittleburgh, G.
H/46374 Cleere, P.
H/93 Pte. Canning, S.
H/18554 Pte. Cressy, W.
H/2069 Pte. Coleman, W.
H/9502 Pte. Clarke, W.
H/27514 Pte. Collingbourne, A.
H/33035 Pte. Catlin, H.
H/27784 Pte. Croft, J.
H/29632 Cpl. Cook, A., M.M.
H/11639 Pte. Carroll, A.
L/11059 Pte. Core, J.*
H/5790 Pte. Derrick, W.
4717 Pte. Davis, H.
3949 Pte. Donovan, T.
H/18973 Pte. Dawson, G.
H/15565 Pte. Deacon, A.
H/4430 Cpl. Dennison, R., M.M.
H/15027 Pte. Dorey, H.
H/19091 Pte. Douglas, H.
H/10338 Cpl. Derrick, C.
H/6688 Pte. Dawson, E.
H/10902 Pte. Dipple, C.
H/1761 Pte. Dwyer, J.
H/8916 Pte. Dennison, A.
H/27764 Pte. Downing, W.

* Beds. Yeomanry attached.

OTHER RANKS—WOUNDED (continued).

H/46371 SS./Cpl. Dobson, J.
H/19597 Pte. Danbury, J.
H/10170 Pte. Eade, W.
H/10574 Pte. Evans, A.
H/46323 Sgt. Evans, W.
H/6689 Pte. Fearon, H.
H/3594 Pte. Frost, A.
H/2939 Pte. Foster, S.
H/9761 Pte. Ferns, E.
H/2783 Sgt. Frost, W., M.M.
H/2784 Sgt. Frost, J.
4410 Sgt. Flight, H.
H/5784 Pte. Fontaine, H.
H/46712 Pte. Flynn, S.
H/1015 Cpl. Fossey, C., D.C.M.,M.M.
H/46651 Cpl. Fordham, B.
H/30948 Pte. Farrington, H.
H/1011 Sdr./Cpl. Goddard, W.
4705 Pte. George, G.
H/426 Pte. Garker, G.
H/9451 Pte. Golder, W.
H/5749 Pte. Goater, W.
H/46283 Pte. Guiney, W.
H/7319 Pte. Gale, W.
H/11035 Pte. Gess, J.
H/7132 Pte. Gregory, E.
H/2890 S./Sgt. Ginn, A.
H/15451 Cpl. Gillies, A.
H/9867 Pte. Grant, E.
H/15433 Pte. Gray, C.
H/734 Pte. Griffiths, J., M.M.
H/33674 Pte. Gradwell, A.
L/30757 Pte. Gearey, P.*
H/27547 Pte. Greenaway, A.
H/2829 Pte. Grainge, A.
H/46403 Sdr./Cpl. Harris, A.
4546 Pte. Horwood, F.
H/9149 Pte. Harris, J.
H/7365 Cpl. Hatto, C.
H/3987 Far./Sgt. Henney, C.
4275 Sgt. Hough, W.
H/8705 Cpl. Haffenden, H.
H/8095 Pte. Hughes, L.
H/1014 Cpl. Harris, J.
H/5947 Pte. Holmes, H.
H/3029 Pte. Haynes, G.
H/16354 Pte. Hannam, T.
H/1017 L./Cpl. Harford, C., D.C.M.
H/10789 Pte. Howell, H.
H/11299 Pte. Hodson, E.
4568 Pte. Hempinstall, H.
H/9130 Pte. Hassell, A.
4709 L./Cpl. Hallowell, L.
H/46359 Pte. Haynes, S.
H/221 Cpl. Hill, A.
H/11033 Cpl. Hawkes, H.
4665 Pte. Hines, G.
H/29799 Pte. Hedges, W.
H/29653 Pte. Harber, A.
H/9712 Pte. Hussey, J.
H/4223 L./Cpl. Harris, F.
H/9737 Pte. Hudson, T.
H/117 Cpl. Harse, A.
H/301068 Pte. Ham, E.
H/15085 Cpl. Haynes, F.
L/31124 Pte. Harding, H.*
L/31109 Pte. Hipwell, E.*
H/18636 Cpl. Holton, E.
H/11234 Cpl. Hartnell, J.
L/30810 Pte. Hall, J.*
H/15409 Pte. Inglis, J.
H/46379 Pte. Jones, J.
H/2570 Pte. Hayward, F.
H/29748 Pte. Jordan, J.
H/498 Pte. Green, R.
H/18914 Pte. John, F.
H/46395 Sgt. Jeffrey, A.
H/226 Pte. Jennings, H.
H/11032 Pte. Jones, D.
H/46326 Pte. Jones, A.
H/29876 Pte. Jones, A.
H/18920 L./Cpl. Jones, G.
L/30120 Pte. James, W.*
H/18700 Cpl. Jordan, R.
4456 Pte. Kent, F.
H/7312 Sdr./Cpl. King, E.
H/7235 Pte. Keen, F.
H/29270 Pte. Kinsey, J.
H/18986 Pte. Kinchin, G.
H/216 Pte. Kelly, T.
H/10199 Pte. Keegan, J.
H/3004 Pte. Knight, W.
H/19159 Pte. Kenward, A.
H/2153 Cpl. Lowen, J.
H/10336 Pte. Lawrence, R.
H/5974 Pte. Latter, W.
H/8708 Pte. Leek, J.
H/15564 Pte. Lambert, F.
H/27324 Cpl. Legate, F.
H/15369 L./Cpl. Lawley, G.
H/2824 Pte. Locke, R.
H/46317 Pte. Lee, T.
H/1006 Pte. Lomax, J.
4433 Cpl. Murphy, J.
H/9652 Pte. McMillan, J.
3501 S.Q.M.S. Mills, J., M.M.
H/46305 Pte. Moore, W.
4750 Pte. Martin, H.
H/5772 Sgt. Mackay, W., D.C.M.
H/1021 Pte. Maylott, W.
H/2425 Cpl. Munn, A.
4413 Sgt. Moss, T.
H/46759 Pte. Marshall, E.
H/1045 Pte. Meadows, W.
H/8609 Pte. Merritt, F.

* Beds. Yeomanry attached.

OTHER RANKS—WOUNDED (continued).

H/19009 Pte. Matthews, J.
H/18302 Pte. Medway, E.
H/7223 Pte. Montague, G.
H/46316 Pte. McEvoy, B.
H/46262 Pte. McCormick, J.
H/5932 Pte. Moore, A.
H/46390 Pte. Meynell, F.
H/46368 Sgt. Medhurst, A.
H/6128 Trptr. McNeill, W.
H/255492 Pte. Moore, C.
H/14621 Pte. Nicholson, G.
H/7296 Pte. Nayler, A.
H/1105 Pte. Nolan, P.
H/46391 Pte. Norman, J.
H/3218 Pte. Neale, G.
H/9698 Pte. Ogden, H.
H/8280 Pte. Orton, L.
H/6015 Trptr. Osliff, C.
L/30700 Pte. Odd, H.*
H/8084 Pte. Perry, W.
H/1052 Sgt. Pike, A.
H/46385 Pte. Peters, A.
H/11222 Pte. Pilgrim, B.
H/990 Pte. Pullen, F.
H/7158 Pte. Poat, J.
H/386 Pte. Pascoe, D.
H/46340 Pte. Pickles, E.
H/27504 Pte. Poole, S.
H/9685 Pte. Price, W.
H/29703 Pte. Payne, G.
H/7230 Pte. Powell, T.
H/7336 Cpl. Page, C., M.M.
H/29627 Pte. Pinnions, F.
H/47340 Pte. Press, A.
H/10922 Sgt. Poole, W., M.M.
H/8922 Pte. Piper, A.
H/1010 Pte. Perryman, A.
H/46299 SS./Cpl. Ryland, A.
H/11190 Pte. Ridge, E.
H/9888 Sgt. Robinson, F.
4680 Pte. Rushworth, W.
H/2936 Pte. Russell, G.
4132 Pte. Richards, T.
4755 L./Cpl. Rayment, J.
H/14017 Pte. Roake, R.
H/21433 Pte. Reynolds, R.
H/27492 Pte. Rogers, S.
H/2401 Pte. Rumsey, S.
H/14606 Sgt. Reynolds, H., D.C.M.
H/14180 Pte. Rogers, W.
H/21346 Pte. Richardson, C.
H/9742 Pte. Spencer, A.
H/29 L./Cpl. Stanyer, S.
H/7328 Cpl. Spicer, T.
H/8279 Pte. Shaw, F.
H/11380 Pte. Stringer, W.
H/7225 Cpl. Stevenson, H.
4653 Sgt. Storey, F.
H/8899 Pte. Sands, F.
H/15635 Pte. Smith, R.
H/9654 Pte. Simpson, R.
H/16680 Pte. Stone, A.
H/3212 Pte. Skinner, C.
H/15461 Pte. Stuchbery, F.
H/18595 L./Cpl. Smouth, S.
H/29930 Pte. Stott, J.
H/8711 Pte. Sartie, W.
H/986 Sgt. Smith, H.
H/27470 Pte. Sexton, A.
H/8094 Pte. Smith, A., M.M.
H/11240 Cpl. Shaw, R.
H/32288 Pte. Stephens, C.
H/7487 Sgt. Turnbull, G.
H/46315 Pte. Tuttlebee, W.
H/46396 Pte. Taylor, E.
H/16315 Pte. Thirkill, G.
H/7149 Sgt. Thorne, A., M.M.
H/107 Sgt. Thompson, C.
H/17158 Pte. Tarrant, G.
H/46399 Pte. Vaughan, T.
H/1012 U./L./Cpl. Vowell, J.
H/15303 Pte. Vaughan, J.
L/30097 Cpl. Vincent, E.*
H/9697 Pte. Winterbottom, E.
H/9499 Pte. Watkins, C.
H/1025 Sgt. Wood, F.
H/9485 Pte. Wass, S.
H/9674 Pte. Waeland, A.
H/9653 Pte. Wade, P.
H/15000 Pte. Wilkinson, V.
H/9662 Pte. Worker, J.
H/15522 Pte. Wright, H.
H/11514 Pte. Watkins, A.
H/8904 Sgt. Witt, W., M.M.
H/10780 L./Cpl. Webb, A.
H/9655 Pte. Webb, P.
H/10919 Cpl. West, W.
H/27531 Pte. Webb, F.
H/21873 Pte. Watkins, A.
H/1616 Cpl. Wilson, E.
H/3871 Cpl. Withey, C.
H/256796 Cpl. Wilshire, R.
H/5853 Cpl. Wall, S.
L/30249 Cpl. White, C.*
L/30269 Pte. Warren, H.*
L/30465 Pte. Warren, P.*
H/27429 Pte. Watkins, A.

MISSING.

H/15375 Cpl. Phoenix, W.
H/29852 Pte. Harris, F.
H/8861 Pte. Hunt, J.
H/9488 Pte. Kemp, W.
H/23222 Pte. Farmer, L.

* Beds. Yeomanry attached.

Appendix C

LIST OF HONOURS AND REWARDS GAINED BY OFFICERS AND OTHER RANKS OF THE 15TH THE KING'S HUSSARS DURING THE GREAT WAR 1914–1919

K.C.B.

Major-General Sir W. E. Peyton, K.C.V.O., C.B., D.S.O.
Major-General F. H. Sykes, C.M.G.

K.C.M.G.

Colonel H. A. L. Tagart, C.B., D.S.O.
Major-General H. W. Hodgson, C.B., C.V.O.

K.B.E.

Major-General Sir F. H. Sykes, K.C.B., C.M.G.
Major-General P. O. Hambro, C.B. C.M.G.

K.C.V.O.

Major-General W. E. Peyton, C.V.O., C.B., D.S.O.

C.B.

Colonel H. A. L. Tagart, D.S.O.
Major and Brevet-Colonel P. O. Hambro, C.M.G.
Major-General H. W. Hodgson, C.V.O.
Brigadier-General Sir F. Meyrick, Bart.

C.M.G.

Brevet-Lieutenant-Colonel F. H. Sykes.
Major and Brevet-Lieutenant-Colonel P. O. Hambro.
Major S. H. Charrington, D.S.O.
Lieutenant-Colonel Lord Kensington, D.S.O.
Brigadier-General Sir F. Meyrick, Bart., C.B.

C.B.E.

Major R. V. Pollok (now Irish Guards), D.S.O.

D.S.O.

Lieutenant Hon. E. C. Hardinge.
Major F. C. Pilkington.
Captain C. Nelson.
Major R. V. Pollok (Irish Guards).
Captain S. H. Charrington.
Captain R. P. Collings-Wells.
Captain H. F. Brace.
Major and Brevet-Lieutenant-Colonel A. Courage.
Captain Hon. J. D. Y. Bingham.

APPENDIX C

BAR TO D.S.O.

Major H. Combe, D.S.O. (3rd Hussars attached).

O.B.E.

Major J. Knowles.
Major W. P. Cantrell-Hubbersty.
Captain R. P. Collings-Wells, D.S.O.
Captain E. C. Coates.
Captain B. Ritchie.
Major G. A. Meakin.

MILITARY CROSS.

Captain A. Courage.
Captain C. J. L. Stanhope.
Lieutenant D. K. L. the Maclaine of Lochbuie
Captain J. Arnott.
2nd Lieutenant J. M. Grant.
Captain and Adjutant H. H. Jackson.
Lieutenant W. P. Alcock.
Lieutenant F. J. Bridges, 15th Hussars, attached Machine-Gun Corps.
Captain J. B. Wheeler, 15th Hussars attached Signals.
Lieutenant J. F. Blakeborough.
2nd Lieutenant J. C. Thomson.
Lieutenant V. H. Bicker-Caarten, Bedfordshire Yeomanry, attached.
Captain F. A. Nicolson.
Lieutenant G. H. Straker.
Captain E. H. C. Bald.
Lieutenant P. P. Curtis
Lieutenant L. J. G. Souchon.
Captain H. F. Brace, D.S.O.
Lieutenant R. F. E. Rhodes.
2nd Lieutenant J. T. Macnab, Bedfordshire Yeomanry, attached.
Lieutenant D. P. Tennant.
Captain and Adjutant R. H. O. Hanbury.
Captain R. H. Tribe, Royal Army Medical Corps, attached.

BARS TO MILITARY CROSS.

Major K. D. L. the Maclaine of Lochbuie.

VICTORIA CROSS.

7368 Corporal Garforth.

DISTINGUISHED CONDUCT MEDALS.

1678 Sgt. Oliver.
3586 Sgt. Blishen.
4633 Sgt. Papworth (Commissioned).
5772 L/Sgt. Mackay (Commissioned).
7311 Corpl. Darley.
2700 Corpl. Potter (Commissioned).
8078 Corpl. Shephard (Commissioned).
728 L/Corpl. Aspinall.
1038 Pte. Neville.
8290 Corpl. Rawlins.
4472 S.S.M. Godden.
4654 Sgt. Burrough (Commissioned).
7341 Sgt. Durnford (Commissioned).
4259 L/Sgt. Dalby.
4111 Sgt. Johnson (Commissioned).
18616 L/Corpl. Thomas (Commissioned).
3801 Sgt. Trptr. Wheal (Commissioned).
9148 Pte. Dable.
578 S.S.M. H. Jordison (Commissioned).
7494 Sgt. Francis, M.M.
4823 Corpl. Holmes (Commissioned).
3158 L/Sgt. Earl.
4516 Sgt. Clark.
1017 Pte. Harford.
9440 Pte. Price.
4506 Trptr. Hopgood.
1020 Sgt. Everest.
1015 L/Corpl. Fossey, M.M.
14606 Corpl. Reynolds.
46377 S.S.M. Hannam.

BAR TO D.C.M.

3586 S.S.M. Blishen.

APPENDIX C

MILITARY MEDALS.

11402 L/Corpl. Berry.
29632 Corpl. Cook.
11409 L/Corpl. Bonner.
734 Pte. Griffiths.
14897 Sgt. Lawlor.
3501 S.Q.M.S. Mills (Commissioned).
21446 Pte. Primmer.
1082 Sgt. Scarterfield.
4823 Corpl. Holmes (Commissioned).
2504 Pte. Gent.
4430 L/Corpl. Dennison.
23411 Pte. Boomer.
10470 L/Corpl. Evans.
7336 L/Corpl. Page.
1030 Corpl. Dobbs.
2883 Corpl. Frost.
1015 Pte. Fossey.
10762 Pte. Swain.
1038 Pte. Neville.
1026 Pte. Prentice.
1025 Corpl. Wood.
11232 Corpl. Dibble.
Sgt. Dunkley (Bed. Yeo. attached).
21002 S.S.M. Cockram.
1832 Pte. Tanser.
14049 Corpl. Goddard.
10922 L/Corpl. Poole.
8347 Pte. Swire.
3766 Sgt. Lee.
3900 S.Q.M.S. Roberts.
8904 Corpl. Witt.
10181 Corpl. Bradford.
4290 Farr. S. Sgt. Davey.
7371 L/Corpl. Bick.
10892 Pte. Ager.
7325 Sgt. Rough.
8337 Corpl. Jeary.
8094 Pte. Smith.
10938 Pte. Carter.
29422 Pte. Cook.
7494 Sgt. Francis.
Sgt. Brawn (Bed. Yeo. attached).
Pte. White (Bed. Yeo. attached).
Sgt. Bugg (Essex Yeo. attached).
7149 Corpl. Thorne.
16945 L/Corpl. Crook.
Pte. Dunkley (Bed. Yeo attached).
7323 Pte. Baker.*
256794 Corpl. Rawle.
286755 L/Corpl. Lee.
21339 Pte. Hodgson.

BAR TO M.M.

298793 Sgt. Brawn, M.M. (Bed. Yeo. attached).
3900 S.S.M. Roberts, M.M.

MERITORIOUS SERVICE MEDALS.

R.S.M. F. Augood (Commissioned).
Sgt. W. Parr.
S.S.M. M. A. Ayrton.
Sgt. C. (O.R.S.) Tay.
S.S.M. A. B. Ryder.
Pte. J. Beaney.
R.S.M. F. Green.
F.Q.M.S. W. Johnson.
S.S.M. T. E. Holderness.
F.Q.M.S. A. Oliver.
R.Q.M.S. A. Purdy.
R.S.M. G. Drew.
S.S.M. A. Flight.
Pte. W. Craig.

FOREIGN DECORATIONS

RUSSIAN ORDER OF ST. VLADIMAR, 4TH CLASS WITH SWORDS.

Major P. O. Hambro.
Captain and Brevet-Lieutenant-Colonel F. H. Sykes.

RUSSIAN ORDER OF ST. ANNE, 4TH CLASS, INSCRIBED "FOR VALOUR IN WAR."

Lieutenant G. H. Straker.

ITALIAN ORDER OF ST. MAURICE AND ST. LAZARUS, 5TH CLASS.

Major J. Knowles.

MILITARY ORDER OF SAVOY, 3RD CLASS.

Brigadier-General Sir H. W. Hodgson, K.C.M.G., C.B., C.V.O.

BELGIAN WAR CROSS.

Major-General Sir W. E. Peyton, K.C.B., K.C.V.O., D.S.O.

* Was awarded the M.M. for a successful escape from Germany when a prisoner of war.

APPENDIX C

ORDER OF LEOPOLD, 3RD CLASS.

Major-General Sir W. E. Peyton, K.C.B., K.C.V.O., D.S.O.

ORDER OF THE NILE, 2ND CLASS.

Major-General Sir W. E. Peyton, K.C.B., K.C.V.O., D.S.O.
Major-General Sir H. W. Hodgson, K.C.M.G., C.B., C.V.O.

ORDER OF THE NILE, 4TH CLASS.

Captain E. H. C. Bald.

MILITARY ORDER OF AVIS, 2ND CLASS.

Major and Brevet-Lieutenant-Colonel P. O. Hambro, C.B., C.M.G.

LEGION OF HONOUR, 3RD CLASS.

Major-General Sir W. E. Peyton, K.C.B., K.C.V.O., D.S.O.
Major-General Sir F. H. Sykes, K.B.E., K.C.M.G.
Colonel Sir H. A. L. Tagart, K.C.M.G., C.B., D.S.O.

LEGION OF HONOUR, 5TH CLASS.

Captain the Hon. F. A. Nicolson.
Captain G. H. Straker.
Captain J. A. S. Balmain.
Major J. Knowles, O.B.E.

FRENCH CROIX DE GUERRE.

Major A. Courage, D.S.O., M.C.
Captain G. H. Straker.
Major J. Knowles.
Lieutenant-Colonel S. H. Charrington, C.M.G., D.S.O.
Major and Brevet-Colonel P. O. Hambro, C.B., C.M.G.

ORDER OF MERIT AGRICULTURE, 3RD CLASS.

Major and Brevet-Lieutenant-Colonel P. O. Hambro.

ORDER OF MERIT AGRICULTURE, 5TH CLASS.

Major J. A. S. Balmain.

MEDAILLE MILITAIRE.

2720 R.S.M. Ellicock (Commissioned).
3586 Sergt. Blishen.
7341 Corpl. Durnford (Commissioned).
1020 Corpl. Everest.
9440 Pte. Price.
4662 Pte. Petter.
388 Sergt. Ryland.
8078 Corpl. Shephard (Commissioned).
4288 S.S.M. Sexton.
14897 Sergt. Lawlor.

FRENCH CROIX DE GUERRE.

4154 Corpl. Crooks.
14897 Sergt. Lawlor.

BELGIAN CROIX DE GUERRE.

482 Pte. Baldwin.
46357 Sergt. Turner.
50714 S.S.M. Flight (serving with Machine-Gun Corps).

APPENDIX C

ORDINE MILITARE DI SAVOIA commendatori.
Major-General H. W. Hodgson, C.V.O. C.B.

MEDAILLE D'OR MOHAMED ALI.
Lieutenant-Colonel R. P. Collings-Wells, D.S.O.

ORDER OF THE WHITE EAGLE OF SERVIA, 5TH CLASS WITH SWORDS.
Captain B. Ritchie.

THE RISING SUN OF JAPAN, 2ND CLASS.
Major-General Sir Frederick Sykes, K.C.B., C.B.E., C.M.G.

RUSSIAN CROSS OF THE ORDER OF ST. GEORGE, 4TH CLASS.
10181 Corpl. Bradford.
7265 Pte. Hatto.
1585 Pte. Watson.

RUSSIAN MEDAL OF ST. GEORGE, 3RD CLASS.
3211 Pte. Pearce.

ROUMANIAN CROIX DE VIRTUTE MILITARIA, 2ND CLASS.
46760 Sergt. Gillies.

NOTE.—The rank of all Officers, N.C.O.'s and Men is the approximate rank held by the recipients at the time of the bestowal of the Honour.

LONG SERVICE AND GOOD CONDUCT MEDAL

Sgt.-Maj. F. Augood.
S.S.M. W. Blishen, D.C.M.
S.S.M. W. Boorer.
Sgt. S. Brown.
S.Q.M.S. W. Bryan.
Pte. H. Bunn.
S.Q.M.S. J. G. Burbidge.
S.S.Farr. O. Cuthbert.
F.Q.M.S. F. Davey, M.M.
Musician N. Duckitt.
Sgt. J. W. Durrant.
R.S.M. E. E. Dyball.
S.S.M. S. W. Foghill.
Bandmaster J. E. Fox.
S.S.M. F. Godden, D.C.M.
S.S.M. R. A. Head.
Sgt. W. Howard
S.S.M. L. S. Jessup.
Sgt. H. H. Johnson, D.C.M.
S.Q.M.S. R. Johnson.
Pte. T. Loughlan.
Cpl. J. Maris.
S.Q.M.S. J. E. Mills, M.M.
F.Q.M.S. A. Oliver, D.C.M.
Pte. R. Parsons.
Sgt. F. Phillips.
R.Q.M.S. A. Purdy.
S.S.M. E. Richardson.
S.S.M. E. Roberts, M.M.
S.S.M. F. Russell.
Pte. J. Squires.
Pte. J. Sullivan.
Pte. H. Symes.
Orderly Room S.M. C. Tay.
Sgt. Tptr. S. Wheal, D.C.M.
S.Q.M.S. J. A. Wooley.

Appendix D

LIST OF OFFICERS OF THE 15TH THE KING'S HUSSARS AND ATTACHED OFFICERS WHO SERVED WITH HIS MAJESTY'S FORCES FROM 1914–1922

(Note.—The rank and honours shown are those held by officers at the end of the war. * Shows officers who actually served with the Regiment in the Field.)

Lt. Sir Robert Abdy*, Bart.
Lt. R. J. Agnew.
Lt. W. P. Alcock*, M.C.
Col. W. Anderson, D.S.O.
Lt. P. Anderson* (Bedfordshire Yeomanry, attached).
Capt. J. Arnott*, M.C.
Lt. T. J. Arnott.
Lt.-Col. R. J. Aspinall, D.S.O. (killed on July 3rd, 1916, whilst in command of 11th Battalion Cheshire Regiment).
Capt. E. H. Bald*, M.C. (also Adjutant, Armoured Car Brigade, Senussi Campaign, Egypt, 1916–17).
Lt. B. J. L. Banks.
2nd Lt. W. G. Bagnell* (3rd Dragoon Guards, attached).
Major J. A. S. Balmain (Camp Commandant, Fourth Army).
Major F. W. Barrett*.
Lt. V. H. Bicker-Caarten*, M.C. (Bedfordshire Yeomanry, attached).
Capt. P. W. Bewicke.
Lt.-Col. the Hon. J. D. Y. Bingham*, D.S.O. (also raised and commanded 16th Battalion Royal Tank Corps).
Lt. J. F. Blakeborough*, M.C.
Major H. F. Brace*, D.S.O., M.C.
Capt. A. E. Bradshaw* (14th Lancers, Indian Army, attached).
Lt. V. C. I. Bradshaw*.
Lt.-Col. H. D. Bramwell*.
Lt. H. Mc. C. Bramwell.
Lt. F. J. Bridges*, M.C.
Capt. J. H. Brigg* (Bedfordshire Yeomanry, attached).
Capt. H. A. Bruen (Adjutant, Reserve Cavalry Regiment).
Lt. H. A. Boyson*.
Major W. P. Cantrell-Hubbersty, O.B.E. (served overseas with Remount Service).
Brig.-Gen. T. O. W. Champion de Crespigny (commanded Reserve Yeomanry Brigade; also Horse Master, VIII Corps, B.E.F., France).
Brig.-Gen. S. H. Charrington, C.M.G., D.S.O. (served on the Staff in Gallipoli, and with the 2nd Battalion Northamptonshire Regiment in France, and commanded a Brigade Royal Tank Corps).
Lt. D. H. Clerke*.
Capt. Sir Edward Clive Coates*, Bart., O.B.E.
Lt.-Col. R. P. Collings-Wells*, D.S.O., O.B.E. (also commanded an Armoured Car Battery during operations against the Senussi in Western Egypt; also Chief Instructor, Anzac Corps, 1917–18).
Lt. C. Cokayne-Frith.
Lt.-Col. H. Combe*, D.S.O. (3rd Hussars, attached).
Lt. W. D. Connochie* (Royal Army Veterinary Corps, attached).
2nd Lt. F. A. Constable*.
Lt. H. J. Cook* (Bedfordshire Yeomanry, attached).

APPENDIX D

LIST OF OFFICERS (continued).

Brig.-Gen. A. COURAGE*, D.S.O., M.C. (also Royal Tank Corps, commanded 2nd and 5th Brigades Royal Tank Corps).
Capt. H. B. CRESSWELL.
Lt. P. G. CROPPER* (14th Hussars, attached).
Lt. the Hon. A. G. CUBITT*.
Major P. P. CURTIS*, M.C. (also Brig.-Major 59th Infantry Brigade and G.S.O.2 29th and 40th Divisions).
Major F. J. DALGETY (3rd Reserve Cavalry Regiment).
Lt. J. A. F. DALGETY*.
2nd Lt. T. L. DEARBERGH*.
Lt. F. E. DE GROOT* (also served with Royal Tank Corps).
Capt. G. V. DOUGLAS*.
2nd Lt. D. A. DUNCAN*.
Capt. SIR HENRY DUNDAS, Bart.
2nd Lt. W. E. ECCLES.
Capt. SIR HENRY FLOYD*, Bart.
Lt. T. F. C. FROST*.
Lt. C. GARRETT*.
2nd Lt. A. M. GASELEE*.
Lt. H. N. GATONBY*.
Lt. F. N. GILBEY*.
2nd Lt. O. H. GILBEY.
Major J. GODMAN* (also Adjutant Royal Gloucestershire Hussars, served in Gallipoli).
Capt. J. M. GRANT*, M.C.
Capt. F. W. GREETHAM.
Lt. SIR JOHN GREY*, Bart.
Lt. J. A. GUTHRIE.
Lt. J. HAGGAS*.
Maj.-Gen. SIR PERCIVAL HAMBRO, K.B.E., C.B., C.M.G. (served on the Staff with the B.E.F. in France throughout the War).
Capt. R. H. O. HANBURY*, M.C.
Lt. the Hon. E. HARDINGE*, D.S.O.
Lt. R. B. HARVIE*.
Lt. J. B. HAYTER*.
Lt.-Col. E. HILL*, D.S.O., T.D. (Essex Yeomanry, attached).
Lt. W. R. HINDE.
2nd Lt. C. M. HOARE*.
Lt. R. B. DE B. HODGE*.
Maj.-Gen. SIR HENRY HODGSON, K.C.M.G., C.B., C.V.O. (commanded a Yeomanry Brigade in Gallipoli and during the campaign against the Senussi; commanded the Western Force in Egypt; commanded the Australian and New Zealand Mounted Division throughout the successful operations in Palestine; commanded at Damascus).
2nd Lt. W. M. Holden.
Major J. W. HUMPHREY.
Capt. L. HUNTER* (14th Hussars, attached).
2nd Lt. A. IRELAND* (Bedfordshire Yeomanry, attached).
Capt. H. H. JACKSON*, M.C.
Lt. H. J. JOEL*.
Lt. R. W. JAMESON (The Worcestershire Regiment).
Hon. Capt. and Qr. Mr. H. JORDISON*, D.C.M.
Major L. E. KENNARD.
Lt.-Col. the Rt. Hon. LORD KENSINGTON, C.M.G., D.S.O. (commanded the Welsh Horse, Gallipoli and Palestine).
Lt. L. N. KINDERSLEY*.
Major J. KNOWLES, O.B.E. (Military Secretary, Second Army).
Lt. L. LATREILLE*.
2nd Lt. H. B. LAUGHTON.

APPENDIX D

LIST OF OFFICERS (continued).

Capt. N. W. LEAF*.
2nd Lt. J. G. LEAF.
Capt. SIR THOMAS LEES, Bart. (died of wounds received in Gallipoli August 24th, 1915, whilst serving with the Dorset Yeomanry).
2nd Lt. R. M. LEIR*.
Major C. H. LIDDELL*.
Lt. S. P. L. LITHGOW*.
Capt. N. J. LIVINGSTONE-LEARMONTH (killed in Gallipoli August 24th, 1915, whilst Adjutant Dorset Yeomanry).
Lt. W. J. M. LOWE*.
Gen. SIR GEORGE LUCK (Colonel, 15th Hussars, died December 10th, 1916).
Capt. K. D. L. the MACLAINE OF LOCHBUIE*, M.C.
Lt. J. T. MACNAB*, M.C. (Bedfordshire Yeomanry, attached).
Lt. E. R. MANNING*.
Hon. Capt. and Qr. Mr. F. C. MARSH*.
2nd Lt. S. J. MARSHALL*.
Major G. A. MEAKIN, O.B.E.
Lt. G. MEGAW (Royal Wiltshire Yeomanry).
Brig.-Gen. SIR FREDERICK MEYRICK, Bart., C.B., C.M.G. (commanded 2/1 South Wales Mounted Brigade and No. 3 Base Remount Depot, France).
Lt. T. F. MEYRICK.
Capt. J. F. MONTAGU*.
Capt. M. A. MUIR (died in Central Africa, 18th July, 1916, whilst Adjutant of 1st King's African Rifles).
Major C. NELSON*, D.S.O. (also served in the Afghan Campaign, 1919).
Major the Hon. F. A. NICOLSON*, M.C. (Lord Carnock).
Lt.-Col. H. E. NORTON, D.S.O. (commanded 7th (South Irish Horse) Battalion, Royal Irish Regiment and 18th Battalion Tank Corps).
Capt. the Hon. W. A. NUGENT*.
Lt. B. OSBORNE*.
2nd Lt. H. W. PALMER*.
Lt. E. G. PEASE*.
Lt. L. V. PEGRUM*.
Capt. C. J. L. STANHOPE*, M.C. (the Rt. Hon. the Earl of Harrington).
Lt.-Gen. SIR WILLIAM PEYTON, K.C.B., K.C.V.O., D.S.O. (commanded 2nd Mounted Division in Egypt; commanded the Yeomanry in Gallipoli; commanded expedition against the Senussi in Western Desert; Military Secretary to Commander-in-Chief in France; commanded Reserve Army X Corps and 40th Division in France; commanded the Cavalry of the Rhine; appointed Col. 15th Hussars, December 10th, 1916).
Lt. W. J. PICKERING*.
Lt.-Col. F. C. PILKINGTON*, D.S.O. (also commanded Corps Mounted Troops in Italy).
2nd Lt. L. PARKER (Temporary Major; served with Royal Air Force).
Lt.-Col. R. V. POLLOK, C.B.E., D.S.O. (served with the Irish Guards throughout the War).
Major C. J. RATCLIFF (Gloucestershire Yeomanry and with Staff in Egypt).
Lt. R. F. E. RHODES*, M.C.
Hon. Major and Riding Master F. A. RICHER.
Major B. RITCHIE*, O.B.E. (also Brig.-Maj. Scottish Horse in Gallipoli).
Lt. G. P. V. ROGERS.
Capt. E. H. ROUSE-BOUGHTON*.
Capt. C. SHAW*.
Lt. R. C. SHELTON* (Bedfordshire Yeomanry, attached).
Lt. R. SMEE* (Bedfordshire Yeomanry, attached).
Lt. A. B. SMITH*.
Capt. L. J. G. SOUCHON*, M.C.
Major G. H. STRAKER*, M.C. (Major J. H. Cradock).
Lt. A. C. STRAKER*.

APPENDIX D

List of Officers (continued).

Maj.-Gen. Sir Frederick Sykes, G.B.E., K.C.B., C.M.G. (commanded R.F.C., France and East Mediterranean, 1915–16; A.A.G., War Office; General Staff Supreme War Council, Versailles, 1917–18).
Maj.-Gen. Sir Harold Tagart, K.C.M.G., C.B., D.S.O. (served on Staff Cavalry Corps and later as D.A. and Q.M.G. Home Forces).
Lt. J. W. Tait*.
Lt. D. P. Tennant*, M.C.
Lt. J. C. Thomson*, M.C.
2nd Lt. F. A. Tilsley*.
Capt. R. H. Tribe*, M.C. (Royal Army Medical Corps, attached).
Capt. the Hon. H. H. S. Tufton*.
Lt. J. M. Tylee*.
Capt. O. B. Walker*.
Major J. B. Wheeler, M.C. (served with Cavalry Corps Signals throughout the War).
Lt. C. H. S. Whittle*.
2nd Lt. G. A. Windsor*.
Lt. J. H. C. Wilson*.
Lt. K. C. North*, 4th Hussars
Lt. D. C. M. Lawrie*, 8th Hussars
Lt. J. H. M. Cornwall*, R.F.A.
} Attached to A Squadron during the Battle of the Marne.

LIST OF N.C.O.'S AND MEN OF THE 15TH THE KING'S HUSSARS WHO OBTAINED COMMISSIONS DURING THE WAR

Appleton, Sgt. J. S., The Cheshire Regiment.
Augood, R.S.M. F., Royal Fusiliers (City of London Regiment).
Banks, S.S.M. B. J. L., 15th (The King's) Hussars.
Bishop, S.Q.M.S. J. J., The Devonshire Regiment.
Blinch, L/Cpl. W., The King's Regiment (Liverpool).
Bromley, Cpl. A., The East Lancashire Regiment.
Bryan, S.Q.M.S. W., The East Lancashire Regiment.
Burrough, Sgt. F. C., The Hampshire Regiment.
Clarke, Sgt. C., The Royal Fusiliers (City of London Regiment).
Collins, R.Q.M.S. L., Royal Army Service Corps.
Danter, S.Q.M.S. W. G., The East Surrey Regiment.
Durnford, Sgt. B., The Royal Fusiliers (City of London Regiment).
Dyball, S.S.M. E. E., Surma Valley Light Horse.
Ellicock, R.S.M. J., No. 1 Base Remount Depot (France).
Holmes, Cpl. D., The King's Own Scottish Borderers.
Hough, Sgt. W., The Royal Munster Fusiliers.
Hounsell, S.S.M. T. H., Northern Bengal Mounted Rifles.
Johnson, Sgt. H. M., The East Lancashire Regiment.
Jordison, S.S.M. H., 15th (The King's) Hussars
Kerton, S.Q.M.S. F., General List.
Kisbey, R.Q.M.S. W. F., Royal Flying Corps.
Knight, S.Q.M.S. S., The Ayrshire Yeomanry.
Lawson, Sgt. Tptr. R. A., 2nd King Edward's Own Gurkha Rifles.
Mansfield, Sgt. J., The Leicestershire Regiment.
Mackay, Sgt. W., The Seaforth Highlanders.
Miller, Cpl. W., The Leicestershire Regiment.
Mills, S.Q.M.S. J., Royal Field Artillery.
Morlidge, S.Q.M.S. A., The Northumberland Fusiliers.
Morris, S.S.M. A. F., The King's Regiment (Liverpool).
Nicholson, Tptr. Maj. J. S., The Royal Marine Light Infantry.
Papworth, Sgt. A. J., The Norfolk Regiment.

APPENDIX D

List of N.C.O.'s and Men (continued).

Pendry, S.S.M. W., The Shropshire Yeomanry.
Ryland, Sgt. C., Prince of Wales Volunteers (South Lancashire Regiment).
Saunders, Pte. A. V., The Royal Berkshire Regiment.
Snelling, S.Q.M.S. C., The Staffordshire Yeomanry.
Tilley, Sgt. A., The Hampshire Regiment.
Wheal, Tptr. Maj. S., The East Lancashire Regiment.
Walsh, Sgt. A., The Norfolk Regiment.

This list is not absolutely accurate. A large number of N.C.O.'s and men left the Regiment for Cadet Battalions, from where they received their commissions direct to the various regiments of the British Army. Of these 15th Hussars there is no record in this history.

Nor is there any record of the rank, the honours and rewards or the fate of the 15th Hussars who obtained commissions from the Regiment. In the histories of the units they joined, their services are fully recorded. A few rose to relatively high rank, many were decorated, and some sacrificed their lives in the service of their country. But all worthily upheld the traditions of the 15th Hussars.

Appendix E

STRENGTHS OF THE 15TH THE KING'S HUSSARS ON VARIOUS DATES

Outbreak of War.	Officers.	Other Ranks.	Riding Horses	Draught and Pack Horses.
Aug. 1914 (each squadron)	6	154	155	12

(This is the establishment as laid down, but there is no record of the actual strength of the squadrons and headquarters until the Regiment was reassembled.)

Regiment reassembled.	Officers.	Other Ranks.	Horses.
April 29, 1915	21	526	529

After 2nd Battle of Ypres.	Officers.	Other Ranks.	Horses.
June 31st, 1915	21	461	549

End of 1915.	Officers.	Other Ranks.	Riding Horses.	Draught Horses.	Pack Horses.
December 31st	25	660	532	80	6

Battle of the Somme.	Officers.	Other Ranks.	Horses.
July, 1916	28	556	579
attached ...	2	6	3
	30	562	582

End of 1916.	Officers.	Other Ranks.	Horses.	Mules.
December 31st	29	592	579	4
attached ...	4	23	16	
	33	615	595	4

Battle of Arras.	Officers.	Other Ranks.	Riding Horses.	Draught Horses.	Pack Horses.
May, 1917	31	589			
attached ...	2	7			
	33	596	451	53	25

Battle of Cambrai.	Officers.	Other Ranks.	Riding Horses.	Draught Horses.	Pack Horses.
November, 1917	30	530			
attached ...	2	11			
	32	541	454	59	25

APPENDIX E

German Attack.	Officers.	Other Ranks.	Riding Horses.	Draught Horses.	Pack Horses.
March, 1918	31	487			
attached ...	2	7			
	33	494	451	58	25

Battle of Amiens.	Officers.	Other Ranks.	Riding Horses.	Draught Horses.	Pack Horses.	Mules.
August, 1918	39	512	463			
attached ...	2	8	3			
	41	520	466	61	24	4

End of the War.	Officers.	Other Ranks.	Riding Horses.	Draught Horses.	Pack Horses.	Mules.
November, 1918	40	516	414			
attached ...	2	13	24			
	42	529	438	58	19	8

January, 1919.	Officers.	Other Ranks.	Riding Horses.	Draught Horses.	Pack Horses.
	37	530	370		
attached ...	3	5	3		
	40	535	373	57	17

Leaving Germany.	Officers.	Other Ranks.	Riding Horses.	Draught Horses.	Pack Horses.
September, 1919	28	399	379		
attached ...	1	176	14		
	29	575	393	59	25

In Dublin.	Officers.	Other Ranks.	Horses.
March 9th, 1920	29	671	299
August 31st, 1920 ...	26	514	363
March 31st, 1921	25	534	340

INDEX

INDEX

INDEX

Printed in the United Kingdom
by Lightning Source UK Ltd.
134506UK00001B/32/A